THE NEW POETS
American and British Poetry Since World War II

THE NEW POETS

American and British Poetry Since World War II

M. L. ROSENTHAL

New York OXFORD UNIVERSITY PRESS 1967

Library of Congress Catalogue Card Number: 67-15134
Printed in the United States of America

For permission to reprint passages from the works indicated grateful acknowledgment is made to the following:

Penguin Books, Ltd., for the Introduction to *The New Poetry* by A. Alvarez.
Faber and Faber, Ltd., and Farrar, Straus & Giroux, Inc., for John Berryman's *77 Dream Songs,* copyright © 1959, 1962, 1963, 1964 by John Berryman, and *Homage to Mistress Bradstreet,* copyright © 1956 by John Berryman.
Paul Blackburn for his 'Good Morning, Love.'
Robert Bly for his *Silence in the Snowy Fields.*
Scorpion Press for Edwin Bronk's *An Attempt at Exorcism* and *With Love from Judas.*
The Macmillan Company for Hayden Carruth's *The Crow and the Heart.*
The Dolmen Press for the poems of Austin Clarke.
Liveright Publishing Corporation for Hart Crane's 'Brooklyn Bridge' from *The Complete Poems and Selected Letters and Prose of Hart Crane,* copyright © 1966 by Liveright Publishing Corp.
Charles Scribner's Sons and Calder and Boyars, Ltd., for Robert Creeley's *For Love,* copyright ©1962 by Robert Creeley.
Routledge & Kegan Paul, Ltd., and Wesleyan University Press for Donald Davie's *Events and Wisdoms,* copyright © 1965 by Donald Davie.
Holt, Rinehart and Winston, Inc., The Dolmen Press, Ltd., and Contessa Maria C. Figarolo di Gropello for Denis Devlin's *Selected Poems,* copyright 1942, 1945, © 1956 by Maria C. Figarolo di Gropello.
Wesleyan University Press for James Dickey's 'The Firebombing,' copyright © 1964 by James Dickey.
Grove Press, Inc., and Robert Duncan for Robert Duncan's *The Opening of the Field,* copyright © 1960 by Robert Duncan; and Charles Scribner's Sons for Robert Duncan's *Roots and Branches,* copyright © 1964 by Robert Duncan.
Ian Hamilton Finlay for his poems.
Holt, Rinehart and Winston, Inc., for Robert Frost's *In the Clearing,* copyright © 1962 by Robert Frost.
City Lights Books for Allen Ginsberg's *Howl and Other Poems* and *Kaddish and Other Poems 1958–1960.*
The Macmillan Company for Paul Goodman's *The Lordly Hudson and Other Poems.*
Faber and Faber, Ltd., for Thom Gunn's *The Sense of Movement;* and Faber and Faber, Ltd., and The University of Chicago Press for Thom Gunn's *My Sad Captains.*
The Macmillan Company for Ramon Guthrie's *Graffiti.*
The Viking Press, Inc., and André Deutsch, Ltd., for Donald Hall's *A Roof of Tiger Lilies,* copyright © 1960, 1964 by Donald Hall.
Harper & Row, Publishers, and Ted Hughes for Ted Hughes's *The Hawk in the Rain,* copyright © 1956, 1957 by Ted Hughes, and *Lupercal,* copyright © 1960 by Ted Hughes; and Ted Hughes for his 'Cadenza.'
Atheneum Publishers for Randall Jarrell's *The Woman at the Washington Zoo,* copyright © 1960 by Randall Jarrell.
Totem/Corinth Books, Inc., for LeRoi Jones's *Preface to a Twenty Volume Suicide Note,* copyright © 1961 by LeRoi Jones; and Grove Press, Inc., for LeRoi Jones's *The Dead Lecturer,* copyright © 1964 by LeRoi Jones.
The Devin Adair Company and MacGibbon & Kee, Ltd., for Patrick Kavanagh's *The Collected Poems of Patrick Kavanagh,* copyright © 1964 by Patrick Kavanagh.

The Dolmen Press and Dufour Editions, Inc., for Thomas Kinsella's *Another September, Downstream,* and *Wormwood.*
The Marvell Press for Philip Larkin's *The Less Deceived,* copyright © 1955, 1960 by The Marvell Press; Faber and Faber, Ltd., Random House, Inc., and Alfred A. Knopf, Inc., for Philip Larkin's *The Whitsun Weddings,* copyright © 1960, 1961, 1962, 1964 by Philip Larkin.
New Directions Publishing Corporation for Denise Levertov's *With Eyes at the Back of Our Heads,* copyright © 1958 by Denise Levertov Goodman, and *O Taste and See,* copyright © 1962 by Denise Levertov Goodman; and New Directions Publishing Corporation and Laurence Pollinger, Ltd., for Denise Levertov's *The Jacob's Ladder,* copyright © 1958 by Denise Levertov Goodman.
Faber and Faber, Ltd., for Robert Lowell's *Poems 1938–1949;* Faber and Faber, Ltd., and Farrar, Straus & Giroux, Inc., for Robert Lowell's *Life Studies,* copyright © 1956, 1959 by Robert Lowell, and *For the Union Dead,* copyright © 1962 by Robert Lowell; Harcourt, Brace & World, Inc., for 'The Dead in Europe,' 'Mary Winslow,' 'The Quaker Graveyard in Nantucket,' 'The First Sunday in Lent,' and 'Winter in Dunbarton' from Robert Lowell's *Lord Weary's Castle* and 'The Mills of the Kavanaughs' and 'Thanksgiving's Over' from Robert Lowell's *The Mills of the Kavanaughs;* and Robert Lowell for his letters.
Scorpion Press for George MacBeth's *The Broken Places.*
The World Publishing Company and Weidenfeld & Nicolson, Ltd., for Vladimir Mayakovsky's *The Bedbug and Selected Poetry of Vladimir Mayakovsky,* edited by Patricia Blake.
Harcourt, Brace & World, Inc., Longmans, Green & Co., Ltd., and Christopher Middleton for 'The Dress' and 'The Thousand Things' from Middleton's *Torse 3;* and W. W. Norton & Company, Longmans, Green & Co., Ltd., and Christopher Middleton for Middleton's *Nonsequences: Selfpoems.*
The Dolmen Press, Ltd., for John Montague's *All Legendary Obstacles* (to be included in *A Chosen Light,* MacGibbon & Kee, 1967), *Patriotic Suite,* and *A Tribute to Austin Clarke on His Seventieth Birthday,* edited by Liam Miller and John Montague; MacGibbon & Kee, Ltd., and Dufour Editions, Inc., for John Montague's *Poisoned Lands;* and John Montague and his agent Harold Matson for Montague's work.
Richard Murphy for his poems.
Howard Nemerov for his poems.
Jargon/Corinth Books, Inc., for Charles Olson's *The Maximus Poems,* copyright © 1960 by Charles Olson; Grove Press, Inc., for Charles Olson's *The Distances,* copyright 1950, 1951, 1953, © 1960 by Charles Olson; and Charles Olson for his works.
The Sunday Times (London) and Harold Pinter for a quotation from Harold Pinter.
Random House, Inc., Alfred A. Knopf, Inc., and Ted Hughes for 'The Disquieting Muses' from Sylvia Plath's *The Colossus,* copyright © 1957, 1958, 1959, 1960, 1961, 1962 by Sylvia Plath; and Harper & Row, Publishers, and Ted Hughes for Sylvia Plath's *Ariel,* copyright © 1966 by Ted Hughes.
New Directions Publishing Corporation and Faber and Faber, Ltd., for Ezra Pound's *The Cantos,* copyright 1948 by Ezra Pound.
Routledge & Kegan Paul, Ltd., for Peter Redgrove's *The Collector* and *The Nature of Cold Weather and Other Poems.*
Doubleday & Company, Inc., for 'Meditation at Oyster River,' copyright © 1960 by Beatrice Roethke as Administratrix of the Estate of Theodore Roethke, 'I waited,' copyright © 1956 by Kenyon College, from *Collected Poems of Theodore Roethke.*
The Macmillan Company for Muriel Rukeyser's *Waterlily Fire: Poems 1935–1962.*
Houghton Mifflin Company for Anne Sexton's *To Bedlam and Part Way Back* and *All My Pretty Ones.*
Random House, Inc., and Alfred A. Knopf, Inc., for Karl Shapiro's *The Bourgeois Poet,* copyright 1962, 1963, 1964 by Karl Shapiro.
Wesleyan University Press for Louis Simpson's 'A Story About Chicken Soup,' copyright © 1963 by Louis Simpson, and 'Carentan O Carentan,' copyright © 1959 by Louis Simpson.

Faber and Faber, Ltd., Random House, Inc., and Alfred A. Knopf, Inc., for *The Collected Poems of Wallace Stevens,* copyright 1923, 1931, 1935, 1936, 1937, 1942, 1943, 1944, 1945, 1946, 1947, 1948, 1949, 1950, 1951, 1952, 1954 by Wallace Stevens.

Oxford University Press for Charles Tomlinson's *A Peopled Landscape* and *American Scenes;* and Ivan Obolensky, Inc., for Charles Tomlinson's *Seeing Is Believing.*

Michael Weaver for his work.

The Macmillan Company for Theodore Weiss's *The Medium.*

New Directions Publishing Corporation and MacGibbon & Kee, Ltd., for 'To a Dog Injured in the Street,' from William Carlos Williams, *Pictures from Brueghel and Other Poems,* copyright 1954 by William Carlos Williams; from Williams's *Paterson IV,* copyright 1951 by William Carlos Williams; and 'This Is Just To Say,' from Williams's *Collected Earlier Poems,* copyright 1938 by William Carlos Williams.

Penguin Books, Ltd., for the Introduction to *The Mid Century: English Poetry* by David Wright.

Wesleyan University Press and Longmans, Green & Co., Ltd., for James Wright's *This Branch Will Not Break,* copyright © 1961 by James Wright.

The Macmillan Company, A. P. Watt & Sons, Ltd., Macmillan & Co., Ltd., and Mrs. W. B. Yeats for the following poems from *Collected Poems of William Butler Yeats:* 'The Road at My Door,' copyright 1928 The Macmillan Company, renewed 1956 Georgie Yeats; 'Meru,' copyright 1934 The Macmillan Company, renewed 1962 Bertha Georgie Yeats; 'Lapis Lazuli,' copyright 1940 by Georgie Yeats; 'Nineteen Hundred Nineteen,' copyright 1928 The Macmillan Company, renewed 1956 Georgie Yeats; 'Her Anxiety,' copyright 1933 The Macmillan Company, renewed 1961 Bertha Georgie Yeats.

Portions of this book in their original form appeared in the following publications: *Approaches to the Study of Twentieth-Century Literature* (Proceedings of the Conference in the Study of Twentieth-Century Literature, Third Session); *Arts and Sciences; Poetry* (from 'New Works on Pound,' first published in the August 1965 issue of *Poetry*) ; *Ramon Guthrie Kaleidoscope* (copyright © 1963 by The Stinehour Press) ; *Salmagundi; The New York Times Book Review* (© 1961, 1963, 1965, 1966 by The New York Times Company; reprinted by permission) ; *The Poetry Review; The Reporter; The Spectator* (London) . Permission to use these materials is gratefully acknowledged.

For my son Alan

Foreword

My main debt in this study, it should go without saying, is to the poets whom I discuss. I mean this in the simplest sense. I am grateful to the poets for their gift to us of their work generally, and to my friends and acquaintances among them with whom I have talked and corresponded over the years and who have so often shown me their work in progress. I am grateful, as well, for their hints, in their poems and in their occasional writings, concerning their artistic practice and theory. Where do our best and clearest ideas about the nature of modern literature come from? First of all, from the works themselves—their very shape and substance. And second, from those hints thrown out by the authors in the process of clearing a little way ahead in their efforts to find their own directions, to touch antennae with their fellow artists, and to point a path for readers.

The 'new poets' who since World War II have emerged in the United States and the British Isles have done so without apologies to their elders, if not without tutelage from them. The new writing is a real presence. It speaks for certain further turns in the sensibility of this age of drastic, candid confrontations. My aim has been to identify a number of the crucial figures and poems and to suggest certain meaningful relationships among them in the light of the whole modern tradition. It is easy to oversimplify issues when one is in the midst of a developing, complex situation, and one must resist an arbitrary fixing on one tendency to the exclusion of most others. For instance, one might almost chance calling the present period of poetry 'the age of Robert Lowell.' It would be difficult, however, to disentangle objectivity from partisanship if one did so, and indeed the issue is not at all that plain. Various schools are battling, not so much with one another as with the challenges of their art. I had thought of naming the book *News from the Front,* but poetic wars are after all not the uppermost ones in public consciousness.

From a large number of poets of interest, I have tried to select those whose work best represents the whole field of poetic force in which it exists. It seems remarkable that this field has defined itself so sharply even while many people have been declaring that modern poetry has come to a dead end—surely the most futile variety of literary prophecy. Though I have given some special attention to certain important but neglected figures, my great regret is the exclusions made necessary by my central purpose and by the structure to which it has led me. To write an exhaustive descriptive catalogue, useful as such a handbook would be, is not at all the aim here. Rather, it is to examine certain key figures in such a way as to intimate the qualitative character of the whole scene as well as I am at this moment able to gauge it. I have tried, incidentally, to avoid overlapping with my book *The Modern Poets: A Critical Introduction* (1960), which deals mainly with the older generations of moderns but does devote a chapter to more recent poetry. This has proved no great problem, both because the act alone of focusing on poetry since 1945 makes a great difference and because so much has happened, and so much more has clarified itself, in the seven years since that book was completed. The main tendencies have, of course, emerged more fully. At the same time, I have come to know the immediate English and Irish situations, and even the American one, more intimately.

My heartfelt thanks are due to Mr. Gordon Ray and the John Simon Guggenheim Foundation, as well as to New York University, for the support they have given this study. I owe a special acknowledgement, finally, to all those poets, editors, scholars, and critics in the United Kingdom and Ireland whose hospitality and friendly communicativeness have helped me to be so much more at home with their current literature than I could possibly have been without their help.

Suffern, New York M. L. R.
November 1966

Contents

THE NEW POETS

American and British Poetry Since World War II

I 'Modernity' and the New Poetry

And I
Am the arrow,

The dew that flies
Suicidal, at one with the drive
Into the red

Eye, the cauldron of morning.
SYLVIA PLATH, 'Ariel'

Modern poetry has a long, tangled history by now. Depending on one's definition of it, one must place its age at somewhere between sixty and one hundred years. I am here concerned with American and British poetry since World War II and with the general question whether, during this score or so of years, modern poetry has not taken a meaningful new turn. As compared with our 'heroic' age of Yeats, Pound, Eliot, and their brilliant rivals and near-rivals, has the poetry of these more recent decades a distinctive character?

Uncertainly and tentatively I say 'Yes.' I propose now to explore this question 'with my bare hands' (as someone has said is his way of reading a poem) and with as much truthfulness to the poetry as I am capable of. I want to begin with a few suggestions about what modernity in literature means, suggestions intended to recall certain directions of the 'modern tradition' and at the same time to see the poetry of the last twenty years in their perspective. Then we shall have a closer look at this poetry in its own right and attempt to take some bearings from that examination.

Our exploration involves scrutinizing the new poetic scene without forgetting the continuing presence of the older masters, some of whom have done significant work since the last war. It demands attention to Robert Lowell, the strongest figure to emerge in the period, and to the 'confessional' poetry that has developed under his influence (though it would be inaccurate to think of him as a 'confessional' poet only). The work of such poets as Theodore Roethke, John Berryman, Sylvia Plath, and Anne Sexton in America and of Ted Hughes and Peter Redgrove in England presents comparable considerations. Outside the magnetic field of this kind of writing, too, there lie other clusters and individuals. Among these we must include the Americans of the Black Mountain and other groups, young and old, of an experimental or 'dissident' cast; and the more conventionally oriented poets associated with the magazine *The Sixties* in the United States and with 'The Movement' and 'The Group' in England. Many figures, including the American poet Howard Nemerov, the English poets Philip Larkin, Charles Tomlinson, and Donald Davie, and the Irish poets Austin Clarke (who at the age of sixty-eight produced one of the memorable long poems of the age in 'The Loss of Memory') and Thomas Kinsella, are independent of movements yet embody important tendencies at the same time. There is no point, here or later, in going mechanically through the whole roster of poets above a certain level of competence, nor should we consciously encourage mediocrity. On the other hand, poetry can be understood one poem at a time only. There is no short cut, and love and respect as well as rigor are needed if one is to come to terms with that one poem. We must, then, take a certain short-run risk, sometimes, of simply being mistaken about the quality of a poem. But then, as Havelock Ellis once put it, life *is* an adventure with risks.

To begin, then, I want to propose that since the war of 1939–45 the most striking poetry in the English language has taken on a new coloration, in effect a new sense of unease and disorder. Behind it is the feeling, perhaps, that the humanistic way, which traditionally educated and romantic modern men still propose to protect, and indeed to project into a Utopian future, has already been defeated and is now no more than a ghost. It is that feeling which Robert Lowell in one of his poems calls, self-ironically, 'our universal *Angst*' — a heart-heavy realization that remorseless brutality is a condition not only of the physical universe but also of man himself. The most telling poem in Robert Frost's very last volume is 'The Draft Horse,' which begins:

> With a lantern that wouldn't burn
> In too frail a buggy we drove
> Behind too heavy a horse
> Through a pitch-dark limitless grove.
>
> And a man came out of the trees
> And took our horse by the head
> And reaching back to his ribs
> Deliberately stabbed him dead. . . .

Frost's poem presents a superbly concentrated symbolic vision, but I might select a less unique instance of the preoccupation of modern sensibility from any one of several dozen poems, at least, by younger writers whose chief adolescent and adult experience has occurred in the years since 1939. As one instance, I cite the first stanzas of Hayden Carruth's 'On a Certain Engagement South of Seoul.'

A long time, many years, we've had these wars.
When they were opened, one can hardly say.
We were high school students, no more than sophomores,

When Italy broke her peace on a dark day,
And that was not the beginning. The following years
Grew crowded with destruction and dismay.

When I was nineteen, once the surprising tears
Stood in my eyes and stung me, for I saw
A soldier in a newsreel clutch his ears

To hold his face together. Those that paw
The public's bones to eat the public's heart
Said far too much, of course. The sight, so raw

And unbelievable, of people blown apart
Was enough to numb us without that bark and whine. . . .

Some of the trite and flat phrasing of Carruth's poem seems to derive from his attempt to make it colloquial in tone while adhering to the *terza rima* scheme. Nevertheless, it is remarkable how the force of his central feeling, or *knowledge,* overbears these weaknesses. I hope I will not seem to be making an oversubtle point when I say that this force comes, to a fair degree, from Carruth's being keyed to the deep, and literal, absorption of our age in the terrors of war — an absorption that informs the literature in the same way as it informs the nature of modern crime and psychic derangement and undercuts the morale of our culture. The awkwardness of Carruth's diction and syntax matters, of course. But because his language has the virtues, too, of its passion and accuracy, the poem does survive. As for its whole substance, the violence and pain reported were first transmitted to the boy, significantly, not on the battlefield itself but in a newsreel. The new technology of communication has rendered it impossible to keep the young from knowing the worst realities far too soon. Even a child's consciousness can no longer be kept very far removed from the state of awareness presented in Lowell's 'Fall 1961':

> Our end drifts nearer,
> the moon lifts,
> radiant with terror . . .
>
> A father's no shield
> for his child.
> We are like a lot of wild
> spiders crying together,
> but without tears. . . .

But at this point I do not wish to stress any further the difference of the new poetry from poetry of the past. Having suggested, for emphasis, as it were, its isolation of the effect of prolonged saturation in traumatic and insolubly depressive experience, I should like to dwell now on characteristics that it shares with the modern literature preceding it. If there is, in fact, one distinctively modern quality in literature, it lies in the centrifugal spin toward suicide of the speaking voice. This movement doubtless began with the embittered isolation of the speaking self in Romantic poetry — who can doubt it? There is no basic difference between the richly pessimistic aestheticism of the 'Ode to a Nightingale' (in which the speaker's transport to the eternal world of the nightingale and its song is finally seen as but an intensification of sensuous existence and the condition of mortality) and the assumptions and modulations of the great twentieth-century masters. Or the difference lies mainly, as with the differences in technique, in making explicit what was formerly implied; and in the sloughing off both of any pretense of a pursuit of the dream as a realizable ideal and of 'interim' solutions, such as Matthew Arnold's hanging the issue on the loss of God and a consequent resort to personal love in 'Dover Beach.' Yeats, who was of more than one era, saw the direction sensibility had taken after the First World War. The best minds — honorable, open, self-critical, unwilling to use brute power, and unready and unskilled to use it — 'lack all conviction' in any dogmatic or self-righteous or even instinctual sense. Personality itself, the great pride of post-medieval man, his great self-transcendent construct, is defeated. In Yeats's 'Meditations in Time of Civil War,' those men who value individual life far more casually than does the poet — first the 'affable irregular' of the intransigent I.R.A., and at another time the 'brown lieutenant' with his Free State soldiers — are seen clearly to be in charge:

> I count those feathered balls of soot
> The moor-hen guides upon the stream,
> To silence the envy in my thought;
> And turn towards my chamber, caught
> In the cold snows of a dream.

Williams, in 'To a Dog Injured in the Street,' after the Second World War, sees the life-principle itself equally betrayed and thwarted; he cannot separate his own personality from it:

It is myself,
        not the poor beast lying there
                yelping with pain
that brings me to myself with a start—
        as at the explosion
                of a bomb, a bomb that has laid
all the world waste.
        I can do nothing
                but sing about it
and so I am assuaged
        from my pain.

A drowsy numbness drowns my sense
        as if of hemlock
                I had drunk. . . .

Just as the speaking self in this poem identifies itself with all that suffers helplessly, so the Keatsian sense of inescapable mortality is identified with the impersonal deadliness of modern technology, brought to its essential nature by the atomic bomb. The thought is another turn on that of Yeats's 'Meditations.' All Yeats says he could do was to return to his chamber, 'caught

In the cold snows of a dream.

The condition was not unlike that of the speaker at the end of the 'Nightingale' ode. Williams misquotes the ode slightly, in the process of recalling that state of incomplete withdrawal from pain preliminary to the effort at aesthetic self-transcendence which he feels he shares with Keats. He did not know his Keats deeply enough to exploit this insight fully. But he saw the link, and felt the difference too. The Self, the subjective side of what used to be called 'civilization as we know it,' has been fragmented by everything that has 'laid all the world waste.' Perhaps it can be reconstructed in the aesthetic process? The predicament and the question seem implicit in the whole curve of modern poetry.

We often think of 'Dover Beach' as a post-Romantic forerunner of the modern, and for good reasons. The culminating figure there of the 'darkling plain' on which 'ignorant armies clash by night' suggests a foreboding of the modern condition more specific than its literal use in the poem would lead us to envisage. Lawrence's 'New Heaven and Earth' might be a revision of 'Dover Beach' in the light of the experience of the First World War. In the Lawrence poem the speaker's predicament has become more drastic because the war-theme has been shifted to a central place in the poem. Now it refers to actual contemporary experience; it is no longer merely a figure for loss of life-perspective. Beginning perhaps with the ending of the 'Burial of the Dead' section of *The Waste Land,* it would be easy to add a number of significant examples of this particular set of thought. Of course, I have been stressing the importance of the modern experience of *war* in giving much of our poetry its special character. I do not want to apologize for this emphasis. War is more than a theme or subject for modern writers. It is a condition of consciousness, a destructive fact that explodes within the literature as without it. Just because the fact is so grossly obvious, we are in danger of overlooking its omnipresence. In another, equally obvious sense, however, it is simply the final step in the technological alienation of sensibility. I have had occasion elsewhere to note the almost identical intrinsic quality of two passages in American poetry, the first in Bryant's 'To a Waterfowl' (1815) and the second in Hart Crane's 'To Brooklyn Bridge' (1926):

All day thy wings have fanned
At that far height, the cold, thin atmosphere. . . .

and:

All afternoon the cloud-flown derricks turn. . . .
Thy cables breathe the North Atlantic still. . . .

In quoting these passages originally, I was concerned only to show the often unconscious continuity between poetry of the past and that of the present. My point was their remarkable closeness in pitch and melody and in their tone of awe at the immensities of time and space brought into focus by bird and bridge. But in the context of our present discussion, it is interesting to observe that, while the Romantic poet Bryant takes his central image from nature, the modern Crane takes his from industrial civilization. *The Bridge* as a whole and its introductory poem of epic invocation, 'To Brooklyn Bridge,' attempt a symbolic projection of the power of man to create his own mystical yet dependable vision of self-transcendence. The alienated spirit will re-integrate himself with the world by way of a symbol of its mechanical achievement, but will assimilate that achievement to the realm of the truly humanistic through the transforming force of imagination. The failure of this conception to prevail by way of the organic structure of Crane's whole sequence is well known. The total impression left by *The Bridge,* despite the beautiful 'Proem' and other passages, is of the poet's defeat by the very motifs in our culture from which he would wrest a conviction of possibility.

Now I am not arguing that modern literature always reveals this alienation. There is no one quality that cuts through the whole of it, except its quality of feeling somehow of its era. The feeling can most often be traced to the language itself — to a certain unpretentious, colloquial edge, say, in much realistic writing; or to a clipped, ironically edged tone of objectivity; or to the combination of these in varying degrees with a highly developed psychological empathy; or, on the other hand, to an extreme subjectivity. An observation on language by the playwright Harold Pinter is an excellent expression of one modern tendency best represented by plays like the author's own *The Caretaker* or Beckett's *Waiting for Godot:*

> The speech we hear is an indication of what we don't hear. It is a necessary avoidance, a violent, sly, anguished or mocking smoke screen. . . . One way of looking at speech is to say it is a constant stratagem to cover nakedness. . . . I think that we communicate only too well, in our silence, in what is *unsaid,* and that what takes place is continual evasion, desperate rear-guard attempts to keep ourselves to ourselves.

To say with Pinter that speech 'is a constant stratagem to cover nakedness' would be easy in one sense for thinkers of all ages; to add that it presents 'desperate rear-guard attempts to keep ourselves to ourselves' is to suggest a vulnerability of the psyche that is unmistakably of this age. The proposition shows Pinter's kinship with the poets. Also, the preoccupation itself with the presenting of these 'rear-guard attempts' is modern. That is a phase, clearly, of the alienation of sensibility, and I had not intended to include more such considerations in this small list of 'other' clues to the specifically modern. But because of the workings of this alienation a drama of ambiguous expectations, relationships, and resolutions has emerged in its own right. All this amounts to a suppression of traditionally conceived personality, both the author's own and that of his characters.

A host of other qualitative differences between aspects of the modern and of previous periods might be adduced, for instance the relation between the awakening to brutality as a condition of existence in writers like Chekhov, Dostoevski, and Flaubert and the cultivation of impersonality in one main stream of our poetry. But I should like to return to the main line of development in the poetry, and particularly in American poetry.

First, then, the point of view that modern poetry expresses toward life in general is that of a Romantic aestheticism. The Self seeks to discover itself through the energy of its insights into reality and through the sensuous excitement generated in it by its experience of reality. Since what is seen or experienced may prove utterly bleak, the poetry is a constant struggle to assert the encompassing validity of the feeling personality in the face of depressing realizations. As Yeats has it in 'Meru':

> Civilisation is hooped together, brought
> Under a rule, under the semblance of peace
> By manifold illusion; but man's life is thought,
> And he, despite his terror, cannot cease
> Ravening, through century after century,
> Ravening, raging, and uprooting that he may come
> Into the desolation of reality. . . .

Secondly, our poetry of political and cultural criticism centers on the individual as the *victim*. In the work of the older aestheticist moderns the poet is generally a sort of cultural hero, by implication (if only negative) at least, fighting for true self-realization in the face of all that victimizes us and, sometimes, fighting for the arts as its greatest source. The relation between this role, of the hero-victim triumphing by way of truthfulness to his sensibility, and the whole Romantic tradition as felt in recent poetry is perfectly embodied in Robert Lowell's 'Words for Hart Crane':

> 'When the Pulitzers showered on some dope
> or screw who flushed our dry mouths out with soap,
> few people would consider why I took
> to stalking sailors, and scattered Uncle Sam's
> phoney gold-plated laurels to the birds.
> Because I knew my Whitman like a book,
> stranger in America, tell my country: I,
> *Catullus redivivus,* once the rage
> of the Village and Paris, used to play my role
> of homosexual, wolfing the stray lambs
> who hungered by the Place de la Concorde.
> My profit was a pocket with a hole.
> Who asks for me, the Shelley of my age,
> must lay his heart out for my bed and board.'

Such a poem is also a link between poems like Masters's 'Carl Hamblin' and 'Editor Whedon' (its tonal echoes of these are, indeed, remarkable), or like Robinson's 'Eros Turannos' and 'Mr. Flood's Party,' and the new poetic movement best represented by Robert Creeley and Paul Blackburn. That is, it has elements of the older 'objectivity' that enabled Masters and Robinson to present for contemplation portraits of defeated but sympathetic personalities, and it also has elements of the new existential subjectivity in which the poet sinks his consciousness deep into his moment-by-moment daily self. In Masters and Robinson, the poet's identification with the central dramatic figures of his poems suggests itself only by implication, by the quality of his concern, the depth of his interest, the sense of the exploration of inwardly compelling ironies through external means. In Blackburn and Creeley, and the general tendency they represent, the poet himself is always at the center of the poem, though most often simply as a consciousness, not in an explicitly defined role as artist. It is the acceptance of this role by Crane and by Lowell that places them with the aestheticist masters and liberates them from the domination of the literal. Without it, we would lack even so disillusioned a variant of self-transcendence as the poem of Lowell's I have just quoted, or as Crane's 'Passage.' On the other hand, deep-diving into the psychology of literal predicament has in the past resulted in such magnificent work as Emily Dickinson's ''Twas like a maelstrom' and Frost's 'The Subverted Flower.'

Thirdly — an extension from the previous point — the private life of the poet himself, especially under stress of psychological crisis, becomes a major theme. Often it is felt at the same time as a symbolic embodiment of national and cultural crisis. Hence the idiom of our poetry can be at once private and public, lyrical and rhetorical. Again, the continuing power of the Romantic tradition is clear, the specifically modern turn being the strongly confessional, literally self-exposing vulnerability characteristic of the statement. Sexual candor, frankness about family life, and confession of private humiliations of varying psychological kinds are not the only kinds of expression this vulnerability entails. The proliferating imagery of failure and self-doubt in 'Mauberley (1920),' the hints of disturbance and confusion in Eliot, the nightmare war-abstractions that ride the psyche in Muir's 'Then' are further instances. It is interesting, as a projection of this tendency of poetic thought, that the classic statement of modernist poetic practice, Eliot's discussion of the 'objective correlative' in his essay on *Hamlet,* links what is essentially the Symbolist and Imagist method of presentative statement in poetry with just this psychological frame. 'The intense feeling, ecstatic or terrible, without an object or exceeding its object, is something which every person of sensibility has known.' * A corollary of the argument in the *Hamlet* essay would be that the image itself, isolated condensation of a moment of realized sensibility

* The character and relevance of a poem depend finally on the accuracy of one man's sense of what actually counts for him at a given moment. They do not depend on what he has been taught, or has himself taught, about the nature of poetry, but upon the clues given him by his sensibility as it informs his intelligence and disciplines that intelligence. For this reason Muir and Williams, though neither of them ever achieved Eliot's heights, are as close to the best poetry of the post-1945 period as is T. S. Eliot. As long as Eliot maintained a sense of the actual feel of contemporary life through his extraordinary suggestibility and ability to be shocked — and even pathologically shocked — he was able to find the language and formal devices necessary for the truly unique body of poetry completed by the appearance of 'Little Gidding' in 1942. His serious philosophical and religious thinking was informed by that deep and exquisite sense of reality that supplied a protective frame within which explorations could occur as the poet sought to overcome a fundamentally depressed state. 'Little Gidding' was, in fact, a belated recrudescence of his original energies of many years before, under the impact of the German bombings of London. It temporarily reversed his 'progress' toward a less sensitive condition in which he eventually succeeded all too well in his early aim of losing the sense of self in something 'greater.' At fifty-seven he had published his last poem of real interest, and the plays that he was to write after the war lacked the intense feeling of *Murder in the Cathedral* and *The Family Reunion.* The exhaustion of feeling in his work suggests to me the fundamental irrelevance to a functioning art of his intellectual commitments, religious, political, and moral, once the tension between them and the naked, vulnerable sensibility with which he came to birth as a poet early in the century had been resolved.

that it is — in Pound's words, 'an intellectual and emotional complex in an instant of time' — is the only clue to private, experientially assimilated meaning. The intensity and purity of a realization are the measure of poetic sense and success. Thus, the alienated sensibility reclaims the world on its own terms.

This is one culmination of a process that began, say, with Poe's fantasies about the sadistic possibilities of a technologically oriented efficiency directed by diabolical logic and about the capacity of sensibility to withstand its pressures and to circumvent them. I am thinking of such a short story as 'The Pit and the Pendulum,' for instance. But we might include in the range of experimentation Emily Dickinson's image of 'a goblin with a gauge' in ' 'Twas like a maelstrom,' that poem about the intolerable pressures of life on the moral sensibility. Ultimately, wherever you have an insight into the unheroic loneliness of human consciousness in an impersonally hostile universe, even such an insight as Longfellow has in his chilling little poem 'The Tide Rises, the Tide Falls,' you have a related motivation, however undeveloped. It is the insistence on the transforming and liberating capacity of personality — the personality behind artistic sensibility — through its power to size up 'things as they are' that restores heroism of attitude if not of a more effectively worldly kind.

> All men have aimed at, found and lost;
> Black out; Heaven blazing into the head:
> Tragedy wrought to its uttermost.
> Though Hamlet rambles and Lear rages,
> And all the drop-scenes drop at once
> Upon a hundred thousand stages,
> It cannot grow by an inch or an ounce.
>
> YEATS, 'Lapis Lazuli'

If her horny feet protrude, they come
To show how cold she is, and dumb.
Let the lamp affix its beam.
The only emperor is the emperor of ice-cream.

STEVENS, 'The Emperor of Ice Cream'

Colour floods to the spot, dull purple.
The rest of the body is all washed out,
The colour of pearl.

In a pit of rock
The sea sucks obsessively,
One hollow the whole sea's pivot.

The size of a fly,
The doom mark
Crawls down the wall.

The heart shuts,
The sea slides back,
The mirrors are sheeted.

SYLVIA PLATH, 'Contusion'

Of Sylvia Plath's last poems, including 'Contusion,' A. Alvarez writes that 'she was systematically probing that narrow, violent area between the viable and the impossible, between experience which can be transmuted into poetry and that which is overwhelming.' I do not know whether this distinction is valid or not; I suspect not. He is partly talking about the suicidal impulse that seems inseparable from the poet's placing his literal Self at the focal point of his work — not that image which, however truthful a reflection in one sense, never forgets its ability to fly on 'the viewless wings of Poesy,' but the essential Self of Lowell's 'Man and Wife,' which begins: 'Tamed by

Miltown, we lie on Mother's bed.' Or the speaking sensibility may seem too big, too real for life — the opposite predicament of Mayakovsky's 'The Cloud in Trousers':

> I feel
> my 'I'
> is much too small for me.
> Stubbornly a body pushes out of me.
>
> Hello!
> Who's speaking?
> Mamma?
> Mamma!
> Your son is gloriously ill!
> Mamma!
> His heart is on fire.
> Tell his sisters, Lyuda and Olya,
> he has no nook to hide in. . . .

But our poetry, oddly, seems to find little room for this sort of marvelous buffoonery of late — it grows too heavy-hearted in the very process. The novel of Joyce and Faulkner perhaps comes closer to it, although we can find a desolate exuberance in Berryman, Roethke, and others (mostly derivative from Joyce, however). The real passion and energy, though, are reserved for works not of buffoonery but of wildly realized madness and suffering, as in Lowell's 'Words for Hart Crane' or, even more, his 'A Mad Negro Soldier Confined at Munich.' An almost unique poem developing out of the Imagist method, Randall Jarrell's 'The Death of the Ball Turret Gunner,' at once achieved a special place in the modern tradition. In it we see the convergence of many of the motifs and developments we have been examining: the alienation of sensibility by modern war and the technological displacement of human values, and the related directions of our poetry, particularly the Romantic and primitivist criticism of these tendencies, the emphasis on the individual as their victim, and the deliberate brutality of the speaking voice at the end to reinforce the impression of utter vulnerability. The fragmentation of the long poem is an aspect of alienation, and I wish to call attention for a moment now to the interesting development of the *sequence* as the characteristic form of the long poem, including the long poem of epic pretensions. Starting with *Song of Myself,* we can make a minimal list in addition consisting of *The Waste Land, Four Quartets, Hugh Selwyn Mauberley* (considered as a single construct of which 'Mauberley (1920)' is but the second part), the *Cantos, The Bridge, Voyages,* and *Paterson.* Poe's attack on the concept of a 'sustained' longer work, that is, one with a continuous narrative or argumentative structure going over many lines, seems to have been borne out by modern practice. Each of the sequences I have mentioned has a number of independent units within it, special points of focus which, taken in order, make for the Poundian *periplum,* or 'image of successive discoveries breaking upon the consciousness of the voyager.' The voyager in each of these instances (including 'Mauberley,' I believe) is the speaking sensibility itself, testing the social and cultural landscape, the lines of continuity with the past, and the prospects of possible reconciliation with the alienating real world at every step along the way. This is a fascinatingly relevant and fruitful line of exploration for the study of literary forms, their evolution, and their relation to the deepest kinds of awareness in our social development. If I do not go into this matter any further here, it is because it is so large an issue in its own right and because a hint of it seems sufficient for our present purposes.

These, then, have been some of the relevant formulations that impress themselves upon me as I try to think inductively over the poetry that I have been rather actively contemplating for some years. Perhaps they are too much dependent on a sense of the working poet's own mentality, and I know that this sense gives me a slight feeling of uneasiness and even guilt, as if I had been betraying the necessary spirit of openness itself — to one poem at a time, as I suggested earlier. Nor do I wish to overlook quieter poetic modes than the ones I have been discussing, though they too, when they work really interestingly, often bear an important relationship to the theme of alienated sensibility. For some time now my thoughts have kept returning to two passages by Yeats of this latter order. One is at the very beginning of 'Nineteen Hundred and Nineteen':

> Many ingenious lovely things are gone
> That seemed sheer miracle to the multitude. . . .

Of course, it is the wonderfully direct, simple, moderately alliterative presentation of the mutability theme that is so taking and moving in these lines; and of course, too, we are going to be led to the magnificently bitter stanza beginning 'Now days are dragon-ridden' that provides a piercing intensification and acceleration of the statement in just the frame of thought we have been discussing. But these lines, and others like them, are modern only in some indefinable quality of idiom. In this respect they resemble the lovely little poem 'Her Anxiety':

> Earth in beauty dressed
> Awaits returning spring.

All true love must die,
Alter at the best
Into some lesser thing.
Prove that I lie.

Such body lovers have,
Such exacting breath,
That they touch or sigh.
Every touch they give,
Love is nearer death.
Prove that I lie.

The poem is more 'modern' in technique than one might think because of the leap of thought required to see the meaning in the opening lines. (How is 'earth in beauty dressed' if spring has not yet come? Apparently it is the earth's nakedness that is beautiful, and perhaps there is an analogy implied of the woman waiting for her lover. That would also account for the further leap of thought to the theme of love, and of its seasons, as it were, in the third line. Traditionally one would not expect the 'conceit' mechanism in combination with such a simply lyrical form.) It will stand by itself in any case, simply because it is so right and fine a lyric poem, though Yeats's daring is an unavoidable consideration — the way he skirts disaster by using language so close to triteness and yet gains immediacy by the very risk. It is 'modern' as well because of its place in the sophisticated 'Words for Music Perhaps' sequence — one kind of note, a traditional one, among many that must be felt in relation to one another.

A poem that takes us first, as 'Her Anxiety' does, by its pure melody and immediacy of feeling seems to do away with any distinction between past and present. The impression is usually only superficial, though, for even the purest lyricism is likely to be marked by the idiom of its moment — an idiom of technique as well as of diction. The Yeats poem, with its tight rhymes and refrain, nevertheless includes a modest off-rhyme ('have' and 'give') that deliberately distorts the patterning and is in its way of a piece with the puzzling beginning, the leaps of implication, and the simple language that is, after all, not so simple. A poem that can carry off this kind of deceptive effort is still a rare achievement, and it is interesting that Yeats brought to bear in it his preoccupations with death, with the self-torment of idealized desire, and with man's desperate need to have the results of knowledge denied in the interest of the will's projections. The method here makes for great compression, and may be compared with the expansive techniques often employed by Pound, Williams, and some of their followers. Thus, Robert Duncan, probably the most gifted of the Black Mountain poets who have made themselves felt since the last war, opens 'A Poem Beginning with a Line by Pindar' with an effect like that at the start of Pound's 'Homage to Sextus Propertius' in its melodic, 'Grecian' character. He holds the poem to this character for some time, then releases it to quite other notes before bringing it closer to the original lyrical level at the very end.

> *The light foot hears you and the brightness begins*
> god-step at the margins of thought,
>   quick adulterous tread at the heart.
> Who is it that goes there?
>   Where I see your quick face
> notes of an old music pace the air,
> torso-reverberations of a Grecian lyre. . . .

The music of its beginning places Duncan's poem in a definite tradition, against which it later moves when it turns into a kind of jeering and then into a political lament. Actually, the poem as a whole does not show Duncan at his best, for the jeering and the political sections are rather weakly rhetorical, with too little meaningful counterpoint to the high lyrical sections. But the poem serves both as an example of a fairly common contemporary practice and as a relatively uncomplicated suggestion of a tendency to use the 'sublime in the old sense,' as Pound put it once, as one element only, though very important, in a *collage* made up of quite varied levels and effects. Enough on these matters for the present, however, I have only wished to note the presence, and the seriousness, of 'other' modes than the ones I have given the most attention to thus far; and also to propose their at least oblique relevance to the main motifs of the age.

II Robert Lowell and 'Confessional' Poetry

1. 'LIFE STUDIES'

The term 'confessional poetry' came naturally to my mind when I reviewed Robert Lowell's *Life Studies* in 1959, and perhaps it came to the minds of others just as naturally. Whoever invented it, it was a term both helpful and too limited, and very possibly the conception of a confessional school has by now done a certain amount of damage.

Any concretely usable suggestion about poetic practice catches on quickly if it is noticed at all. The suggestion may be large or small, and of little or of great importance. It may be almost purely formal, or almost purely attitudinal, though usually it involves the simultaneous acquisition of an idiom of thought and of technique. Among examples of varying significance that one could adduce are William Carlos Williams's flexible three-part rhythmic unit, that 'variable foot' that worked so happily for him in his later work; Robert Bly's reminder that surrealist imagery can be employed effectively in an otherwise straightforward poem; and Robert Creeley's reductionist use of subject matter and poetic style. Such 'discoveries' need only be recoveries of neglected insights or principles, but they always have the effect of innovations when they reappear. On the other hand, their further transmission is likely to be more mechanical than the borrower realizes, especially since one of their chief advantages for him is that they are borrowable without regard to the subjective purposes of their discoverer. In its susceptibility to borrowing, Lowell's discovery of the confessional mode is comparable with the other discoveries I have mentioned. What I want to emphasize now though, is its distinctive contribution. As opposed to the dead echoing and the exhibitionism of some of his imitators, he himself has done what Pound, justifiably, boasts for himself in 'Canto 81.'

> To have gathered from the air a live tradition
> or from a fine old eye the unconquered flame
> This is not vanity.
> Here error is all in the not done,
> all in the diffidence that faltered.

Because of the way Lowell brought his private humiliations, sufferings, and psychological problems into the poems of *Life Studies,* the word 'confessional' seemed appropriate enough. Sexual guilt, alcoholism, repeated confinement in a mental hospital (and some suggestion that the malady has its violent phase) — these are explicit themes of a number of the poems, usually developed in the first person and intended without question to point to the author himself. Accompanying these poems are the long prose-section '91 Revere Street' and a group of related poems presenting the Lowell family background in a manner at once nostalgic, bitter, and psychologically knowledgeable. The mixture of love and loathing, humor and horror, had the impact of a purely personal release, and the softer and more genial notes in the book went mostly unnoticed at first. Lowell had not published a book for eight years before *Life Studies* appeared, and so the term 'confessional' served also to distinguish the new work from the earlier and at the same time to suggest that everything before had been largely a preparation for this development. In a larger, more impersonal context, these poems seemed to me one culmination of the Romantic and modern tendency to place the literal Self more and more at the center of the poem.

In examining Lowell's poetry, therefore, it will be helpful to concentrate on *Life Studies* as his chief volume so far, though we may also look back, if briefly, to *Lord Weary's Castle* (1946) and *The Mills of the Kavanaughs* (1951) and ahead to *For the Union Dead* (1965). (*Land of Unlikeness,* his first book, was published in 1944, but its best poems were for the most part reprinted in *Lord Weary's Castle.*) The earlier collections show his power and enterprise. Their conception and emotional drive are inseparable from his artistry. The technique is rigorous, and poems like 'The Quaker Graveyard at Nantucket' and 'Colloquy in Black Rock' leave no doubt of their author's genius. But despite their explosive brilliance, the books are often musclebound. The awkwardly contained violence of *Lord Weary's Castle* struggles against tight rhymes and a general formal rigidity, as well as against elaborate, stifling overlays of religious and social symbolism, themselves fairly derivative. In the long monologues of *The Mills of the Kavanaughs,* an unspeakably tangled complex of special circumstances and contrived mythical allusiveness hampers the movement, though it provides a protective armor or disguise for Lowell's sensitive reachings out toward confessional statement.

Life Studies, however, is the volume in which the poet at last 'finds himself.' He does so literally, for in most of the poems he himself and his family are at the center, and his object is to catch himself in process of becoming himself. Equally important, in fact more so, he finds himself as a stylist. For the first time he can be casual, simple, and direct throughout a poem, and at the same time he can strike home more tellingly than ever when he wishes. Or, if he desires, he can be transparently clear and *gentle* in his emotional realizations, as he could not have been before. Thus, for instance, the first stanza of 'Grandparents':

> They're altogether otherworldly now,
> those adults champing for their ritual Friday spin
> to pharmacist and five-and-ten in Brockton.
> Back in my throw-away and shaggy span
> of adolescence, Grandpa still waves his stick
> like a policeman;
> Grandmother, like a Mohammedan, still wears her thick
> lavender mourning and touring veil;
> the Pierce Arrow clears its throat in a horse-stall.
> Then the dry road dust rises to whiten
> the fatigued elm leaves —
> the nineteenth century, tired of children, is gone.
> They're all gone into a world of light; the farm's my own.

I have chosen this passage just because it is in one of the less dynamic poems of *Life Studies.* It can be observed without arousing a passion either to cheer it or to do battle with it, yet it is moving on precisely its own terms. The diction is straightforward, accurate but informal. The nostalgic humor of the first nine lines evokes a time in the

1930's when the speaker's grandparents were still alive and dominating his world. Their old-fashioned attitude toward the automobile is remembered with loving irony, darkened by the sadness of the first line. (They who were 'otherworldly' enough in the innocent rituals of their lives are now, in death, *'altogether'* so.) The final four lines of the stanza become consistently, though gently, serious. Their overtones, suggesting the death of an era as well as of two specific people, make themselves felt without calling special attention to the symbolism of white dust, fatigued elm leaves, or even the guilt of the young — their sense that the elders died to punish them deservedly. There is nothing here or in the two stanzas that follow to match the stiffer phrases and the more forced allusions of 'Mary Winslow,' the elegiac poem in *Lord Weary's Castle* that begins:

> Her Irish maids could never spoon out mush
> Or orange-juice enough; the body cools
> And smiles as a sick child
> Who adds up figures, and a hush
> Grips at the poised relations sipping sherry
> And tracking up the carpets of her four
> Room kingdom. On the rigid Charles, in snow,
> Charon, the Lubber, clambers from his wherry,
> And stops her hideous baby-squawks and yells,
> Wit's clownish afterthought. . . .

Now 'Mary Winslow' is hardly a *bad* poem. It begins as naturally and rightly as does the later 'Grandparents.' It has the same compassion without developing it as richly. Lowell brings to bear in it his amazing memory and eye, better than any anthropologist's, for relevant cultural details — though relevance for him is to the pity of the human condition. Both the poems are crowded with such details. 'Grandparents,' however, is in better control of its own direction, for Lowell has outgrown his compulsion to push a symbolic scene so far in search of implication that he is almost led away from the central human insight. In the same way, it is less rhyme-ridden. Rhymes are every bit as operative, but they are far less conspicuous. There is only one exact rhyme ('stick'–'thick'); all the other rhymes are only approximate.* Thus, seven of the thirteen lines quoted echo one another by ending in *n,* each time preceded by a vowel in a syllable that is sometimes stressed, sometimes unstressed. 'Veil' and 'stall' make another such off-rhyme. There is another, more sunken kind of rhyming, between 'now' in the first line and 'own' in the last, and between 'veil' and 'leaves,' for these two pairs are each for the most part simply variant arrangements of the same sounds. This kind of sound-patterning, which is naturally not limited simply to line-endings but saturates a good poem, is one of a poet's major means of reinforcing feeling and thought and of gaining organic structure. Another is the pattern of line-length and stresses. It is easy to see that while both poems are made up of lines tending toward a basic five-stress pattern but with many variations from it, 'Grandparents' is more flexible, with a movement very close to that of normal, somewhat heightened speech.

These are the minutiae of the poem, no doubt, rather than its major qualities. But they seem inseparable from the general liberation of perspective, and of power to call upon his resources, developed by Lowell in the long period

* In 'span'–'policeman' we have a light rhyme (that is, a stressed syllable rhymed with an unstressed one). In any case, the *a* is pronounced differently in the two words.

before *Life Studies* appeared. It is clear now that the shock of the autobiographical sections of that book did not come altogether, as it seemed in 1959, from their self-exposing frankness and the humiliating things said by the poet about his family, especially his father. It came at least as much from the redirection of energy, through the free mastery of these 'minutiae' for a particular purpose that now emerged, toward realizations so intense that at first reading they approached direct experience. Lowell had made a terrifying recovery of his own past, and with it of the lost realities of his parents' and grandparents' existence and of their surrounding life. This recovery did not really happen suddenly. The extraordinary passion of his earlier books is an expression of the search for it, and in *Lord Weary's Castle* we find an almost confessional poem like 'Rebellion' and 'family' poems like 'In Memory of Arthur Winslow,' 'Winter in Dunbarton,' and 'Mary Winslow.' None of these have quite the painful immediacy of *Life Studies.* They are denied the release that would at once have achieved this immediacy and resolved the artificial complexities of the early style. Charged with the same ultimate themes of humiliation, frustration, and unlocated guilt, the earlier books were nevertheless impersonal in a fashion that held the poet himself at arm's length from his true goal (like the early work of Robert Penn Warren).

'Grandparents' is 'terrifying' and 'painful' only in the ultimate sense of any sharp realization of loss. It is, as I have observed, gentler than many other poems in *Life Studies.* Still, it resembles them in its recovery of crucial family experience. Intensity and poignancy are cradled within the gentleness, and the recovery of the past is suddenly converted, in the closing stanzas, into a stricken sense of the present instant. In these stanzas, the lines grow generally shorter and include a number of exclamations, culminating in a cry of childish longing for Grandpa's return and in a reproachful self-characterization. It is the method of *Life Studies* at its simplest that we see in this poem, which forms one brief movement in a series of parallel repossessions of the past, many far stormier. Risking sentimentality, Lowell does not quite avoid it, but the risk is essential to the self-discovery he is after:

> Never again
> to walk there, chalk our cues,
> insist on shooting for us both.
> Grandpa! Have me, hold me, cherish me!
> Tears smut my fingers. There
> half my life-lease later,
> I hold an *Illustrated London News* — ;
> disloyal still,
> I doodle handlebar
> mustaches on the last Russian Czar.

The two confessional sections of *Life Studies* — the title-section of poems and the prose-section called '91 Revere Street' — form the bulk of the book. There are eight poems in addition. An opening group of four, which in a sense sums up the cultural and historical context within which the poet finds himself, precedes '91 Revere Street.' The first two of these poems, 'Beyond the Alps' and 'The Banker's Daughter,' present the failure of the European traditions out of which our classical humanistic ideals were born. The third poem is a severe, tragically tinged, short satire on Eisenhower ('Inauguration Day: January 1953'); and the fourth is a savage, even manic poem called 'A Mad Negro Soldier Confined at Munich.'

This last poem stands as one of the most cumulatively powerful pieces that Lowell has ever written. The progression of the four poems is clear. They move from a general critical summing-up of the state of the civilization — similar in conception though not in style or the specifics of political attitude to that made familiar to us by Pound and Eliot — to an equally harsh comment on the state of the Republic, and then to a close-up of the effect of the last war on one Negro soldier. This final poem in the introductory group shifts our attention from the madness of society to its embodiment in one man. We may assume an intended relationship between this progression and the prose account of his family background, his father's failure especially, that Lowell gives in '91 Revere Street.'

We can see a comparable focusing and progression of intensity in the other nonconfessional group. It too consists of four poems, placed between the prose-section and the fifteen poems of the 'Life Studies' section proper. As with the monologue of the 'mad Negro soldier,' these four poems present figures analogous to the ultimate protagonist of the book, Lowell himself. 'Ford Madox Ford' and 'For George Santayana' are sympathetic but candid portraits of the life-defeated Ford and the dauntless Santayana, 'unbelieving, unconfessed and unreceived.' 'To Delmore Schwartz' is a beautifully engaging, ironic self-portrait of Lowell and his friend and fellow-poet Delmore Schwartz. 'Words for Hart Crane' * is the one poem among these in which Lowell is not himself the speaker, yet it is his strongest personal statement in the book. Hart Crane does the speaking, but of course the 'words' referred to in the title are supplied by Lowell, to underline his identification with Crane. The poem locates the dissident, lyrical, and

* Quoted in full on page 14.

Romantic traditions with which both men are to be associated: Catullus, Shelley, Whitman, the bohemian life of Paris and Greenwich Village. It insists that the poet's outcast state is a failure of America, irredeemable except through unqualified gestures of love:

> 'Who asks for me, the Shelley of my age,
> must lay his heart out for my bed and board.'

It will already be evident, I hope, that although it was the naked, nearly exhibitionistic aspect of *Life Studies* that attracted the greatest attention when the book appeared, this was by no means its only importance. The reductive imitation by other poets of this one aspect results in very different effects from those in Lowell. What I should like to suggest now is the actual character of his achievement in the confessional sections (remembering the symbolic framework created by the eight poems I have just briefly described).

The '91 Revere Street' section starts quietly with an account of Mordecai Myers of New York State, 'my Grandmother Lowell's grandfather.' He is given disproportionate emphasis quite deliberately, it would appear, because he was a Jew. The exotic strain in the poet's nature, the disaffected, anti-New England-granite side of him, is somehow traced back to this respectable New York State political figure: 'Great-great Grandfather Mordecai! Poor sheepdog in wolf's clothing! In the anarchy of my adolescent war on my parents, I tried to make him a true wolf, the wandering Jew! *Homo lupus homini!*' Lowell contradicts the sardonic note in this description of his own adolescent romanticism by the strategic importance he gives to Major Myers at the beginning and at points later on in '91 Revere Street.' This ancestor does in fact play a paradoxical role here, from the time he is first presented as seen in a portrait, fascinating to young Robert, in the Lowell home: 'in his sanguine War of 1812 uniform with epaulets, white breeches, and a scarlet frogged waistcoat.' Lowell contrives this role for him rather insistently:

> There was something undecided, Mediterranean, versatile, almost double-faced about his bearing which suggested that, even to his contemporaries, he must have seemed gratuitously both *ci-devant* and *parvenu*. He was a dark man, a German Jew — no downright Yankee, but maybe such a fellow as Napoleon's mad, pomaded son-of-an-innkeeper-general, Junot, Duc D'Abrantes; a man like mad George III's pomaded, disreputable son, 'Prinny,' the Prince Regent. Or he was one of those Moorish-looking dons painted by his contemporary, Goya — some leader of Spanish guerrillas against Bonaparte's occupation, who fled to South America. Our Major's suffering almond eye rested on his luxurious dawn-colored fingers ruffling an off-white glove.

Thus described, Mordecai Myers is an ambivalent figure and, in a somewhat oblique fashion, becomes the first image of family humiliation in the book. Lowell capitalizes on the slight embarrassment of the stuffier representatives of the family at having this man in their background, though he was a respected public figure, enlightened and patriotic. It is characteristic of him that he should lightly suggest this apparently damped-down anti-Semitic tinge in his very first sentence: 'The account of him is platitudinous, worldly and fond, but he has no Christian name and is entitled merely Major *M.* Myers in my Cousin Cassie Mason Myers Julian-James's privately printed *Biographical Sketches*. . . .' In another sense, though, it is necessary for this particular study of the genesis of a *poète maudit* to suggest as well, however humorously, that there *is* something disreputable in the family heritage. The description I have just quoted is, after all, Lowell's own interpretation,* introducing motifs of madness and subversion, social maladjustment and private suffering, to go with this Jewish strain. Lowell's purpose in all this is psychological, not political; he seems, throughout *Life Studies,* to need to present himself in a degraded or humiliating light, and he is helping to account for the need in '91 Revere Street.' The inspiration to use Mordecai Myers to this end is dubious, perhaps, but in the context of the whole work it is clear that the ancestral figure is but one fixed symbol among many in Lowell's constellation of ambiguous loyalties, shocked memories, and humiliations.

The '91 Revere Street' section is absorbing autobiography, wry, witty, and at once shamefaced and affectionate — full of ambivalence with a purpose. It has a number of symbolic and dramatic centers, around which it is sprawlingly organized. First, of course, there is the house itself whose address furnishes the title. The family moved to this address in Boston when Lowell was seven. In that year, 1924, his father was appointed third in command at the naval yard in Charlestown, Massachusetts, under Admiral de Stahl, and the Boston house was purchased as convenient for both his professional and his social life. Its ambivalence as a home consisted in the fact that de Stahl insisted on Lowell senior's spending every night in a house assigned to him at the naval yard. As a class symbol too, it lacked decisive commitment, 'looking out on an unbuttoned part of Beacon Hill bounded by the North End slums' that

* The portrait itself, writes Lowell, 'has been mislaid past finding.'

were inhabited by Italian immigrant families. Moreover, its section of the Hill had been regained by Yankee families 'from the vanguards of the lace-curtain Irish.' ' "We are barely," ' said Lowell's mother, ' "perched on the outer rim of the hub of decency." ' They lived in this house for three years, until Lowell's father left the Navy for a position with Lever Brothers, the beginning of an unsuccessful attempt to carve out a civilian career. So the house is a symbol as well of the father's inability to realize himself as a man, either professionally or in his family life; and Lowell's mother, insecure, somewhat hysterical, and unsympathetic to her husband's nature, is seen as the dominant household figure. Lowell says that his memory of the *'things'* in the house, unchangeably clear, is 'preserved by that motherly care that one either ignored or resented in his youth.' For these and other reasons, the relationship of masculine and feminine identities is a confused one in the associations of the house.

Though the house and the adults living and visiting there occupy most of our attention in '91 Revere Street,' Lowell himself as a small boy is the central figure. He is the observer throughout, though interpreted by himself grown a generation older. We see him doing unpleasant things or experiencing them — cheating another little boy, being cruel to one who had been his friend, bloodying others' noses, rejoicing in the disgrace of a charming little girl who proved incontinent in the classroom and then, in his 'excitement and guilt,' taking the sopping chair left empty when she fled. The school in which this event took place, he is careful to note, was as female-dominated as his home, for the upper eight grades were limited to girls. 'I wished I were an older girl. I wrote Santa Claus for a field hockey stick. To be a boy at Brimmer was to be small, denied, and weak.' Almost the only counter-note to the impression forced on the boy in so many ways, that it is a woman's world, is the overwhelming one that comes from his father's old friend Commander Billy 'Battleship Bilge' Harkness, who 'despite his rowdiness . . . breathed the power that would make him a vice-admiral and hero in World War II.' This figure stands out in too crude opposition to that of his father to have offered the boy any reassurance; instead, he aroused his resentment on behalf of his father, whose uncertainties and desire for his friend's approval made the son cringe.

In all these details, and in many others of like interest, the poet is really explaining his own personality as it will emerge in the 'Life Studies' group. The rejection of his father's life-style, and the acceptance of the guilt accompanying that rejection, must be shown in the full setting of their origins — only sufficient detail in several emotional dimensions can give conviction to these attitudes. The protagonist must revise his father's life, but that is something that all sons must do to a greater or lesser extent. Here, however, the process seems to the son more frightening and disloyal than usual, and he reports it as violent and as at least in part pathological. And so, in the prose-section, Lowell gives us the information that will account for his personality as shown in the poems and will to some degree justify it aesthetically. As we shall see, however, some of the 'background' information is reserved for the poems themselves. The two sections reinforce one another by presenting overlapping data and motifs in the necessarily different perspectives of direct autobiography and of lyric-dramatic poetry.

In the prose Lowell is a small boy, and though he describes himself as an unintellectual child his sensitivity is clear. The emotional difficulties of the adults around him, their passions and failures, their exciting habits of speech are the meat upon which his intense inwardness feeds. In the poems he is seen at various stages of his life from childhood to middle age, and the characterization is sharpened by his use, for example, of a word like 'manic' to suggest what he was like at the age of seven ('Commander Lowell *1887–1950*'):

> And I, bristling and manic,
> skulked in the attic,
> and got two hundred French generals by name,
> from *A* to *V* — from Augereau to Vandamme.
> I used to dope myself asleep,
> naming these unpronounceables like sheep.

The problem, then, in the work as a whole is to saturate it with a sense of objective reality while making it something more than merely a self-analytical case history. The book's saturation in detail is its chief means of avoiding sentimentality, for its feeling is obviously earned many times over. A corollary fact is that, because the poet deals so accurately with his parents' personalities and his own, he is able to bring his compassion and love to bear side by side with his more negative emotions in a humanly convincing way. We see the brutal anguish of the grown man, in the marriage poems and confession of his 'ill-spirit' that bring the book to its close, both as the result of the family situation and as something to be faced in itself without recourse to special pleading. The prose-section provides a matrix of psychological reality that pervades and illuminates the poems, although the poems exist independently within the matrix. The self-therapeutic dimension of this kind of poetic recapitulation of the relation between one's psychological past and present is unavoidable. What may be harder to see (for the poet as for the rest of us) is how the work gets beyond that dimension — a qualitative matter of its achievement of formal realization and beauty through the impersonal use of its highly personal elements.

Naturally, this is the common poetic task. Words are rooted in private association and take their subjective meaning from the matrix of private experience. (Hence, the importance of '91 Revere Street' and of the recovery of childhood consciousness both there and in the poems: they summon up the relevant associations to be shared with the reader as the poet himself shapes them into his formal structure, which is *his* means of repossessing them.) Words make the complex of subjective awareness 'publicly' available only when taken over by an aesthetic design that seems to transcend them by using them for its own purposes, 'impersonally.' The process repeats in a more encompassing way what happens at a primitive level when a word comes into being as a socially shared symbol of private experience. This is why hostility to formal 'experimentation' or to the artistic use of this or that kind of subject matter or speech is pointless. We can gauge the qualitative meaning of our consciousness only through the paradoxical aesthetic process by which the subjective life is 'tried on' for objective validity. The importance of concrete effects lies in the simplicity of testing their validity and in their rhetorical value as indications that the poet is responding to actuality and is keenly articulate. The importance of wit lies in its similar indication of his alertness to the logical relationships of reality. We are told in '91 Revere Street' that the boy Robert Lowell had the depressed feeling that 'men between the ages of six and sixty did nothing but meet new challenges, take on heavier responsibilities, and lose all freedom to explode.' The first of these phrases ('meet new challenges') is an ironic repetition of his mother's rationalizing explanation of Lowell senior's frequent loss of positions with various firms. The second ('take on heavier responsibilities') is of the same order, but adds the boy's own feeling of the cheerless weight of adult life to the irony of the echoed cliché. The third ('lose all freedom to explode') brings into the open the boy's stifled feeling and driving need for liberation. Altogether, the portion of a sentence I have quoted not only presents a fact about the boy's mental state but also *mimics* it. The self-deception and despair of the atmosphere are evoked through phrasing that reconstructs actual speech and potentially explosive repression.

The echoing of the actual speech of his family and their friends is an essential ingredient of *Life Studies*. In '91 Revere Street' Lowell does a great deal of direct quoting. Thus, he remembers his mother, urging his father to make the move out of the Navy that resulted in a pointless existence for him thereafter: ' "A *man* must make up his *own* mind. Oh Bob, if you are going to resign, do it *now* so I can at least plan for your son's *survival* and education on a single continent." ' Or his father, trying to win his friends' approval for the move: ' "I think I'll put my blues in mothballs and become a *cit* just to prove I still belong to the country. The directors of Lever Brothers' Soap in Cambridge . . . I guess they want me on their team." ' And Commander Harkness, the 'Billy' thus addressed, is heard on the subject of the family's famous literary relative, Amy Lowell:

> . . . He would point a stinking baby stogie at Mother.
> ''Ave a peteeto cigareeto, Charlotte,' he would crow.

> 'Puff on this whacking black cheroot, and you'll be a match for any reeking senorita *femme fatale* in the spiggotty republics, where blindness from Bob's bathtub hooch is still unknown. When you go up in smoke, Charlotte, remember the *Maine*. Remember Amy Lowell, that cigar-chawing, guffawing, senseless and meterless, multimillionheiress, heavyweight mascot on a floating fortress. Damn the *Patterns!* Full speed ahead on a cigareeto!'

Lowell uses remembered snatches of speech much more economically in the poems, but they are if anything more important than in the prose. As with so much else in the poems, they point up what has been established in the prose but absorb it into a mature speaking sensibility that carries it into a different world of statement:

> Each morning at eight-thirty,
> inattentive and beaming,
> loaded with his 'calc' and 'trig' books,
> his clipper ship statistics,
> and his ivory slide rule,
> Father stole off with the *Chevie*
> to loaf in the Maritime Museum at Salem.
> He called the curator
> 'the commander of the Swiss Navy.'
>
> Father's death was abrupt and unprotesting.
> His vision was still twenty-twenty.
> After a morning of anxious, repetitive smiling,
> his last words to Mother were:
> 'I feel awful.'

Here, in the concluding stanzas of 'Terminal Days at Beverly Farms,' we are not really any longer at the level of sheer memory, however significant for the author. The characterization has been purified. There is no reason to think it any less truthfully given than in the prose; but the structure is elegiac now, and the validity of the details of speech and personality depends on their appropriateness rather than on their literal accuracy. 'Calc,' 'trig,' and '*Chevie*' are familiar colloquialisms, but they also help characterize Father as an unsophisticated man who derives his security from external values. His little joke about the curator has the same effect, unoriginal but unmalicious as well. He is dependent on comforts that cannot save him: his new Chevrolet, his engineer's equipment, his 'twenty-twenty vision,' and — despite his two coronaries — his 'vitally trim' and 'newly dieted figure.' Of course, it is moving that the person so described should be the poet's father, but the pathos is largely independent of that fact save for our awareness of the intimacy informing the restrained adjectives of the closing stanza. Their restraint keeps our attention focused on Father's last words, which throw a new light back over the cheerful demeanor he has been showing to the world in this poem ever since the first stanza's ironically incantatory description:

> He smiled his oval Lowell smile,
> he wore his cream gabardine dinner-jacket,
> and indigo cummerbund.
> His head was efficient and hairless,
> his newly dieted figure was vitally trim.

In all these poems, the single words enclosed in quotation marks, the expressions out of common life or philistine vocabulary, and the longer quotations from remembered remarks contribute greatly to their dramatic flexibility and structural dynamics. The first poem of 'Life Studies,' for example, begins with a one-line speech, an outcry by young Robert at the age of five, which sets the poem going to the rhythm of natural speech:

> 'I won't go with you. I want to stay with Grandpa!'
> That's how I threw cold water
> on my Mother and Father's
> watery martini pipe dreams at Sunday dinner.

Lowell has the courage and right instinct to use the trite 'threw cold water' for the sake of naturalness, depending on the small initial explosion to absorb the major attention until the punning 'watery martini pipe dreams' picks up the tone. It should be unnecessary to point out that the 'naturalness' of such a passage as this one in 'My Last Afternoon with Uncle Devereux Winslow' is the result of its achieved artistry. The carefully weighted balance of line-lengths and sound-repetitions is calculated to avoid calling too forcible attention to itself. Thus, the succession of feminine endings, the triple rhyme of lines 2–4, and the initial rhymes of 'that's' and 'watery' are among a number of what I have called 'sunken' effects. When, in the succeeding lines of the stanza, the language becomes more elegantly evocative (though punctuated with momentarily homely notes), it still has the character of active, speech-based phrasing:

> . . . Fontainebleau, Mattapoisett, Puget Sound. . . .
> Nowhere was anywhere after a summer
> at my Grandfather's farm.
> Diamond-pointed, athirst and Norman,
> its alley of poplars
> paraded from Grandmother's rose garden

to a scarey stand of virgin pine,
scrub, and paths forever pioneering.

Each of the four poems in Part III of *Life Studies* makes a comparable use of quoted actual speech. 'Ford Madox Ford' begins with one of Ford's typical compulsive tall stories:

The lobbed ball plops, then dribbles to the cup. . . .
(a birdie Fordie!) But it nearly killed
the ministers. Lloyd George was holding up
the flag. He gabbled, 'Hop-toad, hop-toad, hop-toad!
Hueffer has used a niblick on the green;
it's filthy art, Sir, filthy art!'
You answered, 'What is art to me and thee?
Will a blacksmith teach a midwife how to bear?'
That cut the puffing statesman down to size,
Ford. You said, 'Otherwise,
I would have been general of a division.' Ah Ford!

Here we get the story as Ford told it, given to us without quotation marks until the dialogue Ford quotes is introduced. Lowell is sardonically — if affectionately, as the poem later shows — pretending to believe it. The irony is thus somewhat Chaucerian, at least until the poem's bitter ending. At any rate, the method allows the poet not only to quote but also to parody his subject, and to add his own strongly engaged voice as well without losing pace. In the other poems of this group, the central line in 'For George Santayana' is, again, a typical paradoxical witticism from the philosopher's conversation (' "There is no God and Mary is His Mother" '); the most effective passages in 'To Delmore Schwartz,' except for the brilliant imagistic comedy of the ending, are the wryly whimsical remarks of Schwartz himself; and 'Words for Hart Crane'—though actually *Lowell's* words—is set between quotation marks and full of colloquial turns. So the method has been established, actually, before the 'Life Studies' group itself comes to the foreground in the last, but crucial, part of the book. How much it is a method evolved for the specific uses of this book may be seen, first, in the occasional flashes of it in the earlier books when the context is similar to that of *Life Studies* and, second, in its virtual absence from Lowell's recent collection *For the Union Dead,* which for the most part puts the 'confessional' method firmly behind it.

We may usefully divide the 'Life Studies' group into five sections.* The first section, consisting of three poems, has mainly to do with the child's relation to his grandparents. 'My Last Afternoon with Uncle Devereux Winslow' introduces various motifs that cut through the whole sequence: the child's preference for his grandfather over his father and mother; psychoneurotic tendencies in the family; and an almost hysterically nostalgic pain at the loss of the past, epitomized in this instance in the lament for a young uncle that concludes the poem. After this fierce beginning, 'Dunbarton' (the title refers to the site of the family graveyard) takes up the theme of the boy's special relationship with his grandfather: 'He was my Father. I was his son.' The feeling of betrayal of the real father dramatized in the opening lines of the first poem ('"I won't go with you. I want to stay with Grandpa!"') is sustained in this poem. What would ordinarily seem a de-

* Lowell himself divides it into two more inclusive sections. Section I consists of the first eleven poems (family background and mental breakdown) and Section II of the concluding four (effect on his political experience, marriage, and ultimate relation to life).

lightful and normal relationship is given, if only whimsically, a pathological coloration:

> I saw myself as a young newt,
> neurasthenic, scarlet
> and wild in the wild coffee-colored water.
>
> In the mornings I cuddled like a paramour
> in my Grandfather's bed,
> while he scouted about the chattering greenwood stove.

'Grandparents,' which puts the relationship in another perspective, horror at the irredeemability of the past, brings this opening movement to a sharply nostalgic close.

The second movement, or section, of 'Life Studies' consists of six poems, all having to do with the poet's parents, particularly their deaths. The first of them, 'Commander Lowell *1887–1950*,' plunges us at once into the atmosphere of failure, neurosis, and shame remembered from the child's seventh year:

> There were no undesirables or girls in my set,
> when I was a boy at Mattapoisett—
> only Mother, still her Father's daughter.
> Her voice was still electric
> with a hysterical, unmarried panic. . . .

Most of the poem, however, centers on the father—his failure to impress his fellows in 'the mob of ruling-class Bostonians,' his failure to gain distinction either in the Navy or out of it, his 'piker speculations' that cost him more and more money, his loss of his wife's confidence, his remembered early promise when

> nineteen, the youngest ensign in his class,
> he was 'the old man' of a gunboat on the Yangtze.

'Commander Lowell,' taken by itself, seems full of condescension and contempt for 'poor Father,' 'smiling on all,' 'cheerful and cowed.' In 'Terminal Days at Beverly Farms,' which follows it, the odor of humiliation is even stronger, but is tempered by the same elegiac pain and compassion that were shown in the poem about the death of Lowell's Uncle Devereux Winslow. In this poem we see Commander Lowell at Beverly Farms after his second stroke — 'a two minute walk from the station' and 'half an hour by train from the Boston doctors.' His meekness is given a tragic dignity, and because the main source of pain in this poem is transferred from his failure as a man to the impersonal, invulnerable fact of his death, we see him as a victim of a universally sinister principle rather than as the cause of his son's psychosis. As we can see from the figures used to describe the realms of both nature and artifact, the objective world is now the true enemy:

> They had no sea-view,
> but sky-blue tracks of the commuters' railroad shone
> like a double-barrelled shotgun
> through the scarlet late August sumac,
> multiplying like cancer
> at their garden's border.

Two poignant afterbeats follow the finalities of these two poems. In 'Father's Bedroom' and 'For Sale' we linger over the neat details of the room in which the father died, over an inscription in one of his books that reminds us that he was a hero *manqué,* and over the 'empty, open, intimate' feeling of the cottage afterwards, 'waiting' to be sold. Quietly, at the very end of 'For Sale,' the camera shifts its focus to the mother:

Ready, afraid
of living alone till eighty,
Mother mooned in a window,
as if she had stayed on a train
one stop past her destination.

And the camera remains fixed on her through the next two poems, 'Sailing Home from Rapallo' and 'During Fever.' The first of these takes us to her death and burial four years later. The poet begins with his arrival in Italy to bring her body back to the cemetery in Dunbarton. The first stanza might have stood by itself, a brief 'Chinese' poem that at first seems unconvincing but is actually a sharp, affecting projection of a moment of realization:

Your nurse could only speak Italian,
but after twenty minutes I could imagine your final week,
and tears ran down my cheeks. . . .

Those tears are the only direct image of emotion in the poem. The next two stanzas present the gaudy colors of the *Golfo di Genova* coastline 'breaking into fiery flower' as the ship sails out in which 'Mother travelled first-class in the hold,' and then the freezing contrast of the family graveyard in midwinter, 'dour and dark against the blinding snowdrifts.' On the one hand,

The crazy yellow and azure sea-sleds
blasting like jack-hammers across
the *spumante*-bubbling wake of our liner. . . .

On the other hand,

A fence of iron spear-hafts
black-bordered its mostly Colonial grave-slates.

The dazzling opposition of two entirely different states of concrete existence would be too obvious an ironic effect were it not, in the first place, so anchored in Lowell's extraordinarily keen sense of place, and, more important, were it not so true to subjective experience in action. For this latter reason, as well, the overlay of still another kind of irony — that of the inescapable awareness of considerations of class and status, even in the wake of his mother's death — is absolutely, movingly relevant here. The mother, travelling 'first-class' in a '*Risorgimento* black and gold casket,' is all the more pathetic for this somehow ridiculous fact in the midst of a riotously beautiful nature. This elegiacally tinged absurdity summons up another. After he describes Dunbarton in winter with such Anglo-Saxon somberness, Lowell intrudes one last note on his father:

> The only 'unhistoric' soul to come here
> was Father, now buried beneath his recent
> unweathered pink-veined slice of marble.
> Even the Latin of his Lowell motto:
> *Occasionem cognosce,*
> seemed too businesslike and pushing here,
> where the burning cold illuminated
> the hewn inscriptions of Mother's relatives:
> twenty or thirty Winslows and Starks.
> Frost had given their names a diamond edge. . . .

A brief concluding stanza, paralleling the opening one, adds two further items to the list of absurdities. These are at a level of irony that is simply recognition of life's (or death's) indifference to pride of self or personality. Mother's coffin has 'grandiloquent' lettering, but the name is misspelled 'LOVEL.' Her body 'was wrapped like *panetone* in Italian tinfoil.' One might well ask how an elegiac poem on the death of one's mother could end with these grotesque little items. The reply must be either that the strictly elegiac portion is confined to the first three lines, or that the poem begins with pity and grief for the mother's pain and ends with pity and grief for her degradation when death has reduced her to a mere object that can be put in a package and mislabeled. But there is another consideration: the arbitrariness with which these admittedly relevant and accurate details of humiliation have been selected for special attention from early on in the poem. It *is* a poem of humiliation, and to this fact even the elegiac motive is subordinated. The psychological confession implicit in these grotesque juxtapositions, the suggestion of a psychotic supersensitivity, has been grafted onto the elegiac elements and has produced a different kind of poem. The true elegy 'lets go,' liberated by a reconciliation, grave yet ultimately buoyant, with the deep rhythms and meanings of existence. This poem does not let go, except in the sense of conceding the intrinsic meaninglessness of both social and private presumptions about the self. It will take the whole sequence to reach an affirmation at all comparable with that of the traditional elegy, and the terms of reference will be quite different.

'During Fever' rounds out this second movement of the sequence much as 'Grandparents' rounded out the first movement. It takes us into the present. The poet's little daughter is ill and apologetic for the fact (' "Sorry," she mumbles like her dim-bulb father, "sorry." ') The connection with 'her dim-bulb father's' humiliation at life's 'normal' sufferings illuminates a memory for him, and he addresses his mother in retrospect, recalling how

> as a gemlike undergraduate,
> part criminal and yet a Phi Bete,
> I used to barge home late. . . .

Often with unadulterated joy,
Mother, we bent by the fire
rehashing Father's character —
when he thought we were asleep,
he'd tiptoe down the stairs
and chain the door.

From this touching bit of family comedy the poem moves to a description of the mother's master-bedroom, with its three-colored 'nuptial bed' that was 'as big as a bathroom' — a description to be compared in its lush impression of womanly expectation with the sparse neatness and frustrated manly hopes evoked in 'Father's Bedroom.' Finally, we are taken in imagination (based again, though, on fact) to another scene and another, still earlier generation.

Born ten years and yet an aeon
too early for the twenties,
Mother, you smile
as if you saw your Father
inches away yet hidden, as when he groused behind a screen
over a National Geographic Magazine,
whenever young men came to court you
back in those settled years of World War One.
Terrible that old life of decency
without unseemly intimacy
or quarrels, when the unemancipated woman
still had her Freudian papá and maids!

The exclamation is both flippant and serious. Guilt and repression lie behind the protagonist's present discontents, and he has passed on the guilt, at least, to his little daughter. The mother fades out of the sequence, a textbook case who has brought forth yet another textbook case, who has perhaps carried the process forward unto yet another generation. We have had three innocent-seeming scenes, each with its sinister implications — a design made up of echoes, putting the whole matter of the generations into perspective.

The deaths of Lowell's parents occurred in 1950 and 1954, between his thirty-third and thirty-seventh birthdays, so that the time of the long second movement of 'Life Studies' actually overlaps with that of the concluding movements. The latter seem to take place later, however, because in them our attention is fixed on the poet's own adult life, without reference to his parents. What we may call the third movement consists of two poems ('Waking in the Blue' and 'Home after Three Months Away') about his confinement in a mental hospital and one ('Memories of West Street and Lepke') about his five-months imprisonment during the war as a conscientious objector. Two poems follow, forming a fourth unit. They are 'Man and Wife,' which seems to be about Lowell's second marriage, and ' "To Speak of Woe That Is in Marriage," ' which presents a tormented wife talking about her 'hopped up,' 'screwball' husband. The concluding poem in the sequence, 'Skunk Hour,' stands out independently. It provides a self-loathing close-up for the speaker and with it a dominating image both for his own psychological state and prospects and for the poetic process we have been brought through in this book. The transference of attention in these last six poems from the older figures to Lowell himself makes for great gains in immediacy and concentration — the effect is of having been subjected to successive waves of mounting violence.

If I may consider again the development of these six poems: 'Waking in the Blue' drops us abruptly into the world of the mental hospital. Lowell presents himself as an 'old-timer' there, one of a group of men of patrician ancestry ('thoroughbred mental cases') in their presumably exclusive sanatorium. Their attendants are Roman Catholics with crewcuts, some of them students, who are not altogether sympathetic:

> (There are no Mayflower
> screwballs in the Catholic Church.)

Here is class confrontation again, with an unresolved question of the kind raised by the comments on Mordecai Myers in '91 Revere Street.' Lowell is not free of the illusion of superiority deriving from his family background, but he gives it a special twist by associating it with susceptibility to corruption, degeneration, or hypersensitivity, as if to say to the *polloi:* 'I am more Baudelairean by heredity than you are.' Though assimilating to himself, through the identification of private with public suffering, the problems of the age, he pays little attention to the lives of ordinary men and women who may either experience the same things with as much meaning but in different form or, possibly, offer alternative possibilities if regarded with sufficient empathy. As a result, he also arrogates to himself the embodying through experience of our cultural direction and destiny. (Statistically speaking, there are more neurotic breakdowns in the less privileged classes than there are among the elite, and so the actual cultural situation is distorted by Lowell's assumptions.) I hope that, as before, the point I am making will be seen not as a personal criticism of the poet but as a characteristic assumption implicit in his poetry — true for *it,* contributing to its power and conviction, but not necessarily conclusive in its wisdom or objectivity. Nevertheless, take it for what it is; the bitter vision of 'Waking in the Blue' catapults us beyond the limitations of this assumption:

> Azure day
> makes my agonized blue window bleaker.
> Crows maunder on the petrified fairway.
> Absence! My heart grows tense
> as though a harpoon were sparring for the kill. . . .

'Home after Three Months Away' shows the poet home again after this three months' confinement. He is forty-one now, one of many significant little changes for him. Among others: the nurse attending his baby daughter, a 'lioness' who 'made the Mother cry,' is gone now; the tulips planted a year ago are deteriorating. These are signs of the passage of time while he simply marked time. But something like reassurance comes from the daughter's not having forgotten him —

> . . . After thirteen weeks
> my child still dabs her cheeks
> to start me shaving. When
> we dress her in her sky-blue corduroy,
> she changes to a boy,
> and floats my shaving brush
> and washcloth in the flush. . . .
> Dearest, I cannot loiter here
> in lather like a polar bear. . . .

Restoration from the psychological state in which confinement had been needed, in which 'blue' was associated with a metallic coldness, bleakness, and emptiness, and in which the patients each used 'a locked razor,' lies in these more domestic and gentle variations — the child's 'sky-blue corduroy,' for instance, and the recovered innocence of the ritual of shaving. Lowell's genius in the use of concrete detail is expressed not merely in an ability to create evocative external sense-impressions but also in the higher ability to give body to emotional statement. That is, he builds out an organic, three-dimensional sense of what it feels like physically to be in his skin and having his experiences. Thus, in describing his manic period in the preceding poem, he tells us that

> After a hearty New England breakfast,
> I weigh two hundred pounds
> this morning. Cock of the walk,
> I strut in my turtle-necked French sailor's jersey
> before the metal shaving mirrors. . . .

In 'Home after Three Months Away,' however, the manic phase is ended and he is grateful — in the tender, loving, and humorous fashion that we have seen — for the physical rapport with his little daughter, though his condition has dwindled into a just supportable depression:

> I keep no rank nor station.
> Cured, I am frizzled, stale and small.

'Memories of West Street and Lepke' is an important transitional poem, linked in character to the two just discussed by its literal subject matter but with a much wider frame of reference. In this poem, Lowell is still forty years old, and so the time is presumably shortly before he was committed to the mental hospital. But the period about which the poem is mainly concerned is a decade and a half earlier, when he was sent to prison as a conscientious objector. There is a curiously ambiguous effect in these shiftings and relationships of time. They suggest a simultaneity and interchangeableness of events. In the poem

Lowell is in a deceptively quiet moment during 'the tranquilized *Fifties*,' just before the breakdown that is the theme of the two preceding poems, and during this interval he is vividly possessed by the memory of what he calls the 'manic' state he was in when he made his wartime political gesture. He shared imprisonment with pimps, thugs, and murderers; and the experience is obviously not completely separate in his mind from that in the mental hospital, or for that matter from life in the 'outside world' either. The poem ends with a terrifying close-up of '*Murder Incorporated*'s Czar Lepke':

> there piling towels on a rack,
> or dawdling off to his little segregated cell full
> of things forbidden the common man:
> a portable radio, a dresser, two toy American
> flags tied together with a ribbon of Easter palm.
> Flabby, bald, lobotomized,
> he drifted in a sheepish calm,
> where no agonizing reappraisal
> jarred his concentration on the electric chair —
> hanging like an oasis in his air
> of lost connections. . . .

Czar Lepke certainly resembles the infantile types in the sanatorium, but whereas they have a political meaning only by furthest implication Lepke is given one by deliberately pointed language: 'segregated,' 'the common man,' 'two toy American flags,' 'agonizing reappraisal' (John Foster Dulles's much-satirized phrase). Violence, the reduction of the intelligence to silence, stupefied complacency — all the tendencies in American life against which Lowell and other poets mobilize their resources — are embodied in the terrible figure of the lobotomized leader of the murder syndicate. He stands, for the speaker, as a warning to the country and to the poet himself of possibilities within that may explode at any time. One cannot help thinking of Pound's *Mauberley,* but Lowell's indictment of a civilization is all the harsher for being so brutally, literally concrete. Oddly enough, the rhythmic movement is like that in Poem II of *Mauberley* (1920), in which Pound comes very close, despite the somewhat abstruse and 'difficult' character of the language, to writing a 'confessional' poem himself.

The two painful marriage poems that follow drop this wider reference to close in on a specific private relationship, that of husband and wife. 'Man and Wife' brings the whole background of *Life Studies* into view again in one concentrated opening line: 'Tamed by *Miltown,* we lie on Mother's bed.' The powerful rhyming couplets, in lines of raggedly uneven length, of most of the first stanza follow up this opening and sustain its implications. There is a suggestion that this couple has already been through three mad fits of the husband's and barely avoided a fourth such experience. It is actually a beautiful love poem despite this context, and Lowell's wit was never more evident than in his description of how he first fell in love with his wife. The 'shrill verve / of your invective' against the traditional South had won his love on a memorable evening at a friend's in Greenwich Village, and now her tirade against him in bed, 'loving, rapid, merciless,' excites his admiration again. Yet in another sense this is a humorous treatment of an exceptionally trying situation, and is counteracted by the bitter hopelessness and gross realism of ' "To Speak of Woe That Is in Marriage" ' — a speech invented for the wife of a man at once manic, alcoholic, and satyromanic:

My hopped up husband drops his home disputes,
and hits the streets to cruise for prostitutes,
free-lancing out along the razor's edge.
This screwball might kill his wife, then take the pledge.
Oh the monotonous meanness of his lust. . . .

Again, I shall not attempt to 'psychoanalyze' the verse but only to see it in the context of what has been given. The young man who falls in love with the girl because of her skill in invective and the 'hopped up husband' of the succeeding poem are variant reactions to the wife-ridden father, the failure who had lost all 'freedom to explode,' as we came to know him in '91 Revere Street' and in the preceding poems. These are only two clues among several to the structure of the sequence. The final poem, 'Skunk Hour,' concentrates superbly in its closing stanzas, through the image of the skunks, the motif of self-loathing that has had so many permutations in the sequence. It reminds us, too, of a subtler motif that has been present all along: the poet's power to survive and transcend what he feels to be the destructive, as well as disgusting, character of his own psyche. This latter motif is reinforced by a satirical summing up of the degenerate state of a specific New England community and of the poet's own sick soul 'one dark night.' At the nadir of morale, he looks down upon the town from a hilltop, and the skunk image takes over. Vivid in its own right, it gives us the key to the ultimate interaction between that dogged animal vitality on which everything ultimately depends and the constructive workings of imagination. The *poète maudit* finds a new justification in this image, which points to a more objective artistic exploration in the future:

nobody's here—

only skunks, that search
in the moonlight for a bite to eat.
They march on their soles up Main Street:
white stripes, moonstruck eyes' red fire
under the chalk-dry and spar spire
of the Trinitarian Church.

I stand on top
of our back steps and breathe the rich air —
a mother skunk with her column of kittens swills the garbage
pail.
She jabs her wedge-head in a cup
of sour cream, drops her ostrich tail,
and will not scare.

Looking back over *Life Studies* for its stylistic dynamics, we can see that Lowell has made sophisticated use of the whole modern tradition of the poetic sequence. This tradition includes as its main representatives *Song of Myself, Spoon River Anthology, Hugh Selwyn Mauberley* and the *Cantos, The Waste Land* and *Four Quartets, The Bridge,* and *Paterson.* Lowell has deliberately forgone certain rhetorical heights that his forerunners stormed, and some of their more obvious exploitation of myth (and myth-making) as well. The opening poem, 'Beyond the Alps,' though it hints of these heights and this exploitation, presents the protagonist on a train leaving Rome and its associations behind: 'I left the City of God where it belongs.' Not only the City of God, but the Classical past — 'Minerva, the miscarriage of the brain' — is put behind him as he speeds toward his own theme of the disintegration of the modern embodied in his own life's history:

> Now Paris, our black classic, breaking up
> like killer kings on an Etruscan cup.

Nowhere in *Life Studies* is there eloquence for its own sake, or abstractly developed religious or philosophical symbolism. Lowell had displayed both in his earlier work, but this sequence is stripped down to the immediately relevant. The only, mild exceptions are the two opening poems, which suggest fairly simply the broader historical and cultural relevance of his close-ups of himself and his times, and the four 'documentary' interpretations of a few other modern writers, whose careers throw a clear light on the problems of Lowell himself. The 'myth' that Lowell creates is that of an America (and a contemporary civilization generally) whose history and present predicament are embodied in those of his own family and epitomized in his own psychological experience. It is easy to see how in so doing he parallels some of the important implications of Whitman, Pound, Eliot, Crane, and Williams, and also how he has received clues from these writers' most 'confessional' moments and from Masters's characters at their most disillusioned and nervously disturbed.

But though the stripped-down quality of the work limits its range in one sense, Lowell's virtuosity is such that we get a wide range indeed of effects, most of them functioning appropriately according to what is needed at the given point in the sequence. As his basic formal framework, he tends toward a free use of the heroic couplet, giving the rhymes a hammering emphasis that is supported by concrete, active verbs and well-placed alliteration. The stiffness and straining that often result do mar the earlier poems, and even in *Life Studies* the rhythm can run away with the feeling. In only one poem, though — 'The Banker's Daughter' — does this runaway effect take over for very long. It is, indeed, a dramatic monologue in the earlier style, though it serves, as I have suggested, to broaden the context of allusion in the sequence. It serves, too, to foreshadow the brief, intense ' "To Speak of Woe That Is in Marriage," ' for it too has to do with an unspeakably brutal marriage relationship. The latter poem is equally emphatic and rhyme-dominated, but its brevity, simplicity, and colloquialism give it a far more natural and flexible character. The off-rhymes with which it begins and ends, and its intelligent placing of caesuras, as well as the excitement of what goes on *within* the lines (the sensuous, racy, suffering diction, and the speed of the idiomatic thinking), keep our attention on the whole sense and feeling as it moves along, rather than on the form apart from them. Even when the alliteration and rhymes are most effective, Lowell succeeds in keeping first things foremost:

> My hopped up husband drops his home disputes,
> and hits the streets to cruise for prostitutes,
> free-lancing out along the razor's edge.

Much of the power of these poems derives from Lowell's ability to employ these fundamental resources explosively or (to change the metaphor) to hold them in reserve like a taut bow ready to release the arrow. But given this ability, he modulates his effects in practice in many ways. The third poem, 'Inauguration Day: January 1953,' is in short, four-stress lines, with the rhyme-scheme close to that of a Petrarchan sonnet. The first stanza, of nine lines, rises out of a depressed picture of the mechanical life of New York City in winter to an ironic mimicry of heroic motifs from the past:

> Cyclonic zero of the word,
> God of our armies, who interred
> Cold Harbor's blue immortals, Grant!
> Horseman, your sword is in the groove!

The second stanza, of five lines, begins with an enormous letdown: 'Ice, ice. Our wheels no longer move.' It ends with a bitter taunt to the nation and to President Eisenhower, elected to office at the height of the cold war and in the depths of the national paralysis of morale marked by the influence of Senator Joseph McCarthy:

> and the Republic summons Ike,
> the mausoleum in her heart.

'A Mad Negro Soldier Confined at Munich' follows, speeding manically after the subtly evoked depression of 'Inauguration Day.' Here there is no 'pure music' (even in a form of mockery). It is a highly colloquial dramatic monologue. With one dubious exception, the rhymes are all exact. The verbs are almost all highly charged — 'floored,' 'punch,' 'fumes,' 'squawked' ('lieutenants squawked like chickens in her skirts'), and a half-dozen more of the same order. Stanzas two, three, and four gain enormous speed and pressure by the omission of caesuras and by the language used to show the sexual dimension of the speaker's dangerously excited condition. The metaphors of electric power in the fifth stanza bring this movement to its climax:

> Oh mama, mama, like a trolley-pole
> sparking at contact, her electric shock —
> the power-house! . . . The doctor calls our roll —
> no knives, no forks. We file before the clock. . . .

With equal swiftness, and without transition, the voice takes on a sophisticated but deadly ferocity in the final stanza. It has become the poet's voice speaking for the Negro soldier as later in the sequence it will speak for Hart Crane and still later, in the asylum and prison poems, for Lowell in his own person. (In some important respects, incidentally, John Berryman's *77 Dream Songs,* published in 1964, seems to pick up cues from this poem — especially in its assumption of the tone, and its inconsistent use of the idiom of American Negro speech and its shifting to an alternative self within what is presented as a continuous speech, in quotation-marks, by a single speaker.)

After this introductory group of poems, as we have seen, the prose-section '91 Revere Street' transfers the spotlight to the poet himself, in the setting of his early family life. We have already examined '91 Revere Street' in some detail, and I shall content myself now with a single observation having to do with the use of poetic effects in this section. These come mostly toward the end, in the songs and doggerel humor of Commander Billy Harkness, and in some of his boisterously metaphorical and self-indulgent prose. As the protagonist's embarrassment and shame, on his father's behalf, come more and more into the foreground, these forays of Captain Billy's are more and more in evidence. They add up to the drowning of Lowell senior's deeper but unrealized sensitivity as a man by the extrovert virility of his successful friend who, incidentally and innocently, is at the same time deriding the life of sensibility and its poetic manifestation in particular. Here we have an epitome of the alienating process. The four poems that follow, about Ford, Santayana, Schwartz (and Lowell himself), and Crane, show four results of this process, in a series of subjectivized documentary presentations.

The most brilliantly manipulated of these is 'To Delmore Schwartz,' which fuses casually the compassionate and witty comment and narrative of the poems on Ford and Santayana (with their equally casual yet deft handling of rhyme, sound, and line) with a wild comedy and pain and a more telling imagery. It swings masterfully between shorter and longer lines, depending on the need of the moment, and at the very end breaks into a strange imagist poem, rhythmically tight yet in free verse, with cleverly placed rhymes. The changes of voice — Lowell's own, Schwartz's, Wordsworth's, and then Lowell's again in another mood — make for the liveliest dynamics in the book, encompassing the widest range of emotional tones. After it we have the sonnet 'Words for Hart Crane,' far more concentrated and angry in its passion, in its 'alienated' derangement of a traditional form, and in its piling up of defiantly self-castigating detail.

The fifteen poems of Part IV ('Life Studies' proper) show a similar progression, in general, from a slower, more casually anecdotal, though always moving, style to the highly charged style of the closing pieces. The whole progression is in a sense foreshadowed in the four sections of 'My Last Afternoon with Uncle Devereux Winslow': the leisurely opening section; the bemused second section, so brief and 'odd' in its final effect but still in tune with the first part; the poignant close-up of Great Aunt Sarah in the third section, a little like Masters but more piquantly vivid than his portraits usually are; and then the terrifying ending, in which we see the dying young uncle through the eyes of the five-year old child, guilty and omniscient as 'Agrippina in the Golden House of Nero.' The final fourteen lines are a triumph of projection of this vision. The rigid parallelism has the quality of a black-magic incantation; what appears at first to be humorous description is actually a hair-raising evocation of an apparition, or at least of a living man so near death that he might almost be a wax figure:

He was as brushed as Bayard, our riding horse.
His face was putty.
His blue coat and white trousers
grew sharper and straighter.
His coat was a blue jay's tail,
his trousers were solid cream from the top of the bottle.
He was animated, hierarchical,
like a ginger snap man in a clothes-press.
He was dying of the incurable Hodgkin's disease. . . .
My hands were warm, then cool, on the piles
of earth and lime,
a black pile and a white pile. . . .
Come winter,
Uncle Devereux would blend to the one color.

The next poem in which this kind of 'strangeness' is matched, with a similar grim, climactic effect, is 'Memories of West Street and Lepke.' Both poems prepare us for the startling ending of 'Skunk Hour,' though not for the paradoxical confidence in the future that is part of the picture of the garbage-swilling mother skunk. Lowell has rung many changes within the clearly defined formal range he has allowed himself. I have tried to show enough of these to suggest the intimate relationship between the minutiae of these changes and what is going on in the sequence as a whole. *Life Studies* is perhaps the most functionally shaped and continuously communicative of the great poetic sequences.

2. LOWELL'S NONCONFESSIONAL POETRY

'Writing,' said Robert Lowell in accepting the National Book Award for *Life Studies* in 1960, 'is neither transport nor technique. My own owes everything to a few of our poets who have tried to write directly about what mattered to them, and yet to keep faith with their calling's tricky, specialized, unpopular possibilities for good workmanship.' In a private letter he had written: 'I know what my book intends and what went into its making. Its final character is another matter. I have no way of telling whether there was enough energy and skill behind the projectile to carry it home. Something not to be said again was said. I feel drained, and know nothing except that the next outpouring will have to be unimaginably different — an altered style, more impersonal matter, a new main artery of emphasis and inspiration. Such, such the joy and despair of our profession!'

What I have been trying to show is precisely how *Life Studies* carries through the double program stated in the acceptance speech and implied in the way Lowell wrote about his book some months after it was published. From our consideration, I hope, it will be clear that despite the manifestly intimate importance to him of his subject matter the objective artistry present at every point is at least equally vital. It is, in fact, implicit from the beginning as the shaping motivation that drives the work toward self-transcendence — that is, toward an aesthetic realization that goes beyond the literal subject matter in its resolution. I have also tried to show something harder to state and to demonstrate, the inseparability of the two aspects of the program. The poet's hot pursuit of the realities of his own nature — his 'breakdown' of the family's past and of his childhood relation to it, and his slow reconstruction of an adult self from the depths of that analysis — are aesthetic in character despite their autobiographical relevance. The state of vulnerable but poised openness toward which this pursuit aims has self-destruction as its worst possibility and reintegration on a deeper level as its promise.

To a poet in search of such an openness, the psychological and artistic meanings come together beyond a certain point; and yet he remains sufficiently apart to subordinate the former meaning to the latter one. I was struck, in a conversation with Sylvia Plath in 1960, with her absolute certainty about the transcendence of this kind to be achieved through Lowell's methods, if only one were dauntless enough and gifted enough. And after her posthumous *Ariel,* with its suicidal leap toward a perfection of death-realization, had appeared in 1965, Lowell wrote to me: 'Maybe, it's an irrelevant accident that she actually carried out the death she predicted . . . but somehow her death is part of the imaginative risk. In the best poems, one is torn by saying, "This is so true and lived that most other poetry seems like an exercise," and then one can back off and admire the dazzling technique and invention. Perfect control, like the control of a skier who avoids every death-trap until reaching the final drop.' I am reminded of the passage in Pasternak's memoirs on the suicides of the Russian poets, and of the career of Hart Crane and its relation to his *Voyages.* Lowell is the master who has survived the 'imaginative risk' both in his life and in his art. The reasons are too complex and private to be sought here; but his insistence on remembering the impersonal motivation of his art, even as the private memory threatened to sweep him away from it, made the difference in *Life Studies.*

This self-discipline is manifest in *Lord Weary's Castle* and in *The Mills of the Kavanaughs,* although in these books the motivations that break loose in *Life Studies* are stifled both by the elaborate style and by the characters and situations of the supposed speakers. Though *Lord Weary's Castle* received extravagant praise on its first appearance, it has become dated rather quickly through its 'literary' and 'complex' mannerisms after the example of such post-Eliot writers as Allen Tate and Robert Penn Warren. Most of its poems that show the most passionate conviction are tendentious as well. They attempt heroically but also awkwardly to weld Christian symbolism, social criticism, and an anguished sense of life under unbearable pressure (sometimes deriving from an 'internalized' sense of the pervasive guilt and foulness of men, sometimes out of sheer horror at the war). The first stanza of 'The Dead in Europe' will illustrate Lowell's vices and virtues at this stage. The virtues do make themselves felt, because of the sheer energy that organized the feeling.

> After the planes unloaded, we fell down
> Buried together; unmarried men and women;
> Not crown of thorns, not iron, not Lombard crown,
> Not grilled and spindle spires pointing to heaven
> Could save us. Raise us, Mother, we fell down
> Here hugger-mugger in the jellied fire:
> Our sacred hearth in our day was our curse.

Within this symbol-burdened rhetoric there is a lean, muscular style struggling to be free. It does begin to free itself in sections of these poems, especially the first part of 'The Quaker Graveyard in Nantucket,' despite the overloaded allusions there to *Moby-Dick* and the legend of Orpheus. Lowell's descriptive and narrative skill reveals itself fully in this poem, though he has brought it closer to home in later work. Compare the straightforward syntax and the literal detail of the following lines with the grammatical distortions and the shifting symbolism of the passage from 'The Dead in Europe.'

A brackish reach of shoal off Madaket, —
The sea was still breaking violently and night
Had steamed into our North Atlantic fleet,
When the drowned sailor clutched the drag-net. Light
Flashed from his matted head and marble feet. . . .
The corpse was bloodless, a botch of reds and whites,
Its open, staring eyes
Were lustreless dead-lights
Or cabin-windows on a stranded hulk. . . .

The purity of these lines is a triumph of Lowell's ear and eye, working together so exquisitely that there is no room for symbolical clogging. 'The drowned sailor' is perhaps a distant note from 'The Waste Land.' If so, it is an aesthetically valid recollection evoked solely by the music of the immediate context and entirely dominated by it. The beautifully distributed echoings and re-echoings of the sounds, and the contraction and expansion of the rhythmic units indicated by marks of punctuation and by line-endings, are organically inseparable from the succession of visual and kinesthetic effects. Nothing needs to be added to enhance our sense of the significance of what is shown; it is all there in the straightforward presentation — the terrible and strange character of the death; the human self reduced to sculptured imitation of life in action, and then to a pattern of colors; the relation of man to chaotic nature. It is toward this kind of achievement that Lowell turns in *For the Union Dead,* but this time with the conscious purpose of gaining a new objectivity based on the subordination of his symbol-seeking and autobiographical preoccupations.

Elsewhere in *Lord Weary's Castle,* we can see poems that foreshadow *Life Studies.* I have already noted one of them, 'Mary Winslow,' and suggested that in it Lowell is using private memory and a certain informality of tone, as well as his own special sort of compassionate irony, in ways comparable with his later methods though stiffer in movement and over-encrusted with historical ironies and with contrived allusions and emblems. It is instructive, for instance, to see how, in the two-poem sequence called 'The First Sunday in Lent,' he begins with a fairly simple, clear picture of a March scene from his window, then digresses rhetorically for a moment, and then, in the second stanza, introduces a 'confessional' touch:

> This is the fifth floor attic where I hid
> My stolen agates and the cannister
> Preserved from Bunker Hill. . . .

We are very soon led away, however, from the concrete and personal world sketched in rather beautifully in this stanza. The third stanza takes us to Troy and the Garden of Eden, whence we never return. As for the second poem in this sequence, its locus is a realm of moral and religious allegory far removed from the initial scene. The four-part 'In Memory of Arthur Winslow,' though it occasionally touches a nerve of reality resembling that of *Life Studies,* suffers from the same tendency to lose itself in rhetoric. So, at the very end, does 'Winter in Dunbarton,' but it does, in a minimal fashion, catch some of the sadness of the great 'family' poems of *Life Studies,* through its concentration on the death of a cat —

> . . . Belle, the cat that used to rat
> About my father's books, is dead. All day
> The wastes of snow about my house stare in

Through idle windows at the brainless cat;
The coke-barrel in the corner whimpers. . . .

Three poems in the book come still closer to *Life Studies*. One of them, 'Buttercups,' went almost unnoticed amid the swelling apostrophes and appassionata effects of *Lord Weary's Castle*. The intensity of recollection from childhood in this poem clashes somewhat with its quiet whimsicality, but it could readily have been fitted into the sequence nevertheless. A second poem, 'In the Cage,' foreshadows in its first half the prison and asylum poems of the later book, though the voice of the overly learned preacher takes over at the end. Finally, the longish 'Between the Porch and the Altar,' another sequence, approaches the kind of art we find in *Life Studies* in its guilt-laden, family-centered, sexually self-conscious drive. It is not autobiographical, and it is marred by the usual half-precious reaching after religious portentousness and by the inexorably rhyming couplets. But we can foresee the stripped-down flexibility of *Life Studies* in its four passionate movements, three of them in monologue form.

This last poem, 'Between the Porch and the Altar,' seems a truer start toward the formal realizations of *Life Studies* than the poems of Lowell's next book, *The Mills of the Kavanaughs*. The poem in that book which resembles it most is 'Her Dead Brother,' which centers on a woman's memories of an incestuous involvement. All these poems — there are only seven, though the title-poem is very long — are monologues, and most of them present women speaking of complex marital and sexual relationships. At this stage, Lowell is still overloading his poems with symbolism and allusions based on religion, on the Puritanical traditions and the general history of New England, and on an unresolved problem of creating protagonists through whom he can speak of his preoccupations. We may take his explanatory note at the head of the title-poem as an example of the impossibly cumbersome apparatus some of these poems require:

> An afternoon in the fall of 1943; a village a little north of Bath, Maine. Anne Kavanaugh is sitting in her garden playing solitaire. She pretends that the Bible she has placed in the chair opposite her is her opponent. At one end of the garden is the grave of her husband, Harry Kavanaugh, a naval officer who was retired after Pearl Harbor. The Kavanaughs are a Catholic family that came to Maine in the 17th century. Their house is called *Kavanaugh;* it is on a hill, and at its foot, there is a mill pond, and by it a marble statue of Persephone, the goddess who became a queen by becoming queen of the dead. The Abnakis, or Penobscots, are almost extinct Maine Indians, who were originally converted by the French. Anne comes of a poor family. She was adopted by the Kavanaughs many years before she married. Most of the poem is a revery of her childhood and marriage, and is addressed to her dead husband.

The poem itself begins:

> The Douay Bible on the garden chair
> Facing the lady playing solitaire
> In blue-jeans and a sealskin toque from Bath
> Is *Sol,* her dummy. There's a sort of path
> Or rut of weeds that serpents down a hill
> And graveyard to a ruined burlap mill. . . .

The compulsive need to repossess a vast complex of particular details suggested both by the prose and by these opening lines is one basis of Lowell's power. The details illuminate a personality and a social milieu, but they have also considerable magnetism as emphatically remembered observations. Through their absolute conviction, Lowell (paralleling in his practice an aim of the authors of the *Lyrical Ballads*) encourages himself and the reader to press into the realm of dream and reverie. Anne's memory of her husband is not a simple one; mingled with 'actual' recollections are vivid, psychologically revealing dreams, recent and long past. Erotic motifs enter, by way of her dreams but also by way of the mythical tradition involving Persephone, who learned love in the realm of the dead. Fantasy and vision enter into most of these poems, most economically (and piercingly) in 'Her Dead Brother,' but to great effect as well in the title-poem and in 'Thanksgiving's Over.' Again, Lowell prefaces this last poem as though it were a play:

> Thanksgiving night, 1942: a room on Third Avenue. Michael dreams of his wife, a German-American Catholic, who leapt from a window before she died in a sanatorium. The church referred to in the first and last stanzas is the Franciscan church on 31st Street.

The dead wife's speech is full of reproach and misery, and in the course of it we learn Michael's guilt at his mixed motives in sending her off to the asylum. (Sometimes the language suggests that this poem was a source for Sylvia Plath's 'Daddy.') The climax is the terrifying vision Michael's dream gives him of a lost soul whose suicide has left them both forever bereft of all hope:

> 'You are a bastard, Michael, aren't you? *Nein,*
> Michael. It's no more valentines.' Her hand
> Covered her eyes to cage

Their burning from the daylight. Sleep dispelled
The burden of her spirit. But the cars
Rattled my window. *Where am I to go?* She yelled:
'Let go my apron!' And I saw them shine,
Her eyeballs — like a lion at the bars
Across my open window — like the stars!

As an unresolved image of irrevocable guilt, this hysterical projection is a perfect 'objective correlative' for the emotional turmoil behind all the earlier poems. But it remains an isolated moment, whereas in *Life Studies* the poet's use of his literal self within the curve of fate of his own total experience makes the whole sequence, and each complete poem within it, a complex correlative capable of actual resolution. One of the poems in *The Mills of the Kavanaughs,* 'David and Bathsheba in the Public Garden,' presents interesting evidence of the 'unresolved' character of the work of this volume. Lowell rewrote the poem later and printed the new version in *For the Union Dead* as 'The Public Garden.' His prefatory note about it observes that 'it is a recasting and clarification of an old confusing poem.' The changed title indicates the nature of the clarification: a whole Biblical framework, with motifs of adultery and betrayal flying in the air as thick as the October leaves of the poem, has been cut away. What remains is a nostalgic memory on the lovers' part of an 'Eden' they experienced earlier in the year; otherwise, all is evocation through the sights and sounds of the public garden. There is a vague sense of guilt, but the main feeling is of a passion that has guttered out with the waning of the year.

We drowned
in Eden, while Jehovah's grass-green lyre
was rustling all about us in the leaves

that gurgled by us, turning upside down . . .
The fountain's failing waters flash around
the garden. Nothing catches fire.

This revision is evidence that for Lowell the process of 'recasting and clarification' has continued beyond *Life Studies*. *Life Studies* was the most remarkable poetic sequence to appear since Hart Crane's *The Bridge* and William Carlos Williams's *Paterson*. It may well stand as Lowell's chief accomplishment. At the same time, it presented Lowell himself so vulnerably and humiliatingly that only his extraordinary gifts enabled him to transcend the hysteria behind it. The transcendence made for a revolutionary achievement, but of a sort that can never be repeated by the same poet. In *For the Union Dead,* we are shown that for Lowell at least there is a further way, closer to the 'main stream.' To maintain indefinitely the violent pace of *Life Studies* would be to cultivate a poetry that not only repeated itself but also fed on, and encouraged, suicidal madness. Instead, beyond a certain point at least, Lowell has been working free of the intolerable burden of his self-laceration. The problem is to hold on meanwhile to what he has gained in poetic conception (the painfully alert sensibility alive to the pressure of its own anxieties and those of the age) and in its embodiment in a brilliantly improvised formal technique. We can see in this book how valuable for him have been his translations from poets like Montale and Pasternak (printed in *Imitations,* 1961). They were invaluable in their own right and also in helping him to isolate and use in new ways certain qualities of the earlier work, such as its wry humor and irony. Thus, the boisterous poem to his first wife, 'The Old Flame,' is for him really a gay poem despite the picture of the tormented couple's 'quivering and fierce' life in Maine, 'simmering like wasps in our tent of books.' At the same time, he can project as beautifully as ever that peculiar identification of inward anguish with the public ills of the nuclear age that is the idiom of his genius. Thus (to quote from it again), 'Fall, 1961':

> Our end drifts nearer,
> the moon lifts,
> radiant with terror. . . .
>
> A father's no shield
> for his child.
> We are like a lot of wild
> spiders crying together,
> but without tears. . . .

I would note especially, however, the poems in which something 'quieter' is going on, among them 'Water,' 'The Mouth of the Hudson,' 'The Lesson,' 'Law,' 'The Severed Head,' and 'The Flaw.' In many of these (as in the revised poem 'The Public Garden') everything is put into the concentrated evocation of a scene, within which is locked a tragically relevant personal and historical complex of meaning as well. Perhaps the single most original and surprising piece is the bizarre dream-poem 'The Severed Head,' with its overtones from Crane's 'Passage' and from Dante and the 'familiar compound ghost' episode in 'Little Gidding.' The poetic courage of these new explorations in search of a greater impersonality is to be expected of the man who was able to face the demands that *Life Studies* laid on both his psychic and his artistic resources. As yet, we are only at the beginning of the process, and Lowell has been strengthening himself for its future unfolding, perhaps, through his recent writing for the theater. This evolution, it must be admitted, not only suggests that 'confessional' poetry was an impermanent but indispensable phase of Lowell's development, but indicates as well that only a comparable deployment of energies and resources would justify another poet's trying the same thing. Nothing could be more sterile and obviously self-deceptive than the use of a 'confessional' mannerism in a trivial or immature way. In other words, the method is so demanding, and must be so idiosyncratic in its execution, that its seductiveness may well turn out to be disastrous to others who lack Lowell's very great strengths.

NOTE:

Lowell's latest volume, *Near the Ocean* (1967), appeared just as corrected page-proofs of *The New Poets* were being sent to press. *Near the Ocean* consists of the title sequence (five poems), a brief elegy for Theodore Roethke, a highly private short poem of desolate reminiscence, and a series of free translations from Horace, Juvenal, Dante, Quevedo, and Gongora. Somewhat mandarin in tone, the volume continues the modulation toward a more impersonal style. Indeed, most of the title sequence is unusually 'cool' and contemplative — as much so, at any rate, as Lowell can ever allow himself to be. In the main, the volume is an afterbeat of *Imitations* and *For the Union Dead.*

III
Other Confessional Poets

1. SYLVIA PLATH

On July 30, 1965, the Third Programme of the British Broadcasting Corporation carried a discussion of confessional poetry by a number of poets and critics. It was notable that, while the poems assigned for discussion included two that were genuinely confessional in the special sense we have been developing, the others were so only peripherally. Lowell's 'Skunk Hour' and Sylvia Plath's 'Lady Lazarus' were true examples because they put the speaker himself at the center of the poem in such a way as to make his psychological vulnerability and shame an embodiment of his civilization. At its lowest point of morale, Lowell's poem presents him as for the moment a *voyeur* suffering from a sickness of will and spirit that makes him, literally, lower than the skunks that take over the poem at the end. Sylvia Plath's poem presents the author in the midst of what proved to be her final, and finally successful, suicide attempt. She sees herself as a skilled suicide-artist whose self-loathing the sadistic and voyeurist audience, easily envisioned as the Nazi-tending aspects of the civilization, appreciates all too well. It is perhaps begging the question to suggest that a genuine confessional poem has to be superbly successful artistically if it is to achieve this fusion of the private and the culturally symbolic, but it must at any rate be far more highly charged than the usual poem.

The other four poems discussed by the BBC critics lacked this combination of characteristics. One was Elizabeth Jennings's 'The Night-Mare,' in which the nightmare is not described in detail but is remembered as a psychic experience that would surely prove significant if the speaker were 'laid upon a couch' and psychoanalyzed. Another, 'A Last Poem to My Wife,' is a diatribe by Edwin Bronk against his wife's religious beliefs as a 'dying god' she carries about in her womb. A third was a well-known and rather lovely poem of W. D. Snodgrass's, 'The Operation,' about an operation and the sensations aroused in him by his weakness afterwards. A fourth was Anne Sexton's 'Music Swims Back to Me,' in which the speaker is a woman in an asylum. The reasons behind the producer's choice of pieces seem self-evident: the neurosis implied in Elizabeth Jennings's poem, and her allusion to the analyst's couch; the violation of privacy involved in Bronk's disgusted excoriation of his wife; the fact that Snodgrass and Miss Sexton have been disciples of Lowell's and that her poem, at least, has to do with madness and the asylum. But of these four poems only 'Music Swims Back to Me' can seriously be conceived as confessional. I would not actually so classify it, for it comes closer to the kind of dramatic monologue with a highly melodic strain that we associate with Horace Gregory's work than to the immediately self-revelatory writing of Lowell. (Though because of her other work one hardly doubts that the author bases the speaking character on herself, nothing in the poem specifically points to this conclusion.) One can find many poems of a similar intensity in the past, and with a similar high-pitched anguish. On the other hand, it would be downright pedantic to rule it out entirely, though the absence of any critical 'cultural' dimension is an important consideration. Even Snodgrass's poem, almost purely a musical construction of sensations, sounds, and visual effects, comes closer to the type in this respect.

But the transforming energy of Sylvia Plath's 'Lady Lazarus' is, like that of 'Skunk Hour,' something else entirely than all these private notations. The slow release of this energy, after the self-mocking 'I've done it again' with which the poem begins, builds up in a rocking movement that becomes more powerful as the poem proceeds. At the beginning the speaker is not only mocking but describing herself literally. At the end, having pushed into the depths of her hatred of the whole matrix of family, cannibalistic erotic love, and society that she is destroying symbolically by destroying herself, she promises herself a rebirth. The rebirth is couched as a threat: she will rise in her demonic fury from the grave; she is a witch who 'eats men.'

'Lady Lazarus,' like many of the other poems of the volume *Ariel* (1965), is written out of a strange kind of terror, the calm center of hysteria, the triumphant surge of affirmative projection that comes with a clear perception of despair by an energetically creative spirit. 'These new poems of mine,' wrote Sylvia Plath in an unpublished typescript, 'have one thing in common. They were all written at about four in the morning — that still, blue, almost eternal hour before cockcrow, before the baby's cry, before the glassy music of the milkman, settling his bottles.' That is, at any rate, the symbolic scene of their creation. Some of her comments on the particular poems in the same typescript (prepared for a radio broadcast that was never delivered) give a comparable impression of her sense of an ordered setting or consciousness of motivating elements within which the paradoxically doughty terror of the poems is framed. Of 'Lady Lazarus': 'The speaker is a woman who has the great and terrible gift of being reborn. The only trouble is, she has to die first. She is the phoenix, the libertarian spirit, what you will. She is also just a good, plain, very resourceful woman.' Of 'Death & Co.' (to be discussed shortly): 'This poem . . . is about the double or schizophrenic nature of death — the marmoreal coldness of Blake's death mask, say, hand in glove with the fearful softness of worms, water and the other katabolists. I imagine these two aspects of death as two men, two business friends, who have come to call.' Of 'Daddy': 'Here is a poem spoken by a girl with an Electra complex. Her father died while she thought he was God. Her case is complicated by the fact that her father was also a Nazi and her mother very possibly part Jewish. In the daughter the two strains marry and paralyze each other — she has to act out the awful little allegory once over before she is free of it.' In each of these descriptions we see the confessional being given external order by an artist's balancing of the elements involved, even though the active element in the poems is the suicidal urge and purpose in which they are caught up. In no instance does the poet confine her account of the poem to the interpretation of a purely idiosyncratic psychological state.

Sylvia Plath's range of technical resources was narrower than Robert Lowell's, and so, apparently, was her capacity for intellectual objectivity. As a highly organized woman, intensely absorbed by her children and by the emotional problems of her marriage — 'a good, plain, very resourceful woman,' as she says — the path she took as a poet was perhaps predictable. She chose, if that is the word, what seems to me the one alternative advance position to Lowell's along the dangerous confessional way, that of literally committing her own predicaments in the interests of her art until the one was so involved in the other that no return was possible. It was the old romantic fallacy, if you will, of confusing motive and art, or the real with the ideal. But in this instance the conception has no real meaning because the long, escalating drive toward suicide and the period of extraordinary creativity (comparable in its way to the brief, miraculous period of Keats's most fruitful writing) actually coincided, or were at least two functions of the same process. The commitment was violent, excluding other possibilities—although the poems themselves, because of their artistic character by which private obsession and disorientation become normalized as they are organized into a structure outside themselves, have many doors opening to other worlds. The poems of *Ariel,* written in 1962, were an extraordinary change from the careful, highly promising, but seldom exciting work of *The Colossus* (1960). Contemplation of the meaning of this change can easily arouse fear, for it suggests the dangers of the real thing, as opposed to the safer titillations of what usually passes for artistic and intellectual imagination. *The Colossus* does show some flashes of the long-standing imminence in Sylvia Plath of her final kind of awareness. We see it there, for instance, in one macabre line of her 'Two Views of a Cadaver Room,' with its grisly echo of 'Prufrock':

> In their jars the snail-nosed babies moon and glow.

We see it, in fact, in the whole of this poem, which is divided into two sections. The first is about a girl's visit to a dissecting room, where she sees 'white-smocked boys' working on four cadavers, 'black as burnt turkey,' and where her friend (one of these boys) hands her 'the cut-out heart like a cracked heirloom'—a gross love-token that seems to foreshadow the morbidity of the lover hinted at in 'Lady Lazarus.' The second section describes a Brueghel painting of a war scene, but with a romantic love-scene painted in the lower right-hand corner showing two lovers absorbed in one another and 'deaf to the fiddle in the hands of the death's head shadowing their song.' The attempt to relate by simple juxtaposition a shocking personal experience of the brutal facts of death to the general theme of war represented in Brueghel's 'Panorama of smoke and slaughter' and of a 'carrion army' and to the transcendent character of art points to Sylvia Plath's major preoccupations just a short time later. So does her attempt in 'Suicide off Egg Rock' to reconstruct exactly how the suicide of the poem felt at the moment when he drowned himself (with all the signs of a cheaply commercialized civilization behind him—the sights on the public beach, the gas tanks and factory stacks in the near distance—as well as the normal sights of children, dogs, gulls, and the breaking waves) and how it was with him afterwards when his body was an inert object.

Sylvia Plath was a true 'literalist of the imagination.' When we use the word 'vision' about her poems, it is in a concrete and not a philosophically general sense.* We must place one other sad earlier poem side by side with the two I have mentioned. It is 'The Disquieting Muses,' which gives us a literal report of her 'muses.' These were the 'three ladies' whom from childhood she would see

* This quality is what gives a piece like 'Daddy' a dramatic and political force that is a triumph of active symbolism.

'nodding by night around my bed mouthless, eyeless, with stitched bald head.'

> Day now, night now, at head, side, feet,
> They stand their vigil in gowns of stone,
> Faces blank as the day I was born,
> Their shadows long in the setting sun
> That never brightens or goes down. . . .

After her death, her husband, Ted Hughes, said in a memorial note that in her later poems 'there is a strange muse, bald, white, and wild, in her "hood of bone," floating over a landscape like that of the primitive painters, a burningly luminous vision of a Paradise. A Paradise which is at the same time eerily frightening, an unalterably spotlit vision of death.' *

The evolution of her muse is one sign of the growth and clarification, within a brief span of months, of Sylvia Plath's peculiar awareness of the burden of her life in the whole context of modern existence. In 'Ariel,' the title-poem of her second book, in which 'Lady Lazarus' appeared as well, we see how the exhilaration of swift movement on horseback — or the mere *idea* of it — suggests to her every other kind of ecstatic movement and life-awareness. Just for that very reason, the mood suddenly becomes a desolate realization of the plunge into death that is going on:

> And now I
> Foam to wheat, a glitter of seas,
> The child's cry
>
> Melts in the wall.
> And I
> Am the arrow,

* *Poetry Book Society Bulletin* (London), No. 44, February 1965, p. 1.

> The dew that flies
> Suicidal, at one with the drive
> Into the red
>
> Eye, the cauldron of morning.

The difference between the early flash of ironic knowledge at sight of the 'snail-nosed babies' that so excitingly 'moon and glow' in their jars and the beautiful unfolding in 'Ariel' is very great. It lies in the author's mastery of the dynamics of a poem and in her shedding of self-consciousness after the limited success of her first book. 'She was truly driven,' wrote Lowell in the letter I have already referred to,* 'but with the mercy of great opportunities.' How do we relate this praise to a poem like 'Ariel'? I would point first to its emotional conception. In a single leap of feeling, it identifies sexual elation (in the full sense of the richest kind of encompassment of life) with its opposite, death's nothingness. As with Keats, the more intensely we pursue the exquisite essence, the more swiftly and surely we stare into the eye of mortality. And then I would point to the specifics of what Lowell calls Sylvia Plath's 'perfect control.' These have to do with the rapid exploration and compression of her motifs; with the functional use of rhyme and stanza which are yet ravishing to the ear; with the pulling up short of any tendencies to overexpand, falsify, and comment.

She was, as she says in 'Lady Lazarus,' 'only thirty' when she threw herself into that last burst of writing that culminated in *Ariel* and in her death, now (as in the case of Hart Crane's poems and his suicide) forever inseparable. We shall never be able to sort out clearly the unresolved, unbearably exposed suggestibility and agitation of these

* See p. 68.

poems from the purely aesthetic energy that shaped the best of them. Reading 'Daddy' or 'Fever 103°,' you would say that if a poet is sensitive enough to the age and brave enough to face it directly it will kill him through the excitation of his awareness alone. Sometimes, as I have suggested, in discussing 'Lady Lazarus,' Sylvia Plath could not distinguish between herself and the facts of, say, Auschwitz and Hiroshima. She was victim, killer, and the place and process of horror all at once.*

This is not the whole picture. Though Sylvia Plath may become a legend, we ought not to indulge in oversimplification. Some of her last poems ('Poppies in October,' for instance) are cries of joy despite some grimmer notes. There is rhythmic experimentation looking to the future, in particular with an adaptation of Whitman's characteristic line:

> By the roots of my hair some god got hold of me.
> I sizzled in his blue volts like a desert prophet.
> ('The Hanging Man')

> The tulips are too red in the first place, they hurt me. . . .
> Their redness talks to my wound, it corresponds.
> They are subtle: they seem to float, though they weigh me down,
> Upsetting me with their sudden tongues and their colour,
> A dozen red lead sinkers round my neck.
> ('Tulips')

The buoyant Whitman line and the energetic impression of external forces and sense-impacts invading the private

* See her novel *The Bell Jar* (published under a pseudonym in 1963 and under her own name in 1966) for the light it throws on a personality like her own.

self and taking it uncontrollably in new directions of awareness should remind us that a poem is an aesthetic projection of the psychological motives behind it, perhaps, but is not the same thing as those motives. Artistically, these poems had a destiny not defined by their author's private life and suicide. Apart from the fact that they were all 'written at four in the morning,' she wrote, they were intended 'for the ear, not the eye'; they were 'poems written out loud.' In 'Ariel' alone, despite its tragic dimension, the leap into absolute mastery of phrasing and of the dynamics of poetic movement must be considered an important kind of affirmation. (But there are poems too that are hard to penetrate in their morbid secretiveness, or that make a weirdly incantatory black magic against unspecified persons and situations. These were not resolved by artistic process, and often seem to call for biographical rather than poetic explanations.)

Under all the other motifs of Sylvia Plath's work, however, is the confusion of terror at death with fascination by it. The visions of the speaker as already dead are so vivid that they become yearnings toward that condition. In a later poem like 'Death & Co.,' what I have called her mastery of dynamics enables her to escape the almost inert heaviness of 'The Disquieting Muses.' 'Death & Co.' is one of several nearly perfect embodiments of this deeply compulsive motif of hers. In it, as in 'The Disquieting Muses,' there is a literal vision, this time of the two faces of death: the face of the condor and the face of the revolting but irresistible lover. (These two faces are foreshadowed in 'Two Views of a Cadaver Room,' already discussed, by the lover who hands the girl the heart of a corpse and by the romantic lover in the Brueghel painting.) The faces are seen in relation to a projection of herself as dead, as part of a possibly beautiful series of patterned objects though a series in which she, as her *living* self, no longer exists. The tone shifts from the literalness of almost naturalistic description to passionate contempt to incantation and then to a single death-knell effect. The pictorial shifts, meanwhile, are comparable in variety to those that might be contrived with a motion-picture camera. They move from a disgusted imagery of death the predator and connoisseur of the beauty of dead babies to an equally disgusted yet erotic picture of him as the self-centered would-be lover 'masturbating a glitter,' and at last to such a vision of the speaker's own death as I have already mentioned:

> I do not stir.
> The frost makes a flower,
> The dew makes a star,
> The dead bell,
> The dead bell.
>
> Somebody's done for.

Thinking of this pitifully brief life (1932–1963) and career, it is hard not to ask whether the fine cultivation of poetic sensibility is after all worth the candle. The answer is yes, for reasons that I hope we all know. Yet it seems important to keep raising the question anyway.

2. ALLEN GINSBERG

The initial excitement over Allen Ginsberg's *Howl and Other Poems* when it appeared in 1956 was perhaps mainly the result of its vocabulary. For the first time in the history of serious American poetry with a relatively popular appeal, Ginsberg and some of his 'Beat' associates were writing lines like the following ones in 'Howl,' and there is no question that they brought about certain advances in the age-old fight against private inhibition and public censorship:

> who copulated ecstatic and insatiate with a bottle of beer a sweetheart a package of cigarettes a candle and fell off the bed, and continued along the floor and down the hall and ended fainting on the wall with a vision of ultimate cunt and come eluding the last gyzym of consciousness,
>
> who sweetened the snatches of a million girls trembling in the sunset, and were red eyed in the morning but prepared to sweeten the snatch of the sunrise, flashing buttocks under barns and naked in the lake,
>
> who went out whoring through Colorado in myriad stolen night-cars, N. C., secret hero of these poems, cocksman and Adonis of Denver—joy to the memory of his innumerable lays of girls in empty lots & diner backyards, moviehouses, rickety rows on mountaintops in caves or with gaunt waitresses in familiar roadside lonely petticoat upliftings & especially secret gas-stations solipsisms of johns, & hometown alleys too. . . .

The randy speech of the uncultivated American male has long been available as well to more privileged groups and classes, though reserved by them for 'appropriate' settings and circumstances. Each of the educated generations since the First World War has developed a greater social and literary tolerance for the flat factuality of such speech. It is increasingly cultivated for its power to deflate outworn forms of romanticism, idealism, and puritanism all at the same time, and for its wit and raciness, but also for a more dangerous characteristic — its implied assumption of attitudes traditionally considered vicious and perverse. The open use of such diction in the post-war generations, and particularly in the generations that matured during and after World War II, is linked with an increasingly open acceptance of sexual relationships, including homosexual ones, that are not only frank and easy but inimical to the cultivation of intellectual and moral rigor or fastidiousness. In poetry this development was slowed down less by gentility pure and simple than by considerations of essential taste — that is, by the best poets' sensitivity to the power of language. A single word, sometimes, has the power to subordinate to its own crude force and thus undo a whole structure of phrasing that would otherwise unfold a subtle, perhaps delicate moment of discovery. The first effect of the use, in the passage from 'Howl,' of words like 'cunt,' 'come,' 'gyzym,' 'snatches,' 'cocksman,' 'lays,' and 'johns' is to stun the critical faculties and render them immune alike to the subtleties of the passage and to its stylistic weaknesses. The final effect of their continued usage, in poetry as in everyday life, is at one and the same time to discharge them of their special power to shock or amuse and to devalue the more complex reverberations of language.

Ginsberg's first poetry to come to public notice did rely heavily on rhetorical shock, supported by the reiterated insistence that a generation of Americans had been betrayed and psychically crippled and by a wild and whimsical humor that helped save his work from sentimentality and rodomontade. The shock seemed to come first of all from the gross vocabulary of vulgar speech, but actually Ginsberg never gives us the unadulteratedly elemental speech of the streets, the farm, and the factory. In the passage already quoted, he uses some words that in this context are almost euphemisms — 'copulated,' for instance — and in any case engulfs the more elemental language in deliberately intellectual phrasing ('the last gyzym of consciousness,' 'solipsisms of johns') or rhapsodic lyricism ('sweetened the snatches of a million girls trembling in the sunset'). His mysterious reference to 'N. C., secret hero of these poems,' his allusions to 'visions,' and his mystical identification of joy in the sunrise with joy in sex are similar sophistications of the issue. His imagery of sexual activity, finally, is hysterically frenzied, suggesting a compulsive search for love and acceptance through ceaselessly self-defeating, external, almost automatic activity.

Looking back now to the beginning of 'Howl,' we can see that this motif of intense, neurotically impelled activity is introduced in its very first line: 'I saw the best minds of my generation destroyed by madness, starving hysterical naked. . . .' By 'best minds' (a phrase harped on by hostile critics) I take it that Ginsberg means most vulnerable, or suggestible, sensibilities — best minds in the sense that they are seismographically responsive to the cultural atmosphere. Throughout Part I of the poem, the predicament of this group of the sensitive young being humiliated and destroyed by the 'madness' of the contemporary situation is thrust at us in the most vivid and explosive and comic manner in a series of irregularly parallel constructions, depending for their force on active verbs in the simple preterit and on equally active participial constructions. These syntactically aggressive thrusts underline the poet's assumed spokesmanship for, and embodiment of, his generation.

A revolutionary social and political criticism is implied

in many of the lines. The heroes of 'Howl' appear, for instance, 'on the West Coast investigating the F.B.I. in beards and shorts with big pacifist eyes sexy in their dark skin passing out incomprehensible leaflets'; they have 'burned cigarette holes in their arms protesting the narcotic tobacco haze of Capitalism' and have 'distributed Supercommunist pamphlets in Union Square weeping and undressing. . . .' The more essential rejection of the established order, however, lies in other directions. It centers on psychological breakdown but also on the breakdown of respectable assumptions in the moral sphere, not only concerning sexual behavior but involving generally the whole range of expectation of what will make a meaningful, good, and self-regulated life. Narcotics addiction, the despair of another kind of 'best minds' in modern society, plays an important role, as we can see by turning again to the very beginning of the poem:

> I saw the best minds of my generation destroyed by
> madness, starving hysterical naked,
> dragging themselves through the negro streets at dawn
> looking for an angry fix,
> angelheaded hipsters burning for the ancient heavenly
> connection to the starry dynamo in the machinery
> of night. . . .

The ultimate situation is summed up in one line—'who cowered in unshaven rooms in underwear, burning their money in wastebaskets and listening to the Terror through the wall.' Here an abandonment of normal masculine pride and adult responsibility follows upon the terror created by a mad and brutal world, to whose full cruelty most people have become so well 'adjusted' that they cannot see how irrelevant their lives really are. Nevertheless, the program stated toward the end of Part I is neither escapist nor nihilistic. Like William Burroughs, one of the people to whom the 1956 volume was dedicated, Ginsberg does *not* finally advocate a condition of helpless self-gratification or infantile regression. The program he announces in 'Howl' is after all an aestheticist one, echoing that of Stephen Dedalus in *A Portrait of the Artist as a Young Man*. It is 'to recreate the syntax and measure of poor human prose and stand before you speechless and intelligent and shaking with shame, rejected yet confessing out the soul to conform to the rhythm of thought in his naked and endless head.'

Part II of 'Howl' identifies the hostile universe with which the vulnerable sensibility cannot cope. It is, essentially, our indifferent but man-devouring mechanical civilization. This identification is not really a new idea, but Ginsberg sometimes succeeds in isolating the simple human fact within a familiar theme, as in the second line of the following passage. Most of the fashionable criticism of modern civilization fastens on its affronts to taste and to the values of the educated classes. Ginsberg looks directly at the suffering it imposes on the mass of ordinary people. At such a moment he gets past mere oratory and sentimentality:

> What sphinx of cement and aluminum bashed open
> their skulls and ate up their brains and imagination?
> Moloch! Solitude! Filth! Ugliness! Ashcans and unobtainable dollars! Children screaming under the stairways! Boys sobbing in armies! Old men weeping in the parks!
> Moloch! Moloch! Nightmare of Moloch! Moloch the

> loveless! Mental Moloch! Moloch the heavy judger of men!
>
> Moloch the incomprehensible prison! Moloch the crossbone soulless jailhouse and Congress of sorrows! Moloch whose buildings are judgement! Moloch the vast stone of war! Moloch the stunned governments!

The reiterated scream against Moloch, emblem of a civilization that has wasted millions of individual lives, becomes at the very end of Part II a cry of praise for the destroyed young who 'saw it all' and 'bade farewell' to Moloch's way. Part III then focuses on one person, Carl Solomon, confined in Rockland State Hospital (the New York State mental hospital), with whose madness Ginsberg associates himself:

> Carl Solomon! I'm with you in Rockland
> where you're madder than I am
> I'm with you in Rockland
> where you must feel very strange
> I'm with you in Rockland
> where you imitate the shade of my mother. . . .

Like the first two sections of 'Howl,' the third ends on a note of lamentation combined with affirmation that is both ambiguous and, it may be, openly confused. Not quite satisfied with the three-part structure of this poem, Ginsberg added another poem, 'Footnote to Howl,' that has the effect of a fourth section. It begins with a line that repeats the outcry 'Holy!' fifteen times. It then goes on to specify just what it is that is — not quietly, but always with an exclamation mark — 'holy!' The second line begins the list: 'The world is holy! The soul is holy! The skin is holy! The nose is holy! The tongue and cock and asshole holy!' By the time the final benign outcry is reached ('Holy the supernatural extra brilliant intelligent kindness of the soul! '), all the poet's preoccupations have been recapitulated; like so much else in his work, the series of assertions reflects the barriers of disgust and fear he had to conquer on the way. His incantatory catalogue includes the parts of the human body, Allen Ginsberg himself and his friends, his mother, jazzbands, marijuana, city streets and sights, madmen and 'bums,' the social classes, specific places (Kansas, Los Angeles, New York, San Francisco, Peoria, Seattle, Paris, Tangiers, Moscow, Istanbul), revolutionary politics, visionary experience, and the Christian virtues. Ginsberg brings under the same sign of holiness the tragic, the comic, the ordinary, and the hallucinatory. He does so in part deliberately, in part because his consciously Whitman-like inclusiveness provides no further guidance of perspective.

I have not gone into the structure of 'Howl' in this manner out of a great admiration for the poem, though its vigor and feeling are unmistakable. I have done so, rather, because it is remarkably indicative of the tendency toward the confessional even in a kind of poetry that presented itself at first as rhetorical in purpose. Of course, a rhetorical or extroverted poetry like this would share with confessional writing its hatred or pain at the damage wreaked by 'Moloch.' But the speaker's private allusions point to a significant additional similarity. He refers to himself and his friends by name, and makes a number of private references somewhat baffling to the uninstructed reader. There is the allusion to the indefatigable lover 'N. C.,' for instance; and Carl Solomon, the madman in Rockland State Hospital, is only a name (though apparently the name is of a real person, about whom we learn nothing but his insane condition). Beyond these specific but unpursued identifications, the piled-up details about 'my generation' contain many clues to Ginsberg's private experiences, as William Carlos Williams more than hints in his introduction ('Howl for Carl Solomon') to *Howl.* Among the most interesting of these clues, from our present viewpoint, are the ones suggested in the line of Part III in which Carl Solomon is said by the poet to 'imitate the shade of my mother' and in these lines of Part I:

> Pilgrim State's Rockland's and Greystone's foetid halls, bickering with the echoes of the soul, rocking and rolling in the midnight solitude-bench dolmen-realms of love, dream of life a nightmare, bodies turned to stone as heavy as the moon,
>
> with mother finally * * * * * *, and the last fantastic book flung out of the tenement window, and the last door closed at 4 AM and the last telephone slammed at the wall in reply and the last furnished room emptied down to the last piece of mental furniture, a yellow paper rose twisted on a wire hanger in the closet, and even that imaginary, nothing but a hopeful little bit of hallucination. . . .

One more important clue comes in the 'Footnote to Howl,' when the speaker exclaims: 'Holy my mother in the insane asylum!' These hints about his mother are of a quite different order from Ginsberg's general rhetorical tone, and seem to force themselves into the picture despite it. In the 'Howl' sequence the surface effects, aimed at public recitation, are thus slightly at cross-purposes with a deeper aim, perhaps not altogether conscious, of bringing very personal private concerns to the surface. As with Lowell and Sylvia Plath, the latter aim involves embodying the issues of cultural crisis in the crises of the poet's own life. The poem takes some of its conviction from this incompletely realized tendency, some of its feeling that there is more here than a one-dimensional adaptation of the techniques of Whitman and Kenneth Fearing, humorous and angry or disgusted but not necessarily deeply engaged. He is groping toward a fuller release of his real, private demons. The sense of potentially explosive energy helps him carry through his unresolved sequence, while his inability to give the sections of the sequence inevitability in their ordering and in their diction is an indication that he had not yet found the way to desired release. 'Literally,' says Williams in his introduction, 'he has, from all the evidence, been through hell. On the way he met a man named Carl Solomon with whom he shared among the teeth and excrement of this life something that cannot be described but in the words he has used to describe it. It is a howl of defeat. Not defeat at all for he has gone through defeat as if it were an ordinary experience, a trivial experience.' Williams's remarks are an overstatement. The 'hell' Ginsberg has been through, 'literally,' is not described in the poem. The point is, though, that the effect on Williams at his first reading was that something of the sort had taken place. He knew enough about the Ginsberg family, and in any case had a sufficiently fine sense of what was *behind* the poem, as opposed to what is actually *in* it, to warrant his response. The real 'hell' is not actually presented until 'Kaddish,' the poem in which the madness of the poet's mother holds the center of the stage and is documented in full detail.

'Kaddish,' which appeared in *Kaddish and Other Poems 1958–1960* (1961), is dated 1959 by the author. Its full title is 'Kaddish for Naomi Ginsberg 1894–1956.' (It is just possible that the appearance of *Life Studies* in 1959 may have been suggestive to Ginsberg, despite the very great differences between his style and Lowell's.) The traditional kaddish is the Hebrew lament for the dead, which is at the same time a hymn of praise to God. Modeling his poem on the traditional form, Ginsberg divides it into a sequence of six parts called 'Proem,' 'Narrative,' 'Hymmnn,' 'Lament,' 'Litany,' and 'Fugue.' Of these the second part, the 'Narrative,' is the most important both in substance and in length — it takes up two-thirds of the whole sequence. Here we have the story of Naomi Ginsberg's paranoia, degeneration, and death told in humiliating detail that is far more harrowing in every way than Lowell's accounts. It is not that Ginsberg is a poet of greater power. But his mother's case and its traumatic effect on him were terrible and desperate, and the family's poverty, combined with the hysterical atmosphere, made dignity impossible and deprived the children of any protection against the violence of the experience.

Naomi is the main figure of the poem, but her son Allen is the ultimate speaker and the poem is at least as much his story as hers. In the first part, 'Proem,' he is the omniscient poet and man of feeling. In Part II ('Narrative'), however, he is one of the characters in the tragic account he is writing. Here we see him first as a twelve-year-old boy taking his mother by tortuous bus-route to a 'rest home' in New Jersey. The year is 1938. She is escaping from 'a mystical assassin from Newark,' one of the many agents of Hitler and of her mother-in-law —

> 'The Bitch! Old Grandma! Last week I saw her, dressed in pants like an old man, with a sack on her back, climbing up the brick side of the apartment

> 'On the fire escape, with poison germs, to throw on me — at night — maybe Louis is helping her — he's under her power. . . .'

Louis was her husband, Allen's father, himself a poet as well as a schoolteacher. As with *Life Studies,* we are taken into the involved, irredeemable family myth. Father and mother are virtually estranged by the beginning of the poem, and it has devolved upon the young Allen to look after his mother when she first has this paranoid onslaught. Other scenes, truly shocking, follow: outbursts soon after in the 'rest home' and in a nearby drug store, followed by a brutal ambulance-ride to the state's mental asylum; close-ups of Naomi's behavior at home toward her sons after she has returned three years later as mad as ever, but more gross and indifferent to the effect she is having upon them. Some of Ginsberg's physical descriptions and anecdotes are disgusting, and it is clear that in providing them he is overcoming his own revulsion in order to prevent Naomi's memory from remaining merely an abstraction and in order to achieve aesthetic and spiritual reconciliation with himself: 'By my later burden — vow to illuminate mankind — this is release of particulars — (mad as you) — (sanity a trick of agreement).'

The political aspect of 'Kaddish' is most important for an understanding of the poem itself and for the light it throws on such earlier poems of Ginsberg's as 'Howl' and 'America.' Naomi arrived in the United States as an idealistic immigrant girl who soon became a young Socialist and later a Communist. Ginsberg tells us in the poem that as a boy he had aspired to become an 'honest revolutionary labor lawyer . . . inspired by Sacco Vanzetti, Norman Thomas, Debs, Altgold, Sandburg, Poe — Little Blue

Books.' His aunt Edie, who worked as a bookkeeper in Gimbel's department store, was a union organizer. If we may digress for a moment, the poem 'To Aunt Rose' (dated 1958 and included in *Kaddish and Other Poems*), is useful to contemplate for the way it presents the ambience of left-wing idealism in which the family lived and moved. Written with nostalgic sadness, it lays open the inscape of frustrated hope and desire that defines not only Aunt Rose but Naomi and many others like them as well:

Aunt Rose — now — might I see you
with your thin face and buck tooth smile and pain
of rheumatism — and a long black heavy shoe
for your bony left leg
limping down the long hall in Newark on the running carpet
past the black grand piano
in the day room
where the parties were
and I sang Spanish loyalist songs
in a high squeaky voice
(hysterical) the committee listening
while you limped around the room
collected the money. . . .

Those political memories are inseparable for the poet from those of Aunt Rose's 'long sad face' and 'tears of sexual frustration' and from those of his father's triumphant announcement to the family that his poems had been accepted for publication by Liveright. (The fact that Louis Ginsberg's poetry, while sometimes modestly successful, is generally rather weakly conventional colors the half-sympathy extended to this figure in 'Kaddish,' though Ginsberg never comments on the poetry critically. Louis comes through as a pale, frightened, romantically unfulfilled man, curiously similar to Lowell's father in *Life Studies,* as Naomi bears a very distant resemblance to Lowell's hysterically inclined mother.) The ending of 'To Aunt Rose' has the tone and movement of a true poem in the *Ubi sunt* tradition; its political edge is subordinate to that effect:

Hitler is dead and Liveright's gone out of business
The Attic of the Past and *Everlasting Minute* are out of print
Uncle Harry sold his last silk stocking
Claire quit interpretive dancing school
Buba sits a wrinkled monument in Old
Ladies home blinking at new babies

last time I saw you was the hospital
pale skull protruding under ashen skin
blue veined unconscious girl
in an oxygen tent
the war in Spain has ended long ago
Aunt Rose

The story of Naomi parallels that of Aunt Rose in its assumption of the Communist political ambience as a simple condition of life, rather than as an abstraction of tendentious public debate. 'Kaddish' tells us that the time of Naomi's first nervous breakdown 'was 1919—she stayed home from school,' where she taught retarded children, 'and lay in a dark room for three weeks—something bad—never said what—every noise hurt. . . .' Whatever that first reason was, the paranoia progressed and, under the influence of the rise of Hitler and the internal, passionate struggles within the Communist movement, took the form of a suspicion that she was surrounded by spies and poisoners in the image of the obvious Russian models: 'The enemies approach — what poisons? Tape recorders? FBI? Zhdanov hiding behind the counter? Trotsky mixing rat bacteria in the back of the store? . . .' Clearly, Naomi's unstable personality found the pressures of the 1930's unbearable. Acutely conscious of the Hitler terror and of the ravages of fascism in Europe generally — far more so than the majority of Americans, who were not sensitive to these developments until late in the game — she lived under tensions that were alien to far more sophisticated people. In addition, there were the hysterical obsessions with 'Trotskyism' and with the Russian spy-trials of the Communist movement. Superimposed on the early sexual and other causes that Ginsberg hints at knowingly, and that were doubtless the true ultimate source of her difficulties, these political pressures had a reality that should not be discounted.

Ginsberg's success as a confessional poet in this instance lies partly in his refusal to repress this reality, which is so important to his experience. The refusal clarifies, too, the connection between the allusions to his mother in 'Howl' and the series of outcries against modern civilization in that poem conceived as a speech by an extraordinarily imaginative and sardonic political orator. In *Life Studies*, the 'disgrace' Lowell confesses to, mainly, is his father's failure (and the failure of the culture to save him as a man and his son from breakdown). In 'Kaddish,' the 'disgrace' Ginsberg confesses to is not alone his mother's madness and the pathetic condition to which it reduced every other member of the family. It is also the slightly exotic and generally despised Communist background, which he refuses to apologize for. In the earlier 'America,' indeed, the poet mocks the makers of repressive stereotypes in this country with his sentimental memories of this background, just as he does, in another context, with his homosexual attitudes when he speaks, for instance, of how he is 'putting my queer shoulder to the wheel.' One line especially of 'America' is quite explicit:

> America when I was seven momma took me to Communist Cell meetings they sold us garbanzos a handful per ticket a ticket costs a nickel and the speeches were free everybody was angelic and sentimental about the workers it was all so sincere you have no idea what a good thing the party was in 1835 Scott Nearing was a grand old man a real mensch Mother Bloor made me cry I once saw Israel Amter plain. Everybody must have been a spy.

A good deal of the emotional strength of Ginsberg's poetry lies in its springlike recoil against the repression of radical thought and organization in the United States after the Second World War, the repression generally associated with the word 'McCarthyism.' The virtual sealing off of any legitimacy for revolutionary debate and organization, in the wake of a war that had already — whatever we may say about its inevitability and justification — done immense damage to private personality throughout the Western world, wrought even more psychic than political havoc. The story of Naomi Ginsberg is to some degree a doughty effort to establish the human validity of a retroactively outlawed type of experience. For example, in the line from 'Kaddish' 'Then quiet for months that winter — walks, alone, nearby on Broadway, read Daily Worker — Broke her arm, fell on icy street,' the important fact is not that the woman read the Communist newspaper but that in the midst of a period of quiet recovery and contemplation she suffered an unfortunate accident that interrupted the convalescence, perhaps catastrophically. In another sense, Naomi's story brings out in every possible way the psychopathology of the violence done by modern existence to the most vulnerable among us. The homosexuality of the poet, his use of drugs, and his rejection of squeamishness to the point where he has cultivated a positive addiction to the revolting are familiar motifs of recent literature, but Ginsberg understands, and shows, that they are not the result of spontaneous combustion but highly relevant to the current predicament of sensibility. The barriers of fastidiousness once broken down, the sophisticated intelligence must learn (with Whitman and Blake, to accept sympathetically Ginsberg's identification with these figures) entirely new perspectives of human acceptance and value. That is one important aim, at least, of the revolutionary movement in poetry as it exists today.

No passage of the 'Narrative' brings out more movingly the damaged lives of originally good, sensitive, and simple people than the following one:

> Naomi: 'And when we die we become an onion, a cabbage, a carrot, or a squash, a vegetable.' I come downtown from Columbia and agree. She reads the Bible, thinks beautiful thoughts all day.
>
> 'Yesterday I saw God. What did he look like? Well, in the afternoon I climbed up a ladder—he has a cheap cabin in the country, like Monroe, NY the chicken farms in the wood. He was a lonely old man with a white beard.
>
> 'I cooked supper for him. I made him a nice supper

> — lentil soup, vegetables, bread & butter — miltz — he sat down at the table and ate, he was sad.
>
> 'I told him, Look at all those fightings and killings down there, What's the matter? Why don't you put a stop to it?
>
> 'I try, he said — That's all he could do, he looked tired. He's a bachelor so long, and he likes lentil soup.'
>
> Serving me meanwhile, a plate of cold fish — chopped raw cabbage dript with tapwater — smelly tomatoes — week-old health food — grated beets & carrots with leaky juice, warm — more and more disconsolate food — I can't eat it for nausea sometimes — the Charity of her hands stinking with Manhattan, madness, desire to please me, cold undercooked fish — pale red near the bones. Her smells — and oft naked in the room, so that I stare ahead, or turn a book ignoring her. . . .

The beautiful moment of communion fades quickly into physical revulsion. The next line describes the naked Naomi lying back suggestively in her bed. There is a confused, incestuous atmosphere between mother and son, and Ginsberg confesses that his own attitude was ambivalent despite the ugliness of the situation and of Naomi's fat, operation-scarred body. It is casual, humorous horror. Shortly after this passage, we have other glimpses of the effect of Naomi's madness on her family. There is, for instance, Louis, 'lonely — sitting in the bedroom, he at desk chair turned round to face me — weeps, tears in red eyes under his glasses'; we are told that later he 'reestablished' himself 'in Paterson grimy apartment in negro district — living in dark rooms — but found himself a girl he later married, falling in love again — tho sere & shy — hurt with 20 years Naomi's mad idealism.' There is Allen's younger brother Eugene: 'And Gene lived with her, ate naked fishcakes, cheap, while she got crazier — He got thin, or felt helpless, Naomi striking 1920 poses at the moon, half naked in the next bed.' And there is the story of her treatment of her sister Elanor, sick with a rheumatic heart: 'But started kicking Elanor. . . . And Elanor began dying, upstairs in bed.'

> I pushed her against the door and shouted 'DON'T KICK ELANOR!' — she stared at me — Contempt — die — disbelief her sons are so naive, so dumb — 'Elanor is the worst spy! She's taking orders!'

Such are the joys the poet carries about with him in his memory. Like Lowell's family life, this one strikes us as unique, yet leaves us with the uneasy sense that far more misery is endemic to our contemporary existence than we usually allow ourselves to acknowledge. Implicit in the work of both poets is the idea of liberation through perfect candor — the argument made explicit in Yeats's 'Dialogue of Self and Soul.' The need for this liberation lay behind Ginsberg's early poetry and compelled him to expose Naomi's life, and his family's, to achieve it. The apostrophe to Naomi, toward the end of the 'Narrative,' expresses this need and her meaning for him as a poet:

> O glorious muse that bore me from the womb, gave suck first mystic life & taught me talk and music, from whose pained head I first took Vision. . . .

With the need for liberation is linked the need to expiate his guilt that any such child of such a mother would have, and to discover an ultimate concern for himself and a transcendent beauty in her nature. The 'Narrative' ends with a letter the poet received two days after her death, the phrasing of which provides the tone, with its implications of mystical prophecy, for the 'Proem' (Part I) and the 'Lament' (Part III — actually a hymn of thankfulness for having known Naomi and been able to bring her so fully through the poem into realization).

> Strange Prophecies anew! She wrote — 'The key is in the window, the key is in the sunlight at the window — I have the key — Get married Allen don't take drugs — the key is in the bars, in the sunlight in the window. . . .

I shall not take up the other parts of 'Kaddish' in anything like the detail of my comment on the 'Narrative.' The 'Proem' combines an initial lament and a gesture of consolation by the speaker both to the dead woman and to himself. It reviews briefly the chief points of attention of the 'Narrative' without elaborating on them. Of the various parts, its syntax is closest to normal though it moves for a while into the broken constructions characteristic of Part II. The 'Hymmnn' (so spelled, I assume, to suggest the wailing incantation of the Hebrew prayer) is printed as an afterbeat, or tail, of the 'Narrative.' It is a bitter chant of praise — not intentionally ironic, I think — of God for the sufferings of Naomi and her family, and for the evils and perversions besetting the poet and mankind: 'Blessed be He in homosexuality! Blessed be He in Paranoia! Blessed be He in the city! Blessed be He in the Book!' And: 'Blessed be He who builds Heaven in Darkness! . . .' The 'Narrative,' despite its length, moved rapidly in its shorter, moment-by-moment effects and varied these by intruded echoes of the Hebrew prayer in both Hebrew and English and by occasional passages of rhetoric and soaring exaltation. The 'Hymmnn,' on the other hand, is an astringent coda of eleven lines of fairly strictly parallel construction. Part III, the 'Lament,' is an only slightly longer composition expressing, as I have suggested, thankfulness for having known Naomi and been able to keep the whole truth of her in mind: 'Only to have not forgotten' it all. This part, a sixteen-line single floating sentence that is left incomplete, is a moving effort to contain the stormy, undisciplined emotions that have thrashed through the 'Narrative' within a calmer, more encompassing, cosmic purview. Part IV, 'Litany,' brings us back to the woman herself. Only a few of the lines here are as long as elsewhere; it is a kind of telling over of her characteristics to make sure nothing has been forgotten:

with your sagging belly
with your fear of Hitler
with your mouth of bad short stories
with your fingers of rotten mandolines
with your arms of fat Paterson porches
with your belly of strikes and smokestacks
with your chin of Trotsky and the Spanish War
with your voice singing for the decaying overbroken workers
with your nose of bad lay with your nose of the smell of the
    pickles of Newark . . .

In Part V, 'Fugue,' the song of praise is taken over by cawing crows, with an ambiguous and impersonal energy asserting itself in external nature: crows shrieking, the 'white sun' shining on the graves, and time, the sky, and the wind dominating the visible universe without discernible affect. The 'message' of these forces is beyond human comprehension and constitutes a raucous, disengaged, and unhappy last comment: 'Lord Lord Lord caw caw caw Lord Lord Lord caw caw caw Lord.' The self is lost in the nothingness of God, to be praised at all costs no doubt but also with full recognition of its unanswerable riddles for mortality.

As in Lowell's *Life Studies* the indispensable literal data are given in the prose section primarily, here they are given in the 'Narrative.' The other sections of the sequences constitute a sort of ritual dancing around these central ones. But as a stylistically finished work, 'Kaddish' cannot be compared with *Life Studies*. The long, crucial 'Narrative' is, line by line, careless in diction, syntax, and rhythmic movement. It can be defended, to a reasonable extent, as deliberately having the quality of a series of memories noted down in haste lest the details be forgotten, or snatched up out of the storehouse of the subconscious against the speaker's conscious will. The lines, too, are highly charged with the emotional compulsions underlying the whole of the poem, and there is no denying their gathering momentum. Still, far too large a proportion of the poem relies on short gasps of thought or statement, separated usually by dashes. They have a staccato eloquence that can move us but that contributes little — for there are too few strategic points — to the poetic synthesis. This is achieved mainly through special incantatory passages or through sensational detail at scattered moments. Lines like the following are inadequate:

> I've seen your grave! O strange Naomi! My own — cracked grave! Shema Y'Israel — I am Svul Avrum — you — in death?

and:

> Your last night in the darkness of the Bronx — I phone-called — thru hospital to secret police. . . .

It is a moot question whether twenty pages of such lines (the length of the 'Narrative') piled one on the other can, despite their admitted function of accumulating more and more hysteria and despite the powerful moments contained within them, achieve anything like a poetic triumph. The 'Narrative' cries out to be broken into a small number of related sections, or points of concentration, each serving as sharply defined a function as does the 'Lament.' Nevertheless, by giving free play to the materials of the poem in the manner that he found most convenient, Ginsberg made a poem of sufficient power — the power released by the materials themselves and given improvised, tentative formal structure by the poet's genuine creative spontaneity — to stand as a remarkable utterance.

'Kaddish' seems to have brought Ginsberg to a point beyond which he cannot advance through further drawing on literal memory recollected in manic or hysterical frenzy. The story of Naomi and her family, and of Ginsberg's own sufferings and prepossessions, has carried him a meaningful distance. So have the wit he displays in parts of 'America' and of 'A Supermarket in California' and the attention he pays to the lower depths of American life in a poem like 'In the Baggage Room at Greyhound.' All three of these poems appeared in his first book. Their essential elements reappear in the second book, in 'Kaddish' and 'To Aunt Rose.' The latter poems, however, have explicitly at their centers the body of family experience which is the heart of their emotional power, and so their impact is quite different. The other poems of the *Kaddish* volume, as well as the poems in *Reality Sandwiches* (almost all of them written before 'Kaddish,' though the book was published in 1963) are markedly inferior work. Their buffoonery generally lacks the *telling* character of the earlier exuberant satire, and their seriousness is contrived, unsustained, and pretentious. In other words, they have the weaknesses of the best work without the saving essence. Allusions to the circle of Ginsberg's close friends — Jack Kerouac, William Burroughs, Peter Orlovsky, and others — proliferate. Poems based on drugs ('Laughing Gas,' 'Mescaline,' 'Aether') or exploiting Zen Buddhist and other Oriental religious attitudes serve the same purpose of suggesting a private, special group sharing a valuable kind of knowledge alien to the rest of us. In both instances, as with some of the frankly homosexual passages, an exhibitionistic and self-advertising quality, rarely serving any poetic end, is even more rampant than before. The style of these pieces has generally lost its way. They are for the most part merely derivative from William Carlos Williams and the Black Mountain poets and, except for a very few beautifully inward moments, are uninteresting. These shapeless improvisations spell out the need for this author, the single writer of the 'Beat' poets who has shown outstanding imagination and feeling for a strong poetic line, to restudy his art and make the poems of which he is very probably capable.*

3. THEODORE ROETHKE, JOHN BERRYMAN, ANNE SEXTON

The publication in 1964 of Theodore Roethke's posthumous *The Far Field* and John Berryman's *77 Dream Songs* may well have signaled the end of the confessional move-

* How strongly the poet himself must feel this need is shown in one poem, 'The Change: Kyoto-Tokyo Express,' written in 1963. This poem, unusually tight for Ginsberg in its structure, appears in his *Jukebox All'Idrogeno* (Milan: Arnoldo Mondadori Editore, 1965).

ment in American poetry. I am not sure how well Roethke's memory was served by his very uneven last poems, which he had been readying for the press when he died in August 1963. The poems are touching in at least two ways. First, they refer to his illness and seem aware of imminent death, though he was only fifty-five or younger when they were written. Second, behind their assumption of an achieved, transcendent quietude lies a deeper impression of inability to cope with the old, still unresolved hysteria, which Roethke had unloosed in his earlier work, and of a consequent resort to the stock cosmic pieties of sagedom from Chuang-tzu on down. As V. S. Pritchett has written in another context, 'it is often noticeable that tormented writers who seek a synthesis end by falling into self-complacency.' This was indeed noticeable in Roethke long ago, in the poetic sequences of his early forties whose characteristic structure was based on a progression of psychological states, more or less Freudian in their conception. 'The Lost Son,' for example, took us from the stage of raw terror at the demands of actual life — the brutality of nature and of death, the challenge of adult sexuality — to a phase of self-repossession through identification with the father's daily world and so onward to a final, calmly affirmative, but really unearned resolution.

It is this last phase, unfortunately, at which Roethke was arrested in the poems of *The Far Field.* The vital tension had retreated some distance, leaving the poems free to attempt something like joyous acceptance of things as they are, immersion in nature in the older Romantic sense, before Keats gave nature the special modern twist of being a mirror of man's own mortal predicament. Sometimes Roethke almost achieves what he is after, notably in 'Meditation at Oyster River' and 'I Waited': a certain delicate precision, a light-spirited seriousness such as we are told the early Christians possessed, a sweetness of spirit deriving from a literal rendering of the minutiae of nature and from accepting their meaning without quarreling about ultimates. The 'Meditation' begins:

Over the low, barnacled, elephant-colored rocks,
Come the first tide-ripples, moving, almost without sound, toward me,
Running along the narrow furrows of the shore, the rows of dead clam shells;
Then a runnel behind me, creeping closer,
Alive with tiny striped fish, and young crabs climbing in and out of the water.

No sound from the bay. No violence.
Even the gulls quiet on the far rocks,
Silent, in the deepening light,
Their cat-mewing over,
Their child-whimpering. . . .

It ends:

Now in this waning of light,
I rock with the motion of morning;
In the cradle of all that is,
I'm lulled into half-sleep
By the lapping of water,
Cries of the sandpiper.
Water's my will, and my way,
And the spirit runs, intermittently,
In and out of the small waves,
Runs with the intrepid shorebirds —
How graceful the small before danger!

In the first of the moon,
All's a scattering,
A shining.

Even in these passages, however, although he does convey something like the mystical calm of rapport with elemental being, the effects are finally unearned. 'Elephant-colored rocks' is both obvious and intrusive. 'Moving, almost without sound' is trite. 'Dead clam shells' is redundant. The closing stanzas have a number of derivative echoes and affectations. In between we have, first, a further elaboration of the opening scene, with the speaker retreating to a higher position as the tide rises. Then their is a second movement, an expression of death-longing that begins poignantly ('the self persists like a dying star') before losing itself in a catalogue of the 'shy beasts' and the movements of water with which the speaker yearns to be at one. The third movement assumes that the oneness ('this first heaven of knowing') has been achieved. His flesh having taken on 'the pure poise of spirit,' the speaker's mind turns back to memories of brooks and rivers swelling in early spring, or roaring explosively after the first melting of ice along their edges:

And I long for the blast of dynamite,
The sudden sucking roar as the culvert loosens its debris of
  branches and sticks,
Welter of tin cans, pails, old bird nests, a child's shoe riding
  a log,
As the piled ice breaks away from the battered spiles,
And the whole river begins to move forward, its bridges
  shaking.

This passage, of longing for the great change, is the best in the poem. However, it still leaves unaccounted for the state of longing—of the desire and need for death, and behind it the motives leading to a condition of psychological crisis, itself unclarified, which has in turn led to this statement of reconciliation with existence and acceptance of self-obliteration. The poems of *The Far Field* have a number of lovely effects and interesting passages, though they are often marred by verbosity, cliché, and derivativeness. 'I have tried,' Roethke said of himself in his entry in *Twentieth Century Authors,* 'to transmute and purify my "life," the sense of being defiled by it.' The statement was one clue among others to his struggle with his own self-knowledge, a struggle that comes through as touchingly in some of his prose pieces, almost, and in as unresolved a way, as in his poems. From his student days he seems to have been unusually competitive, and found it difficult to conceal his impatience for recognition as a great poet—an impatience that is one of America's worst literary diseases— and at the same time felt 'defiled' by it. It is striking to see how often he speaks of the 'vulgar' egocentricity of calling attention to one's work, of the dangers of 'exhibitionism,' of 'odious pumping for oneself.' It is equally striking to see how acutely he was aware of the problem of being derivative.

His essay 'How To Write like Somebody Else,' presented as an attack on critics who insensitively and falsely attribute influence on inadequate grounds, obliquely reveals his troubled thoughts about his own overdependence on certain models. Roethke may have fought against the weaknesses he found in himself, but ultimately he yielded to them and tried to make his meanings out of them. Thus, a passage like the following one exposes both the exhibitionism and the imitativeness (in this instance, of Yeats). It is not entirely pleasant either in its style or in its assumptions, yet it does express the conviction of inspiration, or the hot yearning after it, which drives some of his poetry:

> Suddenly, in the early evening, the poem 'The Dance' started, and finished in a very short time . . . I felt, I *knew,* I had hit it. I walked around, and I wept; and I knelt down — I always do after I've written what I know is a good piece. But at the same time I had, as God is my witness, the actual sense of a Presence — as if Yeats himself were *in* that room. The experience was in a way terrifying. . . . At last I was somebody again. He, they — the poets dead — were with me.

Roethke came into his own as a poet in his group of short 'greenhouse' poems published in 1948. (They are to be found, with most of his other work before *The Far Field,* in *Words for the Wind,* his collected edition of 1958.) After a weak start as a conventionally competent versifier, he made his essential artistic advance in these pieces. He had discovered, apparently simultaneously, that his great source of energy was his own uncontrolled, riotous psyche — he called it 'the muck and welter, the dark, the *dreck'* — and that his youthful experience around his father's greenhouse in Michigan provided just the vivid, squirmingly uncomfortable, and concrete focus his poetry needed to channel and concentrate this emotional tumult. The equally exuberant and disgusted earthiness of these poems, their violent rapport with plants and the slimy sublife of slugs and other such creatures, is unique. Although his later work sometimes carries forth their Rabelaisian gusto (see, for instance, 'Give Way, Ye Gates' in the collected volume) and presents searching moments of psychological realization, and though it can jolt us by dropping suddenly from pure manic recklessness to the most painfully gross and disturbing dejection, it seldom carries through with the same absolute conviction. One reason is the greater ambitiousness of the later work, no doubt. More important is the fact that for the most part Roethke had no subject apart from the excitements, illnesses, intensities of sensuous response, and inexplicable shiftings of his own sensibility. The greenhouse poems enabled him to objectify it for a time, but then he had nowhere to go but back inside himself. We have no other modern American poet of comparable reputation who has absorbed so little of the concerns of his age into his nerve-ends, in whom there is so little reference direct or remote to the incredible experiences of the age — unless the damaged psyche out of which he spoke be taken as its very embodiment. But that was not quite enough. The confessional mode, reduced to this kind of self-recharging, becomes self-echoing as well and uses itself up after the first wild orgies of feeling. We are left, at best, with a thin exhausted bitterness or, as at the close of 'I Waited,' with a desire to be cheerful:

> The way grew steeper between stony walls,
> Then lost itself down through a rocky gorge.
> A donkey path led to a small plateau.
> Below, the bright sea was, the level waves,
> And all the winds came toward me. I was glad.

John Berryman, in his *77 Dream Songs* (1964), seriously entered the post-war current of confessional poetry. Except for Allen Ginsberg, whom he resembles more than one might perhaps think likely but whose writing is essentially of a different cast, he was the first poet to pick up Mr. Lowell's cues on so sweeping a scale. The genius of Lowell lies partly in his having that quality, so conspicuously lacking in Roethke, of having absorbed 'the concerns of his age into his nerve-ends.' But he has shown a drastic courage, as well, in the way he speaks in his own person, and of course there is the pure force and virtuosity of his art. We must respect Mr. Berryman's effort to match this achievement in his own way.

The 77 *Dream Songs* were perhaps foreshadowed in the tensions of Berryman's first book of poems, *The Dispossessed* (1948), and in the special quality of his repossession of (and identification with) the psyche of the seventeenth-century poet Anne Bradstreet in *Homage to Mistress Bradstreet* (1956). In this latter book, with its high pitch of intensity, Mr. Berryman presents a kind of dialogue between himself and the woman poet in which their voices sometimes merge, and in a sense the effect is of two voices of a divided self. The technique involved is carried forward in the *Dream Songs,* but this time the character Henry and the other voices are literally of a divided self. 'Unappeasable Henry' and the 'I' of the poem and other voices, often including strong infusions of vaudeville and plantation Negro dialect, are all facets of the central sensibility. In this device, and in presenting his book as 'one version of a poem in progress,' as well as in giving the reader various leads and allusions to be worked on through research on the author's private life and reading, Berryman resembles Ezra Pound. But since the element of innovation here is truly minimal, and since the quality of Berryman's art does not really make him the Pound to Lowell's Eliot, we may decline that part of his gambit which invites us to consider the book a major work and may view it rather as a collection of lyric and dramatic poems all in basically the same form (three six-line stanzas of varying rhyme-scheme and line-lengths). It then becomes a modern equivalent of the traditional sonnet sequence, with a few nuggets of gold among the lesser pieces, witty and interesting but offering no real justification intrinsically for further development. It is 'in progress' in the sense that it would benefit considerably from rigorous reduction and revision, but that is, after all, the common lot of poets when they are preparing to publish a book. (The idea of being a 'great,' or at least a 'major' figure, has doubtless helped push certain poets to the limits of their abilities. More often, as I have already suggested, it is a kind of nagging distraction from the basic thing, which is simply to write real poems, one at a time, each fulfilling itself in a manner appropriate to its conception, regardless of the kind of ready acclaim their work will receive. It can lead to premature birth — presenting unfinished work with a portentous surface — and to imposing one's personality on the reader instead of absorbing it into the poem.)

Of these seventy-seven poems, perhaps a score stand out from the rest, two of them (poems 29 and 53) supremely. These two poems are so much epitomes of what is best in this book that one might almost say — but it would be wrong — that they render the rest superfluous. Poem 29 begins on a deeply moving and beautiful note, stating private misery and unlocatable guilt in the most immediate, humanly accessible manner; and it realizes itself perfectly:

There sat down, once, a thing on Henry's heart
só heavy, if he had a hundred years
& more, & weeping, sleepless, in all them time
Henry could not make good.

Starts again always in Henry's ears
the little cough somewhere, an odour, a chime.

And there is another thing he has in mind
like a grave Sienese face a thousand years
would fail to blur the still profiled reproach of. Ghastly,
with open eyes, he attends, blind.
All the bells say: too late. This is not for tears;
thinking.

But never did Henry, as he thought he did,
end anyone and hacks her body up
and hide the pieces, where they may be found.
He knows: he went over everyone, & nobody's missing.
Often he reckons, in the dawn, them up.
Nobody is ever missing.

Faint echoes of other poets touch these lines — Hopkins and Eliot mostly, yet without the intrusiveness of some others among the *Dream Songs*. It is the essential predicament of the speaker that is presented here, and even the Lowell-like final line does not violate the poem's purity. A fine gift for distorting syntax for emphasis and yet holding on to the clarity of his sentences is one of Mr. Berryman's chief stylistic strengths. What is elsewhere a slightly offensive buffoonery in the use of Negro dialect, and a probably unwarranted assumption that the griefs of the Negro and the griefs of Berryman are aspects of one another, becomes in a few poems like this one a wry effect of childlike vulnerability — 'in all them time,' 'end anyone and hacks her body up.' Even the elsewhere often gimmicky '&' contributes to this effect by helping to compress the statement and make it look less formal. Poem 53, which takes off, as it were, where this one leaves off — 'He lay in the middle of the world, and twitcht' — gives us what might be called the social and cultural correlative of this private condition. It is a poem about the compulsion to shut out what cannot be shut out, the 'outside world':

Kierkegaard wanted a society, to refuse to read 'papers,
and that was not, friends, his worst idea.
Tiny Hardy, toward the end, refused to say *anything*,
a programme adopted early on by long Housman,
and Gottfried Benn
said: — We are using our own skins for wallpaper and we
cannot win.

This poem, as so often here, modulates clearly toward the familiar theme of the *poète maudit*. But unlike, say, Poem 1, it neither sentimentalizes the theme nor oversimplifies it. Nor, as so many of these pieces do, does it commandeer political themes too facilely or fashionably. (See, for example, the easy satire on Eisenhower in Poem 23, or the presumed identification with the Jews of the Warsaw ghetto in Poem 41, or the comment on America's betrayal of Jefferson's meanings in the incantatory Poem 22.) There are many aspects of the book I have neglected — the elegiac group on Frost, the poems about sexual desire, the various autobiographical and self-analytical notations, and so on — which cast a good deal of light on this poet's admirable range and flexibility, and on his own motives and the attitudes of literary and intellectual circles with whom he is associated. A longer discussion would be required to sort out the real thing from the attitudinizing and élite-gossipy chaff. But even this brief examination may suggest that, whatever individually poignant and accomplished poems it may still bring to us, the confessional movement as a startlingly new factor in our art may be just about played out, or more accurately, may now be beginning to be absorbed and taken for granted as part of the extremely varied new poetic scene. With that development comes the danger that its practitioners may be overindulging themselves if they think that every nuance of suffering brought out on the couch or in reverie is a mighty flood of poetic insight or the key to a new aesthetic.

Berryman's effort in *Homage to Mistress Bradstreet* was intrinsically more promising than in *77 Dream Songs.* Disciplined by historical and biographical sources (which, however, we are not required to consult in order to understand the poem) and by the spirit of Anne Bradstreet's poems, he could not so easily rely on a nearly solipsistic clutter of private allusion and willful diction. Not that such allusion and diction, as well as forced syntax and some of the other devices of the later book, are absent from the *Homage.* They contribute a certain compression and vigor and at the same time call too much attention to themselves, as can be seen in the passage or two I shall quote. But they are under a useful restraint. In the same way, the eight-line stanzas of *Homage* have a more self-evident function than the six-line ones of the *Dream Songs.* One can see why Berryman clung to the form he chose for the latter book, but there is a compulsive and mechanical side to the repetition of it so many times. As in many sonnet-sequences, the form itself becomes a tedious excuse, as it were, for proliferation without qualitative development. The stanza of *Homage,* with its shifting placement of rhymes, often inexact, and its varied line-lengths, is similar to that of *Dream Songs* in its essential character. Yet it is employed quite differently. Each of the fifty-seven numbered stanzas is an important unit of the long half-narrative, half-dramatic poem, with its passages of lyric description and of contemplation as well as of imaginary dialogue. The stanza's greater length, too, gives it a useful fullness and dignity, and one accepts it at once as a modern variant in a tradition at least as old as Chaucer. With the curve of the whole work clearly in his purview, Berryman was able to use his stanza flexibly and sensitively, better in fact than he uses the individual line. The significant rhythmic units are related over the course of a whole stanza or more, as should happen in such a work.

The conception itself of *Homage to Mistress Bradstreet* is both moving and engaging. The *poète maudit* of our century, John Berryman, dreams his way back into the life and world of Anne Bradstreet. His prefatory note identifies her: 'Born 1612 Anne Dudley, married at 16 Simon Bradstreet, a Cambridge man, steward to the Countess of Warwick & protégé of her father Thomas Dudley secretary to the Earl of Lincoln. Crossed in the *Arbella*, 1630, under Governor Winthrop.' The rest of the necessary information is suggested in the poem itself or given in a few notes. Some of the notes, for instance, locate the scriptural passages that Berryman quotes or alludes to and cite their original use by Anne Bradstreet. Others supply such essential bits of biography as that her first child was not born until about 1633 and that she suffered from dropsy in her last three years. (They also explain certain *recherché* allusions that would not otherwise be clear and that even so wrench our attention away from the poem.) The modern poet 'summons' Anne from the past, and in the course of his invocation places himself in her time. He makes love to her across the centuries, counting on the kinship of sensibility:

Outside the New World winters in grand dark
white air lashing high thro' the virgin stands
foxes down foxholes sigh,
surely the English heart quails, stunned.
I doubt if Simon than this blast, that sea,
spares from his rigour for your poetry
more. We are on each other's hands
who care. Both of our worlds unhanded us. Lie stark,

thy eyes look to me mild. Out of maize & air
your body's made, and moves. I summon, see,
from the centuries it.
I think you won't stay. How do we
linger, diminished, in our lovers' air,
implausibly visible, to whom, a year,
years, over interims; or not;
to a long stranger; or not; shimmer & disappear.

STANZAS 2–3

There is no need to comment on the affectations, so visible to the casual eye. What is remarkable is that, though they mar it, they do not destroy the poem and that indeed they sometimes enhance it. It is easy to say that Berryman makes heavy use of what he has learned from Hopkins, but he makes deft, bright use of it as well. The third line of the second stanza above is dismal, not only because of the sound but because of the false emphasis it lays on 'it.' It does, however, ground a movement (though threatening to bury it too) that was in danger of becoming sentimentally lilting. The stanzas project a series of concrete effects, rhythmically united in a shifting pattern that the poet, at the risk of being so clever about it all that he becomes precious, never allows to fall into the softly snoring regularity that is the fate of so many poems of ambitious length. After three lines of uninterrupted movement punctuated only by the strong hovering accents, we have a beautifully modulated single line of response to their effect. Beginning 'normally' (i.e. for English pentameter), it ends with a series of three accented syllables that carry the movement begun in the first line to conclusion. Two completely 'normal' lines follow, introducing a thought rather than an active scene and its emotional equivalent, before the idiosyncratic variations begin anew. Again, the method, once noted, becomes clear enough: a shaping of line, syntax, sound to the changing vision and its accompanying realizations. There emerges, in the course of the two stanzas, an astonishingly fresh and sweet-spirited romantic conception. From one point of view, the thought is quite ordinary — the common, naïve thought that might pass through anyone's mind: 'That girl, the poet Anne Bradstreet, was out of her time. If she had known someone like me, we might have felt such sympathy and love as she must, without understanding it, have needed and I have always longed for.' Your husband, says Berryman to her, was not only very much older than you but not the man to be in sympathy with your poetry. You and I must depend on those like ourselves, who 'care' for poetry and what it means for us. We are both of the species alienated artist: 'Both of our worlds unhanded us.' And then the vision, that can so quickly 'shimmer & disappear.' In all this we are always a hairsbreadth only from sentimentality, and Berryman quickly moves in the succeeding stanzas to harsher imagery (including the picture of Anne 'pockmarkt & westward staring on a haggard deck' as the ship approached America) to evoke the calamitous arrival of Winthrop and his group in the New World.

I do not intend to summarize *Homage to Mistress Brad-*

street. It is a serious piece of work, uneven but ingenious and at times exquisitely realized. Lines of description like those already quoted at the start of stanza 2 are an attempt to recapture not merely the scene but the quality of experience in which Anne Bradstreet moved, and to establish the author's sympathetic encompassment of it.

> Outside the New World winters in grand dark
> white air lashing high thro' the virgin stands
> foxes down foxholes sigh,
> surely the English heart quails, stunned. . . .

Here, near the very start (after an expository opening stanza establishing literary and historical points of reference, subtly, by a direct address to Anne), the poet's effort is simply to get us back into the physical world of the colonists. It is only one of countless such efforts, for recovery of the American past is one of the commonest motifs of our literature; but he does it well. It is a question of bringing to bear enough sensitivity, energy, and concreteness. We can see again and again, in Berryman's passages of impressionistic historical narrative, the effects of the modern study of a small number of models — especially Anglo-Saxon verse, as interpreted in Pound's translations and as adapted by him in some of the *Cantos,* and Hopkins:

> By the week we landed we were, most, used up.
> Strange ships across us, after a fortnight's winds
> unfavouring, frightened us;
> bone-sad cold, sleet, scurvy; so were ill
> many as one day we could have no sermons. . . .

A passage like this one (in stanza 5), if not too long, serves well enough for sketching in a general atmosphere.

Berryman wisely does not extend these moments, but moves quickly into the subjective side, as when in the following stanzas he develops an intimately domestic and yet romantic portrait of Anne. A complex womanliness, erotically alert yet repressed and self-disciplining, emerges in the course of the idealized monologue he creates for her.

Winter than summer worse, that first, like a file
on a quick, or the poison suck of a thrilled tooth;
and still we may unpack.
Wolves & storms among, uncouth
board-pieces, boxes, barrels vanish, grow
houses, rise. Motes that hop in sunlight slow
indoors, and I am Ruth
away: open my mouth, my eyes wet: I would smile:

vellum I palm, and dream. Their forest dies
to greensward, privets, elms & towers, whence
a nightingale is throbbing.
Women sleep sound. I was happy once . .
(Something keeps on not happening; I shrink?)
These minutes all their passions & powers sink
and I am not one chance
for an unknown cry or a flicker of unknown eyes.

Chapped souls ours, by the day Spring's strong winds swelled,
Jack's pulpits arched, more glad. The shawl I pinned
flaps like a shooting soul
might in such weather Heaven send.
Succumbing half, in spirit, to a salmon sash
I prod the nerveless novel succotash —
I must be disciplined,
in arms, against that one, and our dissidents, and myself.

STANZAS 9–11

Berryman is at his best at the few moments of identification with the voice and inwardness of Anne as a sensuous, introspective woman. In stanzas 19 to 21 we have a parallel sequence, though much more violent and intense, presenting her in the act of giving birth:

> . . . *Useless.* Below my waist
> he has me in Hell's vise.
> Stalling. He let go. Come back: brace
> me somewhere. No. No. Yes! everything down
> hardens I press with horrible joy down
> my back cracks like a wrist
> shame I am voiding oh behind it is too late. . . .

A case could be made, I think, for the thesis that sexual curiosity and the writer's need to find a self outside his own skin are the driving force behind this poem. It rises to its highest points when his imagination is entirely released toward the satisfaction of his curiosity — that is, when he not only envisions Anne's physical experience but identifies with it and, as it were, finds her language for her. The passionate climax at the center of the poem, in which the two poets are imagined in a transport of discovery of each other, through speech and through love, creates Anne as in a frenzy of desire and guilt. The naïve fantasy in which the poem begins has now become a vision of the torment of religious conscience in conflict with sexual need:

> I fear Hell's hammer-wind. But fear does wane. . . .
> a male great pestle smashes
> small women swarming towards the mortar's rim in vain.
>
> STANZA 37

As I have suggested, the dialogue of this poem is in a sense that of the two voices of a divided self. The physical ardor and stormy melancholy of Anne, and her death-horror that makes itself felt more and more forcibly, are a means for Berryman to objectify his feelings more simply than he does through the several voices of the *Dream Songs* — which are, after all, only private voices despite his attempt to keep them distinct. It is this aspect of the *Homage* that really interests us, and yet the conventional and sentimental plot of the poem has obviously trite and contrived aspects that serve as a formidable barrier. The best things in it are there at strange intervals, and by fits and starts. Nevertheless, unless we are to discount the importance of structure and of the deployment of elements in a work over whose length and proportions the artist exercises at least minimal control, the method of the *Homage* is more promising than that of the *Dream Songs.* In the latter work we must forage too much on our own; it is the occasional high point alone that justifies it at all.

Confessional poetry is a poetry of suffering. The suffering is generally 'unbearable' because the poetry so often projects breakdown and paranoia. Indeed, the psychological condition of most of the confessional poets has long been the subject of common literary discussion — one cannot say gossip exactly, for their problems and confinements in hospitals are quite often the specific subjects of their poems. It is not enough, however, to relegate the matter to the province of the mentally disturbed. A heightened sensitivity to the human predicament in general, for reasons developed in the first chapter, has led to a sharper sense, as a by-product perhaps, of the pain of existence under even 'normal' conditions. Sentimentality, self-dramatization, and the assumption that universal feelings are the private property of the poet himself as a uniquely seismographic instrument are among the manifest dangers of this situation. It is probably inevitable that many of the best practitioners in this age should at times fall into these traps, and that many of them pay for their gifts of sympathy and perception by mental illness. We must, in any case, finally read them as artists. The slogans of the confessional movement are well summed up in the quotations that Anne Sexton uses as epigraphs to her books *To Bedlam and Part Way Back* (1960) and *All My Pretty Ones* (1962). The first is from a letter of Schopenhauer's to Goethe; the second from a letter of Kafka's to Oskar Pollak:

> It is the courage to make a clean breast of it in the face of every question that makes the philosopher. He must be like Sophocles' Oedipus, who, seeking enlightenment concerning his terrible fate, pursues his indefatigable enquiry, even when he divines that appalling horror awaits him in the answer. But most of us carry in our heart the Jocasta who begs Oedipus for God's sake not to inquire further. . . .

and:

> . . . the books we need are the kind that act upon us like a misfortune, that make us suffer like the death of someone we love more than ourselves, that make us feel as though we were on the verge of suicide, or lost in a forest remote from all human habitation — a book should serve as the ax for the frozen sea within us.

'To make a clean breast of it in the face of . . . appalling horror' and to write a book that is 'the ax for the frozen sea within us' is not just a matter of intention but one of art. Force of character, clarity of line, a hard yet sensitive simplicity at the center and in the total outline, however complex the surface detail and the chains of implication may grow, would seem essential.

The poet in this school who comes closest to Lowell and Sylvia Plath at her best in the second and third of these essential qualities is Anne Sexton. A good many of the poems in her first book — as the title, *To Bedlam and Part Way Back,* implies — are explicitly about her experience in mental asylums. They are distinguished by an unambiguous presentation in each of the basic situations, and at the same time by the discovery of an appropriate music for each. At her most successful, as in 'Ringing the Bells,' the harmony of situation and formal embodiment is perfect:

> And this is the way they ring
> the bells in Bedlam
> and this is the bell-lady
> who comes each Tuesday morning
> to give us a music lesson
> and because the attendants make you go
> and because we mind by instinct,
> like bees caught in the wrong hive,
> we are the circle of the crazy ladies. . . .

The nursery rhythm is both true to the condition to which the 'crazy ladies' have been for the time being reduced and to the irony, which is directed at once against herself and against the institutional situation. It enables the poet to present cleanly and economically the pathos of the situation without breaking the rhythm or dissipating the concreteness:

> and this is the small hunched squirrel girl
> on the other side of me

who picks at the hairs over her lip,
who picks at the hairs over her lip all day. . . .

Another poem, 'Music Swims Back to Me,' has already been mentioned as one of the pieces discussed by the critics on the BBC. As I noted at the beginning of this chapter, it illustrates the fact that Anne Sexton's poetry seldom explicitly includes the cultural criticism of Lowell's or Sylvia Plath's. But it is not entirely without it, either. The 'they' of 'Ringing the Bells' refers to the hospital administration, of course, and to what might be called the impersonal tradition of managing the mentally ill. Behind these literal meanings there is at least a faint suggestion of the way the strong and unconsciously brutal folk of the world, and all the institutional structures including the governments, handle the innocents, each lost in his own needs, sufferings, and self. 'Music Swims Back to Me' illustrates this faint but not quite expendable implication a shade more emphatically:

Wait Mister. Which way is home?
They turned the light out
and the dark is moving in the corner.
There are no sign posts in this room,
four ladies, over eighty,
in diapers, every one of them.
La la la, Oh music swims back to me
and I can feel the tune they played
the night they left me
in this private institution on a hill.

'The poetry is in the Pity,' as Wilfrid Owen says — the ultimate referent is the private suffering, whose public dimensions were more self-evident in his poetry of war than in Mrs. Sexton's poems of madness. I do not wish to push this point any further — *poetry* is the issue. Anne Sexton's art is particularly notable for the way it picks up the rhythms of the kind of sensibility with which she is concerned. The examples I have so far given catch the note of the self reduced to almost infantile regression (what hostile critics have called 'baby-talk'), but the mature intelligence of the speaker is ultimately that of one no longer in the literal predicament presented by the poems. The climactic section of 'Music Swims Back to Me,' in which the poet describes how it felt the first night in the institution and how the music that was played became the focus of that feeling, is the discovery of the paralysis of the adult self by way of a brilliant image of its incomplete transference to nature. The image at first resembles the famous one in the second and third lines of Eliot's 'Prufrock,' but the rhapsodic development, the sense of an ecstasy of pain, is peculiarly Anne Sexton's:

> It was the strangled cold of November;
> even the stars were strapped in the sky
> and that moon too bright
> forking through the bars to stick me
> with a singing in the head.
> I have forgotten all the rest.

The relationships, in the poems of *To Bedlam and Part Way Back,* between the tones of mockery and of childlike vulnerability, with appropriate rhythms, and those of rhapsodic realization bring Anne Sexton close to the spirit of Sylvia Plath. These two young women may well have affected one another's styles, for they were certainly aware not only of each other's work but also of their common indebtedness to Lowell. Some of Anne Sexton's images and effects could easily have influenced 'Lady Lazarus' and other poems of *Ariel*. Thus, in 'Lullaby' she forms the kind of ironic and tentative bridge, for just an instant, between a plain fact (associated, needless to say, with her maladies) and a self-contained symbolic image that becomes its own world. Not only the process, but the image of the woman as 'linen,' recalls Sylvia Plath:

> My sleeping pill is white.
> It is a splendid pearl;
> it floats me out of myself,
> my stung skin as alien
> as a loose bolt of cloth.
> I will ignore the bed.
> I am linen on a shelf. . . .

The beginning of 'The Double Image' is still more striking in this respect. The mother is addressing the child from whom she has been separated by commitment to an asylum. The age of the speaker, the attempted suicides, the witch-imagery, even the 'Lazarus' effect are almost the same as in Sylvia Plath:

> I am thirty this November.
> You are still small, in your fourth year.
> We stand watching the yellow leaves go queer,
> flapping in the winter rain,
> falling flat and washed. And I remember
> mostly the three autumns you did not live here. . . .
>
> I, who chose two times
> to kill myself, had said your nickname
> the mewling months when you first came;
> until a fever rattled
> in your throat and I moved like a pantomime

above your head. Ugly angels spoke to me. The blame,
I heard them say, was mine. . . .

Death was simpler than I'd thought.
The day life made you well and whole
I let the witches take away my guilty soul.
I pretended I was dead
until the white men pumped the poison out,
putting me armless and washed through the rigmarole
of talking boxes and the electric bed. . . .

Nevertheless, these poems exist on a narrower scale than Sylvia Plath's. Their high points are not the magnificent fusion of private and universal motifs, but piercing, isolated strains of music and finely compassionate impressions of pitiful life. The former, and greater, kind of success is a purification of the expression of private pain, as in the climax of 'Music Swims Back to Me' or the beginning of 'You, Doctor Martin':

You, Doctor Martin, walk
from breakfast to madness. Late August,
I speed through the antiseptic tunnel
where the moving dead still talk
of pushing their bones against the thrust
of cure. And I am queen of this summer hotel
or the laughing bee on a stalk

of death. . . .

The second kind of success can be seen, in Anne Sexton's first book, in a poem like 'The Waiting Head,' about her mother in a rest home, sitting always at the upper front window and 'watching for anyone from her wooden seat,' and always writing in 'her leather books' that 'no one came'—apparently whether it was true or not. It can be seen in her second book as well, in 'The Hangman,' in which the speaker is the father of an extremely retarded child; and in the title poem, 'All My Pretty Ones,' about her parents, who died within three months of one another in 1959. But again, the highest poetic points are those of private expression, especially the brief, perfect 'The Starry Night.'

> The town does not exist
> except where one black-haired tree slips
> up like a drowned woman into the hot sky.
> The town is silent. The night boils with eleven stars.
> O starry starry night! This is how
> I want to die.
>
> It moves. They are all alive.
> Even the moon bulges in its orange irons
> to push children, like a god, from its eye.
> The old unseen serpent swallows up the stars.
> O starry starry night! This is how
> I want to die:
>
> into that rushing beast of the night,
> sucked up by that great dragon, to split
> from my life with no flag,
> no belly,
> no cry.

All My Pretty Ones has its recognizably confessional poems. Some continue pretty much in the spirit of 'The Double Image,' in the first book. 'The House,' for instance, is a portrait of the poet as an adolescent girl, again with various remarkable resemblances, in its vehement and satirical objectivity of detail and its unforgetting resentments, to Sylvia Plath's work. 'The Flight' is an original, bitterly humorous account of an attempt, hysterical and disorganized at best, to flee to a lover. It was frustrated by the grounding of planes at the airport. Yet there is a growth of new, hardier skin on these pieces, comparable with that in Lowell's *For the Union Dead.* For the most part, the poems are not as vulnerable as before in their self-exposure. 'The Fortress,' though like 'The Double Image' it is an address to a child and a confession of a kind of helplessness, is not autobiographical as much as contemplative. 'Housewife' changes what might have been pure whining into a compelling symbolism of the house as an extension of the body of a woman, underlining the identity that develops between herself and her mother. 'Letter Written on a Ferry While Crossing Long Island Sound' begins as a wrily melancholy account of the end of a love-affair and becomes a magnificently humorous prayer that the four solemn nuns on the ferry with the speaker may become visibly miraculous:

> Oh God,
> although I am very sad,
> could you please
> let these four nuns
> loosen from their leather boots
> and their wooden chairs
> to rise out
> over this greasy deck,
> out over this iron rail,
> nodding their pink heads to one side,
> flying four abreast
> in the old-fashioned side stroke;
> each mouth open and round,
> breathing together
> as fish do,
> singing without sound. . . .

IV

The 'Projectivist' Movement

1. SOME QUESTIONS OF FORM: 'PROJECTIVISM'

Poetic theory, as set forth by poets themselves as an adjunct of their working apparatus, usually has a makeshift air. Their *aperçus,* their occasional comments and reviews, even their more abstract forays take on importance less from what they say literally than from their relation to the qualities of the poets' best work. What Pound has to tell us about Guido Cavalcanti has its real center in, say, his translations of *Donna mi prega* and in his own poetry somewhere between 'The Return' and some of the more complex *Cantos.* What Eliot says about Shakespeare refers to Eliot's own attempt, throughout his career, to 'express the inexpressible,' as he put it. That is to say, the real magnetic center of a poet's criticism lies in his poetry.

Looking broadly at the range of poetry today, and of the related theoretical formulations by its practitioners, one sees the usual raggedly improvisational picture. Robert Lowell, as some of the quotations in Chapter II have shown, has written scattered comments that at times would scarcely interest us save for their incidental illumination of his practice. Yet these remarks, despite their apparent obviousness, do contain clues to Lowell's operational theory. No one any longer denies the organic inseparability of form and content (though I think one could show that certain American schools of poetry do in fact reduce their emphasis to one or the other). Hardly anyone would even deny the absurdity of conceiving, in the juxtaposition of these terms, any significant opposition between them. Yet there is actually a world of difference between Robert Creeley's formula, 'Form is never more than an extension of content,' and Lowell's search for self-transcendence by way of objective artistry as the *shaping* motivation of his work.

Lowell's insistence on remembering the impersonal motivation of his art even while private memory threatened to sweep him away from it made the difference in *Life Studies.* He was, for instance, the one younger poet since Crane to advance the art of the sequence, that single real contribution to the art of the longer poem by the modern age. Indeed, the sequence, with its shorter units and looser structure, has replaced the older forms — or anyway given them a new disguise to fit contemporary sensibility. Then again, he has, we will recall, brought to a certain culmination the evolution of confessional poetry — poetry that uses the poet's literal self, at its most vulnerable, as its central voice and as the major symbol of the modern predicament. Lowell pushed its possibilities to the uttermost limit (for this moment, at least) in *Life Studies.* Even so, he went at the poem's problems as formal ones:

> When I was writing *Life Studies,* a good number of the poems were started in very strict meter, and I found that, more than the rhymes, the regular beat was what I didn't want. I have a long poem in there about

> my father, called 'Commander Lowell,' which actually is largely in couplets. Well, with that form it's hard not to have echoes of Marvell. That regularity just seemed to ruin the honesty of sentiment, and became rhetorical; it said, 'I'm a poem' — though it was a great help when I was revising having this original skeleton. I could keep the couplets where I wanted them and drop them where I didn't; there'd be a form to come back to.*

To which we might add: *Life Studies* gives us the naked psyche of a suffering man in a hostile world. Lowell's way to manage this material, to *keep* it, is by his insistent emphasis on form. The natural heir to Eliot and Pound as well as to Crane, he extends their methods. His talk of 'four-foot couplets' and so on is like Pound's talk, half a century earlier, about 'absolute rhythm' and Eliot's about an 'objective correlative,' but is openly tied in with his own idiosyncratic practice rather than presented as a general poetic principle. Yet implicit in the formal emphasis is the revolutionary formal conception underlying, for instance, 'A Mad Negro Soldier Confined at Munich,' in which an accumulation of pure speed and power is the aim of Lowell's hurtling language. A wild release of psychic energy is catapulted by this poem, sparked off by the speaker's uncontrolled sexual intensity and the confused savagery of the war and its issues. Many other poets, mostly Americans, have had the same aim. One of them, of course, is Allen Ginsberg, who describes his poem 'Kaddish' as 'completely free composition, the long line breaking up within itself into short staccato breath units — notations

* In Malcolm Cowley, ed., *Representative Writers at Work: The Paris Review Interviews, Second Series* (N.Y.: Viking, 1963).

of one spontaneous phrase after another linked within the line by dashes mostly. . . .'

Prosodic and technical theory remains weak and uncertain, however, even among the followers of William Carlos Williams, who are so interested in the subject. 'Who knows what a poem ought to sound like? Until it's thar?' I am quoting Leroi Jones quoting Charles Olson. Yet the one essay by a poet specifically intended to point the new way, as it were, that has achieved any wide currency is by Olson. It is his essay 'Projective Verse,' * which first appeared in *Poetry New York* in 1950. This piece has affected writers as far apart in every way as Williams and the British poet and critic Donald Davie. Williams saw it as an extension and clarification of his own vague but germinative idea of the 'variable foot.' Announcing that 'an advance of estimable proportions is made by looking at the poem as a field rather than an assembly of more or less ankylosed lines,' he linked the essay's importance to the fact that, as he put it, 'the reconstruction of the poem [is] one of the major occupations of the intelligence in our day.' He also saw it as justifying his well-known absorption in local American rhythmic and other values: 'Nothing can grow unless it taps into the soil.' He was quite right to show fatherly pride in Olson's ideas, a direct outgrowth of Pound's influence but also, and more especially, of his own. The cluster of poets usually associated with Olson — Robert Creeley, Robert Duncan, Denise Levertov, and Paul Blackburn, as well as a number of others — bear a

* Reprinted in Donald M. Allen, ed., *The New American Poetry, 1945–1960* (N.Y.: Grove Press, 1960). The quotation from Leroi Jones is taken from the same section of 'Statements on Poetics' at the back of this volume, p. 425. The prose-quotations by Olson in the present section are from the same source, pp. 386–97.

closer relationship to Williams on the whole than they do to Pound.

Davie's interest in Olson is quite another matter. British awareness of the achievements of the great older American masters, including Pound after *Mauberley,* has been long in coming. It is still far from empathy with the violence and intensity, the high valuation put on what I have called cumulative energy, of our most vital work. It tends to isolate the usable externals of approach and technique in American poetry from their original functions and to view them with a far cooler eye than do the practitioners. The connection of the Olson group with the Concretist movement in the United Kingdom, particularly by way of Ian Hamilton Finlay in Scotland, is a strange, extreme example, since not even Creeley in this country denies himself (as Finlay does) the satisfaction of fiery, or at any rate rhapsodic, 'moments.' Indeed, the rhapsodic aspect is an essential value in the practice of the Olson group. The British poet of greatest reputation who has deliberately associated himself with this group is Charles Tomlinson, who took his earliest cues from French Symbolism, though again 'coolly,' and from more deliberately calm and precisionist achievements of Marianne Moore and Wallace Stevens. He has managed to transplant the 'field' approach of Olson in a limited but effective way to the British scene and sensibility, though with none of the reckless self-investment it has demanded of the most successful American practitioners.

To return to Davie. In his study *Ezra Pound: Poet as Sculptor,** he finds Olson's essay a helpful aid to understanding the precise nature of Pound's revolutionary ex-

* Donald Davie, *Ezra Pound: Poet as Sculptor* (N.Y.: Oxford University Press, 1964), pp. 112–16 and *passim.*

perimentation with rhythmic structure. Davie describes this experimentation as aiming 'to reconstitute a longer poetic unit than the line while still holding on to the rhythmical dismemberment of the line from within.' He regards Olson's ideas as support for his own argument that Pound, together with the poets he has influenced, has worked for a poetry of presentative simultaneity rather than of energy and of time sequence. I think he is mistaken. It seems clear that the new poetry has been as much concerned with the one kind of structure as with the other — an illogical equality of concern only when looked at syllogistically rather than aesthetically. After all, the logic of artistic sensibility is precisely involved with the encompassing of paradoxically opposed motifs. Nevertheless, Davie is right to call sharp attention, however lopsided, to the effort toward presentative simultaneity. What he seems to overlook in talking about both Pound and Olson is the relation between Pound's conception of *periplum* — defined by Hugh Kenner as 'the image of successive discoveries breaking upon the consciousness of the voyager' — and Olson's conception of the poetic 'process':

> ONE PERCEPTION MUST IMMEDIATELY AND DIRECTLY LEAD TO A FURTHER PERCEPTION. It . . . is a matter of, at *all* points (even, I should say, of our management of daily reality as of the daily work) get on with it, keep moving, keep in, speed, the nerves, their speed, the perceptions, theirs, the acts, the split second acts, the whole business, keep it moving as fast as you can, citizen. And if you also set up as a poet, USE USE USE the process at all points, in any given poem always, always one perception must must must MOVE, INSTANTER, ON ANOTHER!

> So there we are, fast, there's the dogma. And its excuse, its usableness, in practice. . . .

Olson speaks, of course, as one who is in on the work, rather than as a scholar or pure theoretician. His points of reference are to poetic *action;* hence the resemblance of his language to that of a coach or team captain — almost a literary Casey Stengel. But it is from such clues, thrown out by artists, that critical theory recurrently makes its new starts. Olson, in turn, may have picked up a notion or two from Dylan Thomas's description of his poetry as a 'moving column of words' and from his image of 'blaspheming down the stations of the breath,' as well as from his sexually colored notion of the dialectical process by which a poem grows, finding its own antitheses to the original impulses and then its syntheses beyond that. Olson describes the process as 'composition by field.' Such composition, he says, involves feeling the poem as, 'at all points, a high-energy construct' and at the same time,

> at all points, an energy discharge. . . . And it involves a whole series of new recognitions. From the moment he ventures into FIELD COMPOSITION — puts himself into the open — [the poet] can go by no other track than the one the poem under hand declares for itself.

The principle behind the process is that 'FORM IS NEVER MORE THAN AN EXTENSION OF CONTENT. (Or so it got phrased by one, R. Creeley. . . .)'

It is perfectly true, I think, that what Olson calls 'projective verse' is very far neither from Pound's *periplum* nor, for that matter (however it horrify the projectivists), from Eliot's 'objective correlative.' The terms are shifted, however, from attention to the sequence of images and other concrete effects to any form of externalization of the speaking psyche by way of the medium of language. Davie was somewhat misled because Olson's essay points to some further incidentals of this process of setting the poem in action. Thus, Olson notes the ways in which a poet working by ear rather than by eye suggests the spacing of movements and of silences, his suspension of layers of lines, as it were, in relation to one another, as well as of smaller sweeps of breath and their pauses. Now, British poetry has not for a long time concerned itself very much with such considerations. British poetry is self-conscious but not about the language and its rhythms — only about attitudes and nuances of sensibility. It is for this reason that Olson seems to have taken Davie by surprise with his *spatial* formulations — for instance, his observation that

> it is the advantage of the typewriter that, due to its rigidity and its space precisions, it can, for a poet, indicate exactly the breath, the pauses, the suspensions even of syllables, the juxtapositions even of parts of phrases, which he intends. For the first time the poet has the stave and bar a musician has had. For the first time he can, without the convention of rime and meter, record the listening he has done to his own speech and by that one act indicate how he would want any reader, silently or otherwise, to voice his work. It is time we picked the fruits of the experiments of Cummings, Pound, Williams, each of whom has, after his way, already used the machine as a scoring to his composing, as a script to its vocalizations.

The argument is not revolutionary in itself, though its emphasis sets up the danger of a certain confusion between visual or spatial arrangements on the one hand and the movement of the poem in time on the other. If there is a significant formal weakness in the method of Charles Olson and Robert Duncan, it shows up precisely in this confusion. The avowed intention to 'get on with it, keep moving,' is blocked by a certain narcissism of form, the poet's over-absorption in his own voice not as the embodying element of the curve of the poem but as a reflection of his own self-awareness. Robert Creeley, apparently less ambitious, is able to exploit the formal narcissism without attempting any major constructions. In the preface to his *For Love: Poems 1950–1960,* he writes: 'Wherever it is one stumbles (to get to wherever) at least some way will exist, so to speak, as and when a man takes this or that step — for which, god bless him.' And: 'Not more, say, to live than what there is, to live. I want the poem as close to this fact as I can bring it; or it, me.' The 'modest' tone (and, doubtless, feeling) cannot hide the preoccupation with a personal rhythm in the sense that the discovery of an external equivalent of the speaking self is felt to be the true object of poetry. The transcendence of that self — the great aim of modern romanticism — is not the issue. *That* issue is held in abeyance in this movement, in this crucial respect so very different from its models in Pound and Williams. Yet the rhapsodic side I have mentioned — the structuring so that the poem comes into its own when it most approaches pure melody — is still an important factor. Because certain bearings have been neglected despite the theory, however, the feeling that such a moment is the sacred center or ultimate justification of the poem has been weakened. The richly musical Duncan, with his very considerable natural gifts, resists the whole conception in the interests of a collagist art full of arbitrary interferences with the movement of his poems. We thus have a poetic theory implicitly more vulnerable even than Whitman's — but a trifle less unjustly so accused — to the charge of being anti-aesthetic.

2. ROBERT CREELEY

Creeley, Duncan, and Olson were at one time teachers at Black Mountain College. Hence the name Black Mountain group, attached to these poets, to some of their students, and to others who discovered affinities with them. Creeley's work is the simplest in various ways, and we may consider it, as represented in *For Love: Poems 1950–1960*, first of all.

I have already cited a few sentences of the preface and noted how they suggest Creeley's 'preoccupation with a personal rhythm in the sense that the discovery of an external equivalent of the speaking self is felt to be the true object of poetry.' That speaking self, indeed, is felt to be the center of the poem's universe as well as of the author's private life. Despite his mask of humble, confused comedian, loving and lovable, he therefore stands in his own work's way, too seldom letting his poems free themselves of his blocking presence. Thus, he describes them as 'places . . . stumbled into: warmth for a night perhaps, the misdirected intention come right; and too, a sudden instance of love, and the being loved, wherewith a man also contrives a world (of his own mind).' The result is not so much that we do not get real poems; we *do* get real poems, some of them lovely or touching or at least alive with wit. But the theater of their occurrence is such a minimal one that they are like brief mutterings often, or the few shuffling steps of an actor pretending to dance.

Creeley's *titles* are often portentous enough — 'The Crisis,' 'The Innocence,' 'The Hero.' In fact, this use of an encompassing-sounding 'the' in the titles of poems of great reticence in their statement, so that even the central situation of the poem is never quite clarified, is an irritating mannerism of this group of poets generally. For instance:

THE BUSINESS

To be in love is like going outside to see what kind of day

it is. Do not
mistake me. If you love

her how prove she
loves also, except that it

occurs, a remote chance. . . .

The attraction of the minimal *can* be considerable, however. Its essential rhythm is of self-ironic reverie, momentarily self-forgetting and then catching itself up short, as Creeley does at the end of 'The Business':

. . . But barter for
the Indian was a means of sustenance.

There are records.

The witticism, like the one with which the poem began, is wry but made of some vanishing substance. It depends, not on its own veritable wittiness, but on the author's winking presence. That is, a poem of this sort is a kind of attractive incidental effect created out of casual introspective tones from an undefined speaker whom, for want of greater energy on the poet's part, we must consider to be the poet himself. It resembles one particularly delightful little moment in William Carlos Williams's *Paterson*, Book Four, the section beginning the fifth of the mock-pastoral exchanges called 'Corydon and Phyllis.' In this section Williams discovered for himself a way of intermingling racy, natural speech and poetic effects of the 'casual introspective' sort just seen in Creeley. It is very possible that this kind of subordinated rhythmic play in Williams is the main source for Creeley's method. What is remarkable, though, is the way that Williams's firmer structure and clearer use of dramatic voice make even his minor effects reverberate further than Creeley's into a formally vibrant fulfillment, independent of any sense of the poet's own shadow hanging over the whole.

In this passage, as Williams's readers know, the speakers are an older woman, Corydon,* and a younger one, Phyllis, whom she has employed as her masseuse. Corydon speaks first:

> Phyllis, good morning. Could you stand a drink at this early hour? I've written you a poem . and the worst is, I'm about to read it to you . You don't have to like it. But, hell take it, you damn well better listen to it. Look at me shake! Or better, let me give you a short one, to begin with:
>
> If I am virtuous
> condemn me
> If my life is felicitous
> condemn me
> The world is
> iniquitous

* The humorous sympathy of her conception is reflected in the parody of the pastoral tradition that suggests to the poet his giving such a name to a Lesbian character.

Mean anything?

Not much.

Well, here's another:

You dreamy
        Communist
where are you
        going?

To world's end
        Via?
Chemistry
        Oh oh oh oh

That will
        really
be the end   .
        you

dreamy Communist
        won't it?
Together
        together

'With that she split her girdle.' Gimme another shot. I always fell on my face when I wanted to step out. But here goes! Here it is. This is what I've been leading up to. It's called, *Corydon, a Pastoral.* We'll skip the first part, about the rocks and sheep, begin with the helicopter. You remember that?

Williams sets the one magnificent little stanza of wistful nonsense beginning 'You dreamy/Communist' within the dramatic framework of the relationship of the two women. In the structure of *Paterson* as a whole, the scene has its place as part of the panorama of America's search — or at least, need — for a 'language' to overcome its inarticulateness and its distortions of love through repression and blocked communication. The little stanza itself, like the awkwardly charming (but serious, too) stanza beginning 'If I am virtuous' and like the echoing passage between 'That will' and 'won't it' that follows a little further on, takes a greater 'risk' than the Creeley poem by its freer improvisational character. The one phrase 'dreamy Communist,' suggesting nothing more than an unpredictable waywardness or indifference in the person being made love to, has this quality in particular. It leaves behind its structural motivation in the general purposes of *Paterson* I have just described. Even Williams's very short pieces, in which he sometimes introduces himself in his own person — for instance in 'This Is Just To Say,' in which he confesses eating the breakfast plums that were in the icebox — manage to break away from their private origin as the poet loses himself in the language itself, or in the sheer sensuousness of the projected picture or expression:

> Forgive me
> they were delicious
> so sweet
> and so cold

The dryly minimal character of Creeley's poetry stands in sharp contrast, usually, to these examples from Williams. Corydon's rhapsodies and the plum-thief's apology are a richly absurd clowning with comparably minimal materials. They have an emotional and physical forthrightness at the same time, because those materials are literally realized. One further contrast may be seen in the treatment of love. We have already seen the self-evident appeal of Corydon's painful but amusing romantic Lesbian yearnings, but that is an exceptional topic for Williams. More characteristically, he has written straightforward love poems and has also attempted, with rare candor and disregard for the personally awkward or unbecoming aspects of his own relation to his subject, to present the turbulent frustration of certain kinds of erotic experience.

> Look at us! Why do you
> torment yourself?
> You think I'm a virgin.
> Suppose I told you
> I'd had intercourse. What
> would you say then?
> What would you say? Suppose
> I told you that .
>
> She leaned forward in
> the half light, close to
> his face. Tell
> me, what would you say?
>
> Have you had many lovers?
>
> No one who has mauled me
> the way you have. Look,
> we're all sweaty. . . .
>
> I don't know why I can't give myself to you. A man like you should have everything he wants . I guess I care too much, that's the trouble .

Compare Creeley's 'The Riddle':

> What it is, the literal size
> incorporates.

The question
is a mute question. One is
too lonely, one wants
to stop there, at the edge of

conception. The woman

imperative, the man
lost in stern
thought:

give it form certainly,
the name and titles.

'The Riddle' is a riddle simply because the poet does not close with his themes. There is a concrete dramatic center —

. . . The woman

imperative, the man
lost in stern
thought. . . .

Presumably the dramatic center of the poem (unstated, as so often with Creeley) is the ambiguous, purely potential power of the moment preceding sexual commitment — whether to the implications of love and marriage generally or to the act of conception. A dangerous moment either way, admittedly, but so abstracted here that the very elements of the issue are in doubt. A refusal to accept defined human relationships on their own terms is implicit in each of the three assertions preceding the simple concession that after all a man and a woman are involved in the poem. The first assertion vaguely suggests a physical fact, possibly a fact of physical relationship — the 'literal size' of an undefined 'it' is said to incorporate 'its' identification. Is it the relation of man and woman, reduced, say, to genitalic proportions? But 'The question / is a mute question.' In a sense, it is the question of what the whole future, and the self's whole identity, will be. Why a 'mute' question? Possibly because the whole issue is instinctual, of the body, rather than intellectual; or because, in the heat or the emotional intensity of love-relationship (if that, indeed, enters) ultimate issues are present but impossible to state explicitly. 'One is too lonely,' the poem says further — a poignancy, but how to be taken? Too lonely to withdraw now? Too lonely in the sense that one feels one's inadequacy so keenly that one cannot bear to take the risks of love and procreation? It sounds like the latter —

> . . . One is
> too lonely, one wants
> to stop there, at the edge of
>
> conception. . . .

Yet there is also a minimal affirmation at the end, as though after all the divine gift of creation must indeed be exercised — the 'conception' be 'given' its right 'form' and its 'name and titles.' Almost a kind of *noblesse oblige.*

By holding off from commitment to the statement of his theme, Creeley makes the poem bear the weight of many possible orientations of thought and feeling, of which I have suggested only the most obvious, perhaps. It can be read, too, either solemnly or wryly, a poem of the cosmos held in abeyance, then almost flippantly released. The touchstones of 'interpretation' are these: that the poet has a riddle for us (and himself) to solve; that he is dealing in the inexpressible; that he is lonely and afraid but self-ironic too; that sex is involved, a little comically in the contrast (at once literally accurate and reversing the usual assumptions of romantic tradition) of 'imperative' woman and bemused man; that he has power of 'conception' and also of formal authentication, an oddly bureaucratic turn to the rhetoric at the very end. These Prufrockian notes might be hints, as well, of the poet's uncertain relation to his Muse and to publication, but such connotations are dim shadows of the primary effect.

Creeley's refusal to give the poem a more concrete force seems derived from a fear of giving the personal game away. At the same time, he clearly has a desire to suggest the universal dimensions of the issue. The short-cut he adopts, of extreme implication through a kind of Delphic reserve, limits the possibilities of success to the symbolic and emotional carrying power of a few understatements. Though avoiding the difficulty that Williams ran into from unsympathetic critics who insisted that his poems carried no meaning beyond the literal sense-impressions and notes from experience that form their exuberantly concrete basis, the unreverberative inwardness of a poem like 'The Riddle' muffles its own possibilities. The form that Creeley employs is not so much an 'extension of content' as an underlining of it — for instance, in the isolation of the unmemorable three-word line 'conception. The woman.' The effect does point up the dramatic situation of the poem and 'extend' it visually. That is, the line hangs in the air, the focal center of the poem, its well-framed 'riddle.' It has considerable magnetism, in that special sense; the reference is ultimately to the poet staring at the riddle, not to the intrinsic mystery itself.

In 'A Form of Women,' the title-poem of the Creeley collection, there is a more conventionally melodic treatment of a similar theme. The speaker here is addressing a beloved woman to whom he has been cruel and unresponsive. Again, there are curious suggestions of 'The Love Song of J. Alfred Prufrock' and even of Robert Frost's 'Acquainted with the Night' as the speaker sings, sometimes in doggerel, of his fearful, lonely walking, his too adaptable nature, his terror of loneliness and of life's challenge. As the song progresses, it drifts from motif to motif, not really relating them. First there is the speaker's terror of the unknown, of 'things / looking in at me through the open door' and

> . . . shapes more fearful
> because I feared
> what I did not know
> but have wanted to know. . . .

Then comes an explanation of the speaker's inability to act to comfort the woman, somehow leading to his mystification concerning his own personality:

> I could not touch you.
> I wanted very much to
> touch you
> but could not. . . .
>
> My face is my own.
> My hands are my own.
> My mouth is my own
> but I am not.

Addressing the woman as his 'Moon,' he says that when she leaves him he is in utter darkness that is 'a pit of fear' and 'a stench,' and he pleads in the closing stanza:

> But I love you.
> Do you love me.
> What to say
> when you see me.

The 'form' of women, then, is like that of the changing moon, a 'form' on whose mythical, cyclical movements the speaker's own reality hangs, though at the very end syntax and such clarity as has so far been present disintegrate in a limply indefinite clause. A compost of derivations (there are echoes of Lawrence amid the others) and a loose sequence of notes on the woman-theme all stated as reflexes of the indeterminate self, the poem is actually less firm than 'The Riddle' though emotionally more suggestive. The jigging doggerel effects and the broken phrasing in several of the stanzas seem a deliberate interference with the lyric movement and the potentially sustained and organic curve of feeling. That Creeley actually knows how to create such a movement and curve is shown in at least three poems — 'Kore,' 'The Rain,' and 'Jack's Blues.' The first of these is an exquisite poem in which the disintegrating or alienating effects are few and so located that they enhance the music instead of breaking it. The second is a simple love poem in which the sense of deep loss and the need for sexual reassurance underlying 'A Form of Women' are made earthily explicit. The third is an imaginative yet subdued improvisation on the theme of opting out. Its title is exactly right, and its language sadly, aptly American:

> I'm going to roll up
> a monkey and smoke it, put
> an elephant in the pot. I'm going out
> and never come back. . . .

Creeley's humor, especially in his complaints about married life, seems to me too often obvious and easy, though in 'Sing Song' we get a splendidly exasperated bit of mock praise for a wife to whom bed means one thing only: sleep. This impression of work demanding too little from its author, though the author demands a good deal of attentive sympathy and faith from the reader, is equally true of his more serious writing. Yet he can be hilarious or strangely moving, when he has things right. Poems like the title poem and 'The Hero' touch an authentic nerve of suffering, and a poem like 'The Riddle' touches a different kind of pain, the ironic irreversibility of the life-process which human will can hardly find a way to hold off or get around. The 'field' approach in his poetry has something to do, at times at any rate, with Creeley's best effects. That is, his best poems characteristically establish certain phrases of intenser life than the language around them projects. These phrases float within an otherwise rather flat or undirected context, but by their strategic placement they seem to accumulate an emphasis fraught with suggestiveness. Thus they induce in the reader an empathy with the speaker's subjective state of inward pain and alert awareness protected by an apparently confused and nonintellectual disorientation. If a last stand were necessary (it does not seem to be), one could say that this sort of poetry, like René Char's work in France during the Occupation and like some of the post-World War II poetry of England that makes a point of restraint and cool control, is the last stand of genuine sensibility against the violence and ruthlessness of twentieth-century civilization. But genuine sensibility cannot give up its passion quite so tamely; it all seems a little too confined to settle for just yet.—Perhaps after World War III? If so, Creeley is indeed ahead of his time.

3. CHARLES OLSON

Charles Olson's poems, largely collected in two books published in 1960, *The Distances* and *The Maximus Poems,* have the typographical appearance of work influenced by Ezra Pound's *Cantos.* The very first line of the former book, in the poem 'The Kingfishers,' bears a Poundian sort of brand: the slant line that Olson uses to impose a caesura where it would not naturally occur:

> What does not change / is the will to change

This poem is a somewhat lopsided sequel in three parts, of which the first is itself subdivided into four sections. Perhaps more strikingly Poundian, though, is the interlacing of parallel motifs by the technique that Davie called 'the rhythmical dismemberment of the line from within':

> I thought of the E on the stone, and of what Mao said
> la lumière"
> but the kingfisher
> de l'aurore"
> but the kingfisher flew west
> est devant nous!
> he got the color of his breast
> from the heat of the setting sun!

Isolating this brief passage from its context in Part I, Section 2 of 'The Kingfishers,' we see in it a representative sampling of Olson's general practice. Certain motifs run through the whole poem — the ancient symbol 'E,' cut rudely on an old stone; an inspirational and activist quotation from Mao Tse-tung; and the over-all symbol of the kingfisher, in this case presented in sensuous action. The mystery of the 'E' is the mystery of the changed use of identical symbols and objects. The kingfisher, too, was valued for its feathers, which, in earlier Mexican cultures, 'were wealth.' The feathers were exported at one time, and worked into golden ornamental sculpture whose totemistic meaning exalted the bird and other animals. Like Pound, Olson weaves snatches of quotation and speech from other languages into his fabric. (Whether Mao actually composed in French or whether he is being represented by a French translation would seem to be a relevant though not a crucial question.) The passage as a whole sets going simultaneously two directions of movement, related yet diametrically opposite. The speaker, thinking both of 'the E on the stone' and of Mao's words, links the remote, all but forgotten past to the still ungrasped present and future. Similarly, the double movement of looking toward the dawn (*la lumière de l'aurore est devant nous!* — to reassemble the French quotation) and of flying toward the sunset (the kingfisher's westward flight) suggests the historical pressures on man at any given moment. Yet the passage is simple in construction, direct in its tone and impressions. Despite its larger implications, it is held together by the echoing *r*'s * of *lumière, kingfisher* (repeated two lines later), *l'aurore,* and *color,* and by the central rhyme of *breast* and *west,* which echo *said* and are echoed by *setting.* There are other echoes of importantly placed sounds, such as *stone* and *sun,* supporting this main pattern, and the two exclamations create another kind of

* They are French *r*'s and English *r*'s, unless Olson intends to Anglicize (or rather, Americanize) the pronunciation of the French words. His omission of the *accent grave* in '*lumière,*' which I have taken to be a typographical error and therefore 'corrected,' is conceivably a sign of this intention.

echoing and balance, as do the two sets of incantatory effects.

The influence of Williams, Pound, and sometimes Cummings is obvious in the split lines, extensive quotation, varied line-lengths, shifts from one poetic mode to another, and plasticity of syntax and punctuation throughout the poem. Olson's voice is nevertheless his own. That is, it is *finally* his own. The following passage, for instance, starts out as pure Williams but ends as pure Olson:

> He woke, fully clothed, in his bed. He
> remembered only one thing, the birds, how
> when he came in, he had gone around the rooms
> and got them back in their cage, the green one first,
> she with the bad leg, and then the blue,
> the one they had hoped was a male. . . .

This particular personal note, whether couched in the first or the third person, is never found in Pound, nor does Williams—though fond of effects like the sudden introduction of himself as 'he' in a specific, concrete setting—have quite this pattern of informal, ramblingly detailed narrative.* Olson, like Creeley, deliberately skirts tediousness of style. The passage follows the poem's opening line, already quoted, which is set off by itself as a clue that it is the major motif: 'What does not change / is the will to change.' The memory of the recaging of the birds summons up another memory, of the remarks of an effete fellow at a party—an altogether unsuitable person to be in any sense the carrier of exciting ancient values—concerning the kingfisher's loss of meaning, as wealth or as symbol, for the modern world.

* One finds comparable effects in Williams's prose, however—for instance, in *A Voyage to Pagany* or in *Kora in Hell.*

We have already looked at the opening stanza of the second section of 'The Kingfisher,' Part I (beginning 'I thought of the E on the stone'). After the extremely active projection there, this section moves, in the manner of Hugh MacDiarmid's more pedagogic forays, into a short lecture on the 'features' of the kingfisher — serrated bill, inconspicuous tail, 'syndactylism of the 3rd & 4th digit,' and so on — and then into a subtle balancing of the legendary or prophetic uses of birds against the peculiar nesting habits of kingfishers. Olson wants to make clear his point that it was not the literal characteristics (except for the feathers) that had anything to do with the changed attitudes toward the kingfisher, but a dying out of its symbolic meaning for the Indians. On the other hand, the birds lay their eggs on fishbone pellets, 'rejectamenta,' which they throw up after feeding, and as the nestlings 'are fed and grow, this nest of excrement and decayed fish becomes a dripping, fetid mass.' The birth and growth of the new out of the decay of the past illustrates the continuing condition and challenge of life stated at the poem's start: 'What does not change / is the will to change.' Olson restates the principle at the end of Part I, Section 2, in a form that once more picks up the quotation from Mao already referred to:

Mao concluded:
          nous devons
                    nous lever
                              et agir!

The activist Marxian perspective implicit in the Mao quotations is somewhat modulated by Olson throughout 'The Kingfisher' toward a more purely qualitative notion of dialectical process and change. Yet he too is program-matic, though not politically so. His attempt is to isolate and resurrect primal values that have been driven out of sight by the alienating force of European civilization. Thus, the third section of Part I has to do with the moment when the wrecking of the Indian religious and cultural structure began, and when the invaders' assaults put a sudden end to peace, 'sweet brotherhood,' and 'the tilled fields.' The fourth and final section then contemplates, in lines that move tonally between the extremes of intellectual exposition and of mystical incantation, the question of personal identity in relation to the dialectics of change. Parts II and III recapitulate, in the manner of the *Cantos,* the motifs already developed. Part II does so through a sharply contrasting picture of Indian burial-rites and the actions of the conquistadors, and through a consideration of the violence and filth underlying all public order and decency. Part III does so through an apology by the poet speaking in his own right. He says humbly (ironically so, as Pound does in the opening poem of *Hugh Selwyn Mauberley*) that as he is neither Greek nor Roman the artistic 'risk' he is taking does not matter, but that he must stake himself as he is on his language and native traditions. The roots of artistic and personal meaning are here, in this hemisphere where the Indian tragedy occurred and where the American present defines the speaker:

> . . . if I have any taste
> it is only because I have interested myself
> in what was slain in the sun
>
> I pose you your question:
>
> shall you uncover honey / where maggots are?
>
> I hunt among stones

So the poem ends. It has a remarkable lyrical buoyancy and sureness of movement for a piece of writing that is so intellectually oriented, with so many 'points' to be made. An occasional gawky Creeley-note creeps in, but it seems almost lost in the wider sweep of Olson:

> But I have my kin, if for no other reason than
> (as he said, next of kin) I commit myself, and,
> given my freedom, I'd be a cad
> if I didn't. Which is most true.

Olson can also lapse into the commonplace or silly *without* benefit of Creeley. Indeed, his method is to focus his purer writing on vivid points of attention that, from the point of view of his self-indulgent aesthetic theory, justify a disregard for incidental imperfections. Sometimes he revels in a certain kind of bad line: 'I am no Greek, hath not th'advantage'; or 'I offer, in explanation, a quote.' The second of these lines can be defended as, at any rate, a natural enough Americanism. But 'I am no Greek, hath not th'advantage' is emptily tricky. It is memorable for its weak grammar in the manner of certain advertisements, but functionally it is indefensible.

I have gone into 'The Kingfisher' at some length because it is characteristic of Olson both in method, including its large structural technique, and in its over-all tone and attitudinal set. Olson feels in this poem that he is dealing with a crucial issue by way of the kingfisher symbol: the issue of the betrayal of humanly meaningful modes of life that were discovered before the emergence of the modern state. The European perfection of the state was a triumph of the abstract and impersonal over man as a rationally and aesthetically oriented being. The first section of Part I introduces the theme obliquely, as incidental to the curious memory of someone's odd remarks and early departure from a party. The section is casual, subdued; we hardly notice the large historical implications of the opening line about 'the will to change,' or the special emphasis implied in the slant line in the middle of that line. Each of the three longer stanzas actually calls attention to the kingfisher motif, one by abruptly shortening the lines in which it is introduced, another by a device of spacing (' "The pool the kingfishers' feathers were wealth why. . . ." ') not employed elsewhere in this section. The second and third sections then throw a very heavy weight on it, beginning with the passage that connects it with both the 'E' motif and that of the Mao quotation. These reorient the context. The kingfisher was at first a mere subject for contemplation, somehow allied with the mystery of historical change and the depressed sense of the diminution of personality in our age. Now it is related to the continuing, archetypal processes of nature, to the realization of our loss of a whole qualitative mode of civilization, and to the large philosophical question of the relation of human will to historical fatality. Section 4 brings the first part to conclusion by moving into abstract, incantatory statement. Part II then tries to sharpen the general focus by relating it to a new concrete emphasis (on Indian burial rites), and Part III does so even more by bringing in the poet himself, awkwardly apologizing for his presumption and defining the present condition of society as one of 'maggots' rather than of 'honey,' where one must perforce 'hunt among stones.'

There is no escaping the strongly didactic tone of Olson's larger constructs, which is at variance with the intrinsically lyrical self-containment of his best passages and, to some extent, with his professed poetic theory. On first reading, the didacticism stands in the way of a response to the genuinely poetic orchestration going on. Afterwards, it *still* stands in the way, but is sufficiently subordinated to the over-all curve to be less of a barrier. Feeling for the American past is a powerful force in this writer, helping to overcome incidental weaknesses of rhythm and phrasing at points where the vision or the ear falters. The grimly funny narrative 'There Was a Youth Whose Name Was Thomas Granger,' about the trial and conviction of Tom Granger for sodomy in Plymouth Plantation, revels in the language and the psychology of colonial Puritanism. 'At Yorktown' broods over the soil of Revolutionary memory, cherishing that memory like a revelation:

> At Yorktown the long dead
> loosen the earth, heels
> sink in, over an abatis
> a bird wheels
>
> and time is a shine caught blue
> from a martin's
> back

Both these latter poems, the one by relying on documentation (except for one or two transitional and unobtrusive comments by the author), the other by focusing on the local scene and the simplest of evocations, avoid the tendentious note that mars poems like 'The Kingfishers.' As long as Olson is able to keep a shorter poem anchored in such concrete and unified materials, he can avoid tendentiousness — though in too many of even the shorter poems he fails to do so. In fact, imprisoned within the tendentious poet is a pure lyric poet of the finest imaginative power. One has only to pick up the half-surrealist 'The Moon Is the Number 18' to see that a talent comparable with that revealed in Dylan Thomas's 'In My Craft or Sullen Art' is locked up in Olson's expansions and arguments. The desolate death-vision of 'The Moon Is the Number 18' goes far beyond most of Olson's other work in sheer quality of poetic statement:

> The blue dogs rue,
> as he does, as he would howl, confronting
> the wind which rocks what was her, while prayers
> striate the snow, words blow
> as questions cross fast, fast
> as flames, as flames form, melt
> along any darkness. . . .

Avoidance of tendentiousness is not one of Olson's purposes, however. This is unfortunate, yet one can only admire his determination to have his say, at length, and to develop a practicing aesthetic to match this determination. Intellectual directness and steadfastness are virtues in art as elsewhere. We forgive and even admire Milton for risking his readers' boredom at times, though in part we do so because his art is never entirely dormant while he is trying us. Moreover, a sufficient number of the greatest works of our own age have a clear didactic purpose among their motivations. In *The Maximus Poems* the purpose is rather overwhelmingly belabored. The sequence consists of thirty-eight poems, or 'Letters,' * a great many of which repeat the accusing theme of the

* Some of the poems are called 'Letters' in their titles; others are not. Thus, the first poem is called 'I, Maximus of Gloucester, to You,' the second 'Maximus, to Gloucester: Letter 2,' the third 'Letter 3,' the fourth 'The Songs of Maximus,' and the fifth 'Letter 5.' After 'Letter 23,' all the remaining poems have individual titles without reference to 'letter'-numbers.

triumph of 'pejorocracy' in American life. Another theme, of the persistent, intrinsic meaning of the place that is the locale of the poem — Gloucester, Massachusetts, and the whole adjacent region and its history — is equally familiar in its implications. One must recognize the fact that we have now a modern tradition of poetry that makes certain assumptions concerning American capitalism and its eroding effect, from the days of the mercantilism and 'nascent capitalism' of the early seventeenth century (about which Olson writes, for instance, in 'Letter 23') to the 'corporative murder' ('Good News') of our own day. The nativist emphasis, brought into the foreground especially by Williams, but in fact powerful in American poetry for a century and a half, is equally an established tradition. After Masters and Williams, one might even call it a 'set theme.'

The problem, then, for poets working within these traditions, is to fasten on a region one knows intimately, to possess through whatever study is necessary its literal history and idiosyncrasies, and to realize its felt meaning for those who have most intimately shaped their lives within it. Betrayal of original possibilities of the land and the people is of the essence of much modern history — the motif will unfold itself in its own particular way. The theme is a fall, not so much from original bliss as from golden, if hard-to-be-wrung, possibility. Though we may call it a sequence, *The Maximus Poems* is not the structured work as a whole that it at first promises to be, but is mainly a series of variations on this complex traditional theme, built around Gloucester, Massachusetts: its origins, its economic history in relation to the nation's, its peculiar landscape, its cultural needs and deprivations, and the poet's literal and symbolic place in it. The connection with the scheme of Williams's *Paterson* should be clear.

I shall not examine *The Maximus Poems* in depth, for a number of the individual poems require more detailed explication than we have space for, and their characteristic structure resembles that of 'The Kingfishers.' Letter 1, for instance — 'I, Maximus of Gloucester, To You' — is divided into six sections which seek to project and correlate the recognizable Olson motifs by way of the technique of moving verbal energy espoused in his essay from which I have quoted. Although the name the poet invents for himself, 'Maximus,' is a bit presumptuous, we may justify it on the grounds that it is less his literal self to which he gives this name than his symbolic, functional self as an embodiment of the potentialities of full self-awareness and keen sensibility of the region. He is 'a metal hot from boiling water,' tempered and sharpened by all the meanings in which he has been immersed. A note on the device printed opposite the title page, a 'glyph' vaguely analogous to the Chinese ideograms printed in Pound's *Cantos,* tells us that this is 'Olson's "Figure of Outward," striding forth from the domain of the infinitely small; and, also, a written character for Maximus himself — the Man in the Word.' The mystical, incantatory language prefacing the first section of the poem suggests that the poet uses Maximus as Williams uses his figure of 'Dr. Paterson' or Pound his figure of Odysseus *redivivus.* In Maximus, the creative process acts to transmute the poet's private sense of the life-force, his affection for Gloucester, his own erotic nature, and his prophetic insight into the organically aesthetic dimensions of a poem. The brief first section, which follows below, is one of Olson's finest 'projective' flights:

the thing you're after
may lie around the bend
of the nest (second, time slain, the bird! the bird!

And there! (strong) thrust, the mast! flight
(of the bird
o kylix, o
Antony of Padua
sweep low, o bless
the roofs, the old ones, the gentle steep ones
on whose ridge-poles the gulls sit, from which they depart,

And the flake-racks
of my city!

This passage, I think, is as good an example as any of the remarkable individual achievement of Olson in a number of these poems. One would think that the burden of the derivativeness of his general framework of ideas and materials would drag down his writing hopelessly. But he finds his own way of launching the poem into action again and again. It is as if one man were to undertake to sail a huge old ship all by himself, a man moreover with a Chaplinesque gift for entangling himself in the rigging whenever possible — one who does everything the hard way. And the point is that, despite the entangling and stumbling and waste of effort, he does sail the ship and sometimes, as in the passage just quoted, does so beautifully. In 'The Songs of Maximus' (Letter 4), he describes himself as a kind of serious tramp clown. He says that the issue for him is not to take advantage of modern conveniences and efficiency but to avoid them as much as possible. The position is almost a parody of that of Thoreau; the literal reality, the 'meanness' that he must grapple with, lies not in the outside world but in himself somehow. Olson's comic tone is rather like Creeley's:

> Holes
> in my shoes, that's all right, my fly
> gaping, me out
> at the elbows, the blessing
> that difficulties are once more. . . .

Again, in 'Maximus, to Himself' (Letter 12), the role is presented and contemplated less defensively. A certain confessional note enters, perplexed and dismayed:

> I have had to learn the simplest things
> last. Which made for difficulties.
> Even at sea I was slow, to get the hand out, or to cross
> a wet deck.
> The sea was not, finally, my trade.
> But even my trade, at it, I stood estranged
> from that which was most familiar. . . .

Once more a comparison with Creeley suggests itself. These notes of humility are like Creeley's paradoxical self-minimizing. They are paradoxical because accompanied by an effort to rearrange the universe around a shrunken vision of the self. Olson's elaborate formal outworks share with Creeley's ambiguities of noncommitment an insistence on that almost hidden, untranscended self as the key, after all, to value.

The three passages just cited are variants of Olson at his best, either as a highly original lyric poet, or as a comic performer, or as a possibly ironic delineator of his own sense of inadequacy. What they have in common, besides their literary quality, is that they all point to simple acceptance of reality as it is, whether of place or of the self, so long as it is idiosyncratic reality in its natural conformations. As Maximus says in the unpunctuated, slightly Delphic utterance closing 'Maximus, at Tyre and at Boston' (Letter 21):

> . . . we are only
> as we find out we are

Many of the 'letters' are directed against the prevailing tendencies of the age, or are highly specific pursuits of local history, with their emphasis on the recurrent undercutting of the economic prospects of the region and the erosion of the status of the fisherman. There is a passionately polemical side to *The Maximus Poems,* obviously comparable with what we find in the sequences of Pound and Williams but, again, quite original within the context of that comparison. For the most part, Olson is most successful, even in this aspect of his sequence, when he is being most personal. A good instance is 'Maximus to Gloucester, Letter 19 (A Pastoral Letter),' largely the account of a personal encounter with a local minister who tried to pin down Olson's church allegiance and was rebuffed:

> For I am no merchant.
> Nor so young I need to take a stance
> to a loaded
> smile.

In the complex proliferations of this sequence, it is these moments that illuminate the intensity behind the entanglements of attitude and information. They redeem the work from its ponderousness by providing clues to the private tone within the expansive expositions.

4. ROBERT DUNCAN

As I suggested earlier, at the end of the first chapter, Robert Duncan is probably the figure with the richest natural genius among the Black Mountain poets. His work lacks Creeley's consistent surface simplicity and Olson's familiar cluster of localist and radically critical attitudes, and is consequently less well known than their writings. Also, it is cluttered by certain 'interferences,' partly stylistic and willful, partly related to his mystical and private attitudinal assumptions. The most interesting of his pieces have been collected in two books, *The Opening of the Field* (1960) and *Roots and Branches* (1964). Though it seems clear now that Duncan's art is to some degree self-defeating, one has only to leaf through these books to find poems and passages that mark him as a modern romantic whose best work is instantly engaging by the standards of the purest lyrical traditions.

The first poem in *The Opening of the Field* is a perfect example. This poem, 'Often I Am Permitted to Return to a Meadow' (the title is also the first line), carries us, beautifully and simply, into the dual realm of the child-mind's mythopoeic reveries and of the poet's own symbolic transmutation of reality.

OFTEN I AM PERMITTED TO RETURN TO A MEADOW

as if it were a scene made-up by the mind,
that is not mine, but is a made place,

that is mine, it is so near to the heart,
an eternal pasture folded in all thought
so that there is a hall therein

that is a made place, created by light
wherefrom the shadows that are forms fall. . . .

Often I am permitted to return to a meadow
as if it were a given property of the mind
that certain bounds hold against chaos. . . .

None of the other Black Mountain poets, and few other poets of our day, can match the exquisite workmanship and mystical directness of these lines at the beginning and near the end of the poem. The tone is complex — humble, sweet, sad — yet makes for a single curve of feeling. This effect is created partly by a varied incantatory pattern of parallel constructions, so that there is a falling movement at the beginning of lines that shifts, imperceptibly, into a rising movement created by a new turn at the end. Thus the first line (the title) begins with an abstract statement that is a gracious acknowledgment, courtly and bearing a sense of prayer akin somehow to the poetry of the Court of Love tradition. It ends on a concrete note, summoning up a magically remembered place. That note is held at the beginning of the fifth line ('an eternal pasture'), which in turn is followed by an encompassing new phrase, half image, half abstraction ('folded in all thought'), preparing us for the extended vision of an earthly paradise that follows. Affinities with parallel passages in the tradition as old as Dante, at least, and as recent as Eliot and Pound, will suggest themselves readily. The last three quoted lines, on the other hand, embody the program of modern aestheticism; that is, of art as a holding against chaos and a projection of human meaning in the face of it. They do so, not programmatically but as part of the pursuit of the meadow image.

At the center of the poem the sources of its vision are

suggested in two key passages, each concretely projected. These reinforce one another as clues both to the poem's sense of mystery and to its claims for the function of art. They may be summed up, I suppose, as recollections of the lost but still powerful earth-mother, and of the lost self-entrancement of childhood. The first source is the 'First Beloved,' 'the Lady':

> She it is Queen Under The Hill
> whose hosts are a disturbance of words within words
> that is a field folded.

The second is revealed in a children's game:

> It is only a dream of the grass blowing
> east against the source of the sun
> in an hour before the sun's going down
>
> whose secret we see in a children's game
> of ring a round of roses told.

The incantatory movement of the poem as a whole conveys a gravely contemplative spirit, as of one who is being instructed by a scene he himself has conjured up. Motifs that elsewhere in Duncan's poetry are forced and contrived assert themselves in this brief masterpiece with absolute authority. Even the idea of a poem as 'a field folded,' 'a disturbance of words within words,' is easily contained within the structure of the pursuit of the inward vision that drives the poet toward the discovery of his own meanings — or, as he puts it, of 'all architectures that I am.' He realizes his own and Olson's shared aesthetic here with the utmost grace and economy. Apart from everything else, the poem makes an ideal invocation of the Muse at the beginning of a volume of verse.

Very often Duncan's poems are inspired by other poems or by works in another of the arts. He has, for instance, been strongly influenced by the collages of his friend Jess Collins, who designed the title page of *The Opening of the Field.* Similarly, much of his work is touched off by his own and others' thinking about the nature of artistic process; Duncan is in many ways the most intellectual of our poets from the point of view of the effect upon him of a wide, critically intelligent reading. He shares with Malraux the belief that art is not the imitation of nature but her rival, though his insistence is deliberately oriented toward the irrational in a way that Malraux would perhaps find abhorrent. What they would agree on is the fertile significance of the insight that the realm of art is a 'made' reality, as the opening poem has it. The subject is pursued in a series of poems called 'The Structure of Rime.' According to the second of these poems (the overall object of which is to assert the mystical character of the discovery of 'the unyielding Sentence that shows Itself forth in the language as I make it' — a punning indication of the kind of revelation these pieces are after), *'An absolute scale of resemblance and disresemblance establishes measures that are music in the actual world.'* Duncan's italics here are an effort to stamp on the reader the revealed character of what he is saying. In actual fact, the formulation has probably been adapted from Wallace Stevens's essay 'The Realm of Resemblance,' which plays with the relation between 'the structure of poetry' and 'the structure of reality.'

However that may be, there is a clear connection between this line of Duncan's thought and Olson's association of his art with an allegiance to the human prospect at the moment of history before the development of the modern state, and also between it and Creeley's allegiance to the private sensibility at an ambiguously uncommitted stage. In another very simple poem, 'Ingmar Bergman's *Seventh Seal,*' Duncan finds in the Bergman film a clue to the poet's role. At first glance the poem may seem 'escapist.' Its real implication, however, is of the irrelevance to man's essential nature of the 'issues' created by the pursuit of power abstracted from the subjective needs and visions of the self. In a passage such as the following one, Duncan speaks for the sensibility of the age, as we have seen it in the whole body of post-war poetry we have been examining, and gets clear for the moment of his special preoccupations:

> our age! It's our age!
> and the rage of the storm is abroad.
> The malignant stupidity of statesmen rules.
> The old riders thru the forests race
>   shouting: the wind! the wind!
> Now the black horror cometh again.
>
> And I'll throw myself down
> as the clown does in Bergman's *Seventh Seal*
> to cower as if asleep with his wife and child,
> hid in the caravan under the storm.
>
> Let the Angel of wrath pass over.
> Let the end come.
> War, stupidity and fear are powerful.
> We are only children. To bed! To bed!
>   To play safe!
>
> To throw ourselves down
> helplessly, into happiness,
>   into an age of our own. . . .

The poem requires no special comment, but its theme of the 'black horror' suggests the emotional range of Duncan's work. It has its very 'dark' side, often uninhibited in its acceptance of personal depression and worse, as in 'A Poem of Despondencies.'

> It's the fearful rising where the cock
>   won't rise
> that sickens the eyes, tricks
>   the domestic poseur to self-loathing.
> Black bile not blood drips
>   from the enclosure.
>
> This is the way the land lies. . . .
>
> A man held so, up-
> held we see in staind unmoving
> sea moved, sustaind in
> Hell,
>   mannd against calm.

Another poem of this order is 'Out of the Black,' though in this one the movement is a downward plunge through the theme of 'black desolation' toward a vision of the experience as a way of assimilating 'the cry of all grievous being' and thereby finding the way 'upward' again — 'a going up of pestilence into the crown.' Perhaps the most accurate way of describing Duncan's emotional range is to stress his remarkable virtuosity, which enables him to encompass opposite states of awareness and feeling through the interplay of both traditional and highly personal modes of expression.

The virtuosity is best seen in certain purely technical achievements, such as 'Shelley's *Arethusa* Set to New Measures,' the opening section of 'A Poem Beginning with a Line by Pindar,' and 'After a Passage in Baudelaire.' In each of these the initial problem is of the mastery of rhythm and idiom consonant with and expressive of the original. The problem in each instance is set by the opening line: 'Now Arethusa from her snow couches arises'; *'The light foot hears you and the brightness begins';* 'Ship, leaving or arriving, of my lover.' From these beginnings, the complex interplay takes off. The Shelley poem adheres most strictly to the movement of the original, while the one that takes off from Pindar is guided by the original only at the very beginning. Duncan's rhythmic recasting of 'Arethusa' gives more emphasis than does Shelley's version to the swift downward action and resurgence afterwards that, in a purely formal way, parallel the swoon and rise of feeling of 'Out of the Black.' The repossession of Baudelairean complexities is sufficient, in the poem that attempts it, to achieve a comparable end — the sense of tragic and insoluble frustration of need yielding, in a special way, to the debonair dismissal of suffering once the artist's perspective has taken over. The process is examined in the Pindar poem, a sequence of four movements, at far greater length. The sequence begins exquisitely, evocative of the whole lyric tradition and its human meaning. (As I noted in the first chapter, in quoting this opening stanza, its movement is reminiscent of the beginning of Pound's *Homage to Sextus Propertius.*)

> *The light foot hears you and the brightness begins*
> god-step at the margins of thought,
>   quick adulterous tread at the heart.
> Who is it that goes there?
>   Where I see your quick face
> notes of an old music pace the air,
> torso-reverberations of a Grecian lyre.

From this stanza the first section moves swiftly to a contemplation of Goya's painting of Cupid and Psyche — the sensual physicality and rapture of their love, surrounded by envy and by the atmosphere of their coming pain. The second section contemplates for some lines the meaning of the 'magic' and the 'passionate dispersion' portrayed in the painting: the tragic nature of time, and the contradictory fact that 'it is toward the old poets,' among the living, that we go for guidance, to their

> words shed like tears from
> a plenitude of powers time stores.

It may be Williams especially that this passage pays tribute to, for there are certain clues in the language, allusions perhaps to his 'variable foot' and to the strokes he suffered toward the end of his life. In any case, we hover for a moment over the theme of the stored power of the artist with which a great, aging poet is entrusted. It is a brilliant moment in the poem, and then, grotesquely, the poet cuts into it with a series of clownish puns and a long attack on the failure of the country to find one president since Lincoln with the imagination and spiritual power to move a people toward its best possibilities. The third section returns to the theme of Eros and Psyche, linking it to the lost myth of America and the whole struggle of man through the mysteries of science and of art to encompass and deal with the disintegration of vision and with death. The final section then reasserts the mystery, recalling the motifs of the opening poem and celebrating the human mind. Only at a few points of the latter sections is the high poetic achievement of the first one matched, but the pattern of soaring movement, depressive scattering of energies, and reintegration demands that this be so.

I have touched on some of the main qualities of Duncan's poetry, but only barely upon the particular complexities and difficulties that his work presents. His mysticism, certainly, deserves further study. Its particular points of reference and its affinities need clearer outlining than they have yet received. It is less a system (if that at all) than a set of partially private, partially literary, and partially traditional occultist interests, derived from sources as diverse as the cabala, Blake's writings, and the hermetic later writings of H. D. The appendix of 'Statements on Poetics' in Donald M. Allen's *The New American Poetry* contains useful statements by Duncan on this subject, and the poetry itself naturally provides many hints and clues. Some familiarity with cabalistic lore reveals itself, for instance, in the charming poem 'What Do I Know of the Old Lore?' Beyond the cabala and the pagan mysteries, of course, Duncan has invented a fragmentary mythology out of his private life and interwined it with his erotic-aesthetic mystique, sometimes intruding it quite abruptly in a poem but sometimes, as we have seen, using it effortlessly and naturally.

The intrusions constitute a special problem. Until their bearing in a particular poem becomes clear and is seen to be artistically relevant as well, they are barriers to any reader. Duncan employs them at times arbitrarily, to break his own spell, as it were. He does not want to subordinate the freedom of the poem's movement to any sort of formal expectation, and the art of the collagists has suggested an aesthetic of the mixture of modes by which he guides himself on occasion. Another sort of intrusion is present in his work as well, in the allusions to his private attitudes concerning — among other matters — love and friendship and to autobiographical details unknown to the uninstructed reader. Like Ginsberg, he brings in the names of his own San Francisco coterie and introduces autobiographical data as though these names and data were items within a sacred text or covenant. In a number of the poems, too, an acceptance of homosexual love is taken for granted; that is, it is assumed that everyone will share the poet's felt meanings. The assumption is at times far too easy, as at the beginning of 'A Sequence of Poems for H. D.'s Birthday':

The young Japanese son was in love with a servant boy.
To be in love! Dont you remember how the whole world is
    governd
by a fact that embraces
                    everything that happens?

I will not say that such a passage is an imposition on the heterosexual reader. It is only one instance among many in our modern literature of the freedom of sexual expression; one can find cognate passages in writers otherwise as unlike Duncan and each other as Ginsberg and Paul Goodman. But the shift from the literal statement of the first line to the girlish outcry and sentimental philosophizing of the ensuing lines is emptily facile. At best it will induce a certain depression in most of us at the exploitation of what is anyway a romantic cliché in such a context. Some of the other writing on the same theme by Duncan is far better, though. One poem especially, 'Sonnet 1,' is moving and indeed painfully so:

Now there is a Love of which Dante does not speak unkindly,
Tho it grieves his heart to think upon men
    who lust after men and run
    — his beloved Master, Brunetto Latini, among them —

Where the roaring waters of hell's rivers
Come, heard as if muted in the distance,
    like the hum of bees in the hot sun. . . .

Both these poems, the first one in the H. D. sequence and the sonnet that opens a group of three sonnets, are initial notes (in the sequences that they begin) toward a self-definition. The dream imagery of the Japanese boy's love story fades into autobiography at a later point in the sequence when Duncan tells of his childhood, of the loss of his real father, who could not support him, and of his adoption and search for a masculine identity. The factitious feeling of the lines on the Japanese boy and his love soon disappears. The brief sonnet-sequence has a similar, though not so explicit, movement toward revealing the poet's literal life-relationships. Interesting as this aspect of Duncan's writing may be to people who have developed an awareness of his vivid personality and artistic talent, there is little question that even the sympathetic and sensitive reader of poetry will find it hard to come to sympathetic terms with everything that Duncan writes. At any rate, the 'interferences' from all these different sources have to some degree hidden from readers the beauty and original force of his work.

5. DENISE LEVERTOV, PAUL BLACKBURN, LEROI JONES

Few such barriers exist between the work of another Black Mountain figure, Denise Levertov, and her readers. She is closer to Creeley than to Olson or Duncan in her desire to keep her poems uncluttered both in their formal movement and in their literal statement. One cannot accuse her of cultivating a 'minimal' style, however. She does at times let the thought trail off in a kind of inaudible ambiguity in her effort to keep the rhythm and the associations off-handedly natural. And a number of the poems lose their definitive outlines for the same reasons. Poetry may be, as Auden once declared, 'heightened speech'; perhaps, though I doubt it, that is *all* it is. For my part, I very much enjoy reading Miss Levertov's work even when it becomes simply a running brook thinking aloud as it runs, and doing so musically and charmingly. But work that goes too far in this direction does threaten to dwindle into mere 'heightened speech,' and on the whole that result is far from Miss Levertov's intention.

Her earlier work, before *With Eyes at the Back of Our Heads* (1959), involved a slightly painful process of dissolving a tendency toward over-complexity by imitation of the colloquial simplicities and the rhythmic discoveries of Williams. Her more recent work, beginning with the volume just noted and including *The Jacob's Ladder* (1961) and *O Taste and See* (1964), reveal her as freed from that struggle. Her characteristic expression had been, earlier, the indirect formulation of an abstract thought, perhaps set off by a literary allusion, and then its resolution in some concrete piece of narration or image. The obtrusive tendency of the whole Black Mountain group to call attention in their poems to the fact that they are writing poems, or to offer some nugget of aesthetic wisdom as the cream of a poem on a quite different subject, is present in Miss Levertov's work as well. But in *With Eyes at the Back of Our Heads* she begins to give us some vivid, simple impressionist poems, such as 'The Five-Day Rain' and 'February Evening in New York.' These show her able to catch the essential details of sensuous experience and to relate them so as to organize a world of insight and of emotional response with great economy and objectivity. In the same book, the poems 'Terror' and 'The Wife' introduce a confessional frankness and psychological immediacy that, together with the refined impressionist technique, have marked most of her best work ever since.

One might well take one poem in *O Taste and See*, 'Losing Track,' as an example as good as any of the 'best' Levertov, neither too lost in the obvious nor trammeled by theoretical literary dicta. It is a poem of married love, a recurrent theme in these later books. 'The Wife' too is such a poem, but lacks the consistent erotic realism and rich density of 'Losing Track.' It begins half-humorously, with an exciting initial image too difficult to sustain, and soon loses itself in generalities. (Though happy and attractive enough, the subsequent language has only minimum energy and dissipates itself.) Here are the first two stanzas of 'The Wife':

> A frog under you,
> knees drawn up
> ready to leap out of time,
>
> a dog beside you,
> snuffing at you, seeking
> scent of you, an idea unformulated. . . .

Compare the beginning of 'Losing Track':

> Long after you have swung back
> away from me
> I think you are still with me:
>
> you come in close to the shore
> on the tide
> and nudge me awake the way

a boat adrift nudges the pier:
am I a pier
half-in half-out of the water? . . .

The difference is an accurate measure of Miss Levertov's development.

Two poems in *The Jacob's Ladder* will suggest other dimensions of that development. One is the five-part piece called 'A Sequence.' It is at first a remarkable attempt to evoke a dramatic situation, apparently a bitter marital misunderstanding, by way of external images deliberately without emotional charge. But these very images, literal as they seemed, suddenly undergo a stormy change as if they, not the couple, were full of wild feeling:

A changing skyline.
A slice of window filled in
by a middle-distance oblong
topped by little
moving figures.
You are speaking
flatly, 'as one drinks a glass of

milk' (for calcium).
Suddenly the milk
spills, a torrent of black milk hurtles
through the room, bubbling and
seething into the corners.

The rest of the poem is not quite up to this beginning; sustaining a sequence of any length is not Miss Levertov's forte. She is good at a dramatic focusing that amounts to an appreciation of a situation or relationship, and gets in her own way when trying to build out thematically and abstractly (while lacking the bulldozing persistence of an

Olson that helps him get through his problems with a ruthless rhetorical drive). It seems likely that her most durable work will be that which combines her dramatic sureness and frank sensuality, as a number of the marriage poems do. Nevertheless, another sequence of hers, 'During the Eichmann Trial,' is in part a triumph of concrete imagination with materials she has not herself personally experienced. This is the concluding section of the poem, called 'Crystal Night' after an infamous moment in the Nazi terrorization of the Jews. The best part of this section is completely alive and realized, a fine example of 'field' composition:

> The scream!
> The awaited scream rises,
> the shattering
> of glass and the cracking
> of bone
>
> a polar tumult as when
> black ice booms, knives
> of ice and glass
> splitting and splintering the silence into
> innumerable screaming needles of
> yes, now it is upon us, the jackboots
> are running in spurts of
> sudden blood-light through the
> broken temples. . . .

Two other 'allied' poets are Paul Blackburn and Leroi Jones. Both present certain difficulties of access, as it were. Blackburn is simply unavailable to the general reader, for most of his publication has been of a fugitive nature.*

* Some of his work may be found in the Allen anthology already referred to, and in my anthology *The New Modern Poetry* (N.Y.: Mac-

Like Miss Levertov's, his basic talent makes for a simple lyric poetry, inwardly directed and existential in its preoccupations. He too, more often than not, deals in deep-sunken moments of awareness that absorb or 'internalize' details of sense experience. His ear for American speech has been sensitized, like hers, by the lessons of Williams and others, but his colloquialism is usually racier, more energetic and masculine, than hers. He has a sharper ear for the American lingo than the British-born Miss Levertov:

> if it's the light & gas man
> announcing himself as "EDISON!
> Readjer meter mister?"
> For Christ sake yes
> read my meter
> Nothing can alter the euphoria
> The blister is still on one finger
>   There just are
> some mornings worth getting up
>   & making a cup
> of coffee that's all

If his poem 'The Watchers' is any indication, he is better able to sustain a long poem with a theoretical bearing akin to that of Olson's 'The Kingfishers' than any of his Black Mountain fellows, because better able to sustain a complex pattern of motifs without losing rhythmic and emotional momentum anywhere along the line.

Leroi Jones, too, has a natural gift for quick, vivid imagery and spontaneous humor, and his poems are filled with sardonic or sensuous or slangily knowledgeable

---

millan, 1967). 'Good Morning Love'—quoted below—and 'The Watchers' are both published in the latter collection.

passages. His first book, *Preface to a Twenty Volume Suicide Note* (1960), was interesting — as much of our newer poetry is — for the structural similarity of some of its pieces to jazz improvisation. Thus, the ending of what is perhaps the best poem in that volume, 'Way Out West':

> . . . Insidious weight
> of cankered dreams. Tiresias'
> weathered cock.
>
> Walking into the sea, shells
> caught in the hair. Coarse
> waves tearing the tongue.
>
> Closing the eyes. As
> simply an act. You float

The spiraling, dreaming movement of associations, spurts of energetic pursuit of melody and motifs, and driftings away of Jones's poems seem very much an expression of a new way of looking at things, and of a highly contemporary aesthetic, of a very promising sort. The perspectives include traditional directions and symbols, yet are not dominated by them. Jones, a Negro intellectual and playwright, at first seemed to be finding a tangential way of making use of Negro experience and its artistic and psychological aspects in such a way as to enable himself, at the same time, to develop within the normal context of American poetry of this period. As he came into some prominence, however, and, for the time being at least, began to ally himself with the new tendencies toward intransigent hostility to the 'white' civilization, his poetry became more militant in its projection of that hostility. The earlier work had often lacked a certain clarity. It was not usually well resolved. This was the 'difficulty of access' to which I referred at first, and it is the kind of problem with which 'field' theory is not as centrally concerned as it is with other matters. Jones's second book, *The Dead Lecturer* (1964), still suffers from difficulty in focusing on its controlling insights, except in the pieces that fall back on the politics of racial enmity, often in obvious sexual disguise. The sequence called 'Black Dada Nihilismus' is a characteristic expression of these tendencies. On the other hand, poems like 'I Substitute for the Dead Lecturer' and the 'Crow Jane' poems, and scattered passages throughout the book, show not only Jones's art of rhapsodic inwardness in full growth (very much under Robert Duncan's influence) but also his capacity to keep aloof from easy political self-identification. Again, we may look at an ending, the final stanza of 'I Substitute for the Dead Lecturer':

> For all these wan roads
> I am pushed to follow, are
> my own conceit. A simple muttering
> elegance, slipped in my head
> pressed on my soul, is my heart's
> worth. And I am frightened
> that the flame of my sickness
> will burn off my face. And leave
> the bones, my stewed black skull,
> an empty cage of failure.

Because the scope of the Black Mountain movement is essentially American, I shall leave to the next chapter a few notes on British poets who have been affected by it. I should add here, though, the plain observation that it is this movement alone which has taken seriously the revolutionary formal theory advanced by Pound and his contemporaries early in the century and has tried to adapt it in the light of Williams's concern with the idiosyncratically American. The result has been a slow flowering of new manifestations of the modern tradition, and a coming together under its influence of the most varied personalities and interests. The movement has by its nature encouraged, as well, new expressions of nonconforming thought and of observed psychological realities. The actual poems, one by one, must be weighed by their particular poetic qualities as all poems have always had to be weighed, but something in our life has been cracked open as a result of all the energies that the movement has directed and encouraged.

V
Contemporary British Poetry

1. THE BRITISH POETIC SCENE GENERALLY (THE WARS OF THE ANTHOLOGIES; CONCRETE AND CONFESSIONAL POETRY; DAVIE, REDGROVE, BRONK, ENRIGHT, AND OTHERS)

In the introduction to his Penguin anthology *The New Poetry* (1962), A. Alvarez wrote:

> Sometime in the twenties Thomas Hardy remarked to Robert Graves that '*vers libre* could come to nothing in England. All we can do is to write on the old themes in the old styles, but try to do a little better than those who went before us.' Since about 1930 the machinery of modern English poetry seems to have been controlled by a series of negative feedbacks designed to produce precisely the effect Hardy wanted.

By 'negative feedbacks' Alvarez meant the reactivation of the anti-experimental, anti-intellectual, and anti-emotional 'sets' or prejudices in English sensibility. He hoped to counteract this renewed conservatism by leading off his anthology with two fiercely emotional Americans, Robert Lowell and John Berryman, and by giving more space to

Ted Hughes, a writer of highly charged if beautifully contained and directed violence, than to any of the other seventeen Britons represented. He included, as well, the nervously energetic Peter Redgrove, the American influenced Charles Tomlinson and Christopher Middleton, and the intellectually intense Donald Davie, among others who could to a greater or lesser degree be said to represent modulations toward the kind of vigor and relevance he advocates. Alvarez praised Philip Larkin's talent but discounted his tone and his concerns. He included Thom Gunn without comment, as an acknowledgment (I would surmise) of a latent power that has only very recently begun to find its right formal expression.

Since the Alvarez anthology appeared, there have been other signs of new orientations. The poetry of William Carlos Williams has belatedly begun to take hold on the English ear and imagination, partly in the wake of the impact of Allen Ginsberg and of a revival of interest in Pound. This development parallels a new attention to Russian and other European poetry and a vast proliferation of public readings, one culmination of which was a highly publicized affair at the Albert Hall in London, in 1965. Not only did a wide array of Americans from Ginsberg to much lesser known figures read there, but some quite unexpected Continental and English poets did so too. George MacBeth, for instance, took part. Though he is a lively, witty young poet, there is nothing in his work that could in any sense be called revolutionary. He is associated with the usually somewhat inhibited movement called The Group, and his involvement in such an affair was partly an obvious example of the renewed acceptance of both oratorical poetry and, with it, the idea of the poet as performer. Partly, however, it reveals the new openness to hitherto unwelcome poetic modes as well.

There are many signs of this openness besides the ones I have already mentioned. For instance, the international Concretist movement has come into wider recognition. Here the efforts of the Scottish poet Ian Hamilton Finlay, editor of the magazine *Poor. Old. Tired. Horse.* and publisher of the Wild Hawthorn Press, have been quite effective. Another, especially telling sign was the extraordinary response to Sylvia Plath's posthumous volume *Ariel.* This book by a young American, wife of the British poet Ted Hughes, appeared in England more than a year before its American publication. It brought home to many British readers the savage energies and full involvement of experience of which poetry is capable. For the first time, there is serious discussion in England as to whether or not such energies and such poetry are what a realized poetry *demands,* and one can see a forcible wrenching of opinion into new channels.

Thus, one result of the response to *Ariel* was the publication by Turret Press in 1965 of a nineteen-page booklet, in a limited edition, of pieces by Sylvia Plath called *Uncollected Poems.* Turret Press is under the general direction of the poet and critic Edward Lucie-Smith, around whom The Group has centered during much of its existence. At first unenthusiastic about Sylvia Plath and the confessional tendency in poetry (as a glance at his *A Group Anthology,* published in 1963, would inevitably lead one to predict), Mr. Lucie-Smith seems to have been swung around by recent developments. Shortly afterwards, Turret Press courageously published a booklet of poems, *Sussicran,* by Harry Fainlight, a young poet of the Anglo-

American *avant-garde* (he is American, but has lived in England for some years) who had appeared in various magazines but never in a book even as small as this one. The dozen or so poems in the collection center about the title-piece, a description of ritualized masturbation performed in view of mirrors in such a way as to approximate a literally narcissistic act of love. (Hence, the reverse, or mirror, spelling of the title.) Some of the poems deal with homosexual and exhibitionistic encounters, and one of them with the experience of failure in normal sex. Whatever one's feeling about such themes, and about the personality that finds them natural and inevitable, the poems themselves are touching, sometimes anguished, sometimes in search of a self-reordering, sometimes ironically mocking, or self-mocking. 'Shameless' in their assumptions, they nevertheless strike notes of pathos and lyrical reverie, and at times shows unusual rhythmic sensitivity and life.

The publication of these two booklets by Turret Press is only a minor, and perhaps even an accidental, ripple, but it is the sort of thing that would not so easily have happened only a few years ago. It is hard to believe that out of so much ferment, so many readings, so much response to the outside world's doings, the English are not on the verge of a brilliant new period. The signs are still inconclusive — a single stray poem here and there (such as Ted Hughes's 'Cadenza,' which I shall discuss briefly in the next section of this chapter), the serious critical contributions by Ian Hamilton and his magazine *The Review,* the largely neglected work of Charles Tomlinson, and some of the more recent directions of poets like Christopher Middleton and Donald Davie. These indications are all still exceptional, and an American reader of British poetry is still on more alien ground than he may at first realize. He is likely to be repelled by what looks a morass of petty cleverness — effetely knowledgeable, spongy and talkative, and often derivative — that seems quite dead at the center. The poetic act, on many occasions socially rather than aesthetically oriented, seems taken for granted, and a tolerance for facile mediocrity at times pervades every level of poetic activity. An American needs the experience of much re-reading, and if possible of hearing the poets and, indeed, of getting used to contemporary British speech in general to correct this over-all impression to a significant degree. The nuances and pitch and style of thought and speed of movement in British speech are obviously, and significantly, different from those in American speech and do make a great difference. Behind them lies another world of common experience and background, a reaction against violence and overstatement in the wake of the last war, a highly European political sharpness and class-feeling, and some decisive differences in the character of both mass and elite education. That education encourages greater articulateness than the American, but not necessarily greater originality.

Old-fashioned British insularity is on the wane, in about the same proportion, I suppose, as American self-entrancement is, but it is hardly dead yet. It is most winningly represented, probably, in the anthology *The Mid Century: English Poetry 1940–60* (1965), edited by David Wright, a South African poet whose long sojourn in London has made him as ethnocentrically opinionated as it is possible for someone to be and yet remain an amiable and sensitive spirit. His genial discounting of American poetry, in an introduction to the anthology dated March 1962, is an excellent example of literary pub-talk of the kind that goes on in England endlessly:

> There are no American poets in this anthology. American and English poetry is no longer homogeneous, though written in approximately the same language. Contemporary American poetry — which, thanks to the excessive interest taken in it by American universities, is now an industry rather than an art — seems to be wandering off in the direction of the decorative, where style and technique is all and thought, if anything, a peg on which to hang a Chinese box of semantic ingenuities. It is not that the artist must not be craftsman, but that craftsmanship is not all.

The mind staggers at the thought of all the American poetry of this period that is anything but obsessed with the 'decorative' and with 'semantic ingenuities.' However, the Wright anthology has its own valuable purpose, in reminding readers not only of the continuing presence of well-established figures like Auden, Graves, Betjemann, and Empson but of the importance for English poetry of such 'outsiders' as the Scottish Edwin Muir and Hugh MacDiarmid, the Irish Patrick Kavanagh, and the Welsh Dylan Thomas. In these latter figures, and in George Barker's autobiographical poem 'The True Confession of George Barker,' Wright by strong implication takes a stand for a certain widening of horizons after all, by way of the revolutionary, recalcitrant, and bohemian attitudes toward life that these poets express in their several ways. A bardic or hortatory style, particularly with a large infusion of satire (some of it, unfortunately, more facile than telling), is favored by Wright's group, the poets once associated with the now defunct magazine *X*. The astringent musings of poets like C. H. Sisson, John Heath-Stubbs, and sometimes Wright himself — though he is at his best in simply exploring a feeling — lend more of the same kind of coloration. One discovers an intensely local orientation in this collection, the very flavor of a certain set of thought in Wright's 'Soho' group — at once provincial and radical, with little interest if any in rhythmic experimentation or the concerns of either 'projectivism' or 'confessionalism'; a sort of holding operation, rather, of an attractively nonconformist, willful, somewhat dogmatic spirit of poetic thought, rather hostile to liberalism and science as well.

The most highly publicized conservative tendency in recent British poetry, though, has been that called 'The Movement.' It arose in the mid-1950's, around the work and thought of three young men who had been students at St. John's College, Oxford. They were Philip Larkin, Kingsley Amis, and John Wain, poets very unlike one another and yet sharing certain wry perspectives and a distrust of flamboyant mannerisms or Romantic attitudes. With the publication of the *New Lines* anthology, under the editorship of Robert Conquest, in 1956, The Movement became identified not only with these names and those of the other poets in the collection (Elizabeth Jennings, John Holloway, Thom Gunn, D. J. Enright, Donald Davie, and Mr. Conquest) but with the explicit principles laid down in the editor's introduction. Basically, Mr. Conquest called for a renewed attention to the 'necessary intellectual component' in poetry, viewed from a commonsense standpoint. 'Great theoretical constructs' and the 'agglomeration of unconscious commands' were to be rejected in favor of 'reverence for the real person or event,' and versification was to be tightened up in accordance with the conventional English norms — the iambic pentameter or tetrameter line. A reaction against the hysterical tone of war literature and against the memory of the emotional life of that period was apparently felt to be in order. Philip Larkin's two novels *Jill* and *A Girl in Winter* and Kingsley Amis's better known fiction express the same sort of reaction, and the same resistance to literary attitudinizing.

The Movement naturally engendered the opposition of the poets it snubbed and of others who resented either its anti-romanticism or its arrogation of concern for honesty of technique to itself. *New Lines* was followed almost at once, in 1957, by the *Mavericks* anthology, edited by Howard Sergeant and Dannie Abse, attacking The Movement's 'lack of motivating impulse' and the whole English tendency to form poetic cliques. Abse's own poetry is marked by a warm involvement in private and public concerns and, at the same time, by a European rather than an insular outlook. Ultimately the sensibility is Romantic, although the form reaches toward a free colloquial structure while holding pretty much to the traditional line. A more telling assault came from those critics who recognized that, whatever the merits of a renewed Neo-Classicism, England had yet to complete its discovery of the full possibilities of the Pound-Eliot-Yeats revolution in poetry, now over a half-century old — let alone of the important recent developments in the wake of that revolution. The most cogent arguments were summed up in the introduction to A. Alvarez's *The New Poetry,* though more than a third of Alvarez's poets had already appeared in the Conquest anthology. (English talent was, and still is, concentrated into fairly genteel and conventional channels.) 'The great moderns,' he wrote, 'experimented not just to make it new formally, but to open poetry up to new areas of experience.' As for the *New Lines* poets, what they wrote was

> academic-administrative verse, polite, knowledgeable, efficient, polished, and, in its quiet way, even intelligent. . . . The pieties of the Movement . . . are summed up at the beginning of Philip Larkin's 'Church-Going':
>
> Hatless, I take off
> My cycle-clips in awkward reverence.
>
> This, in concentrated form, is the image of the post-war Welfare State Englishman: shabby and not concerned with his appearance; poor—he has a bike, not a car; gauche but full of agnostic piety; underfed, underpaid, overtaxed, hopeless, bored, wry. This is . . . an attempt to show that the poet is not a strange creature inspired; on the contrary, he is just like the man next door—in fact, he probably *is* the man next door.

Mr. Conquest replied to the strictures of Mr. Alvarez and others in his introduction to *New Lines 2* (1963). He claimed he had been misinterpreted but restated his basic position sturdily. The anthology, however, was broadened to include Ted Hughes, Thomas Kinsella, and others who did not quite fit the original Movement approach. In addition, a few of his original cast had evolved toward a more open or experimental position, or taken very much to heart Mr. Alvarez's insistence that English poets could not ignore the terrifying side of recent history and the breakdown in psychic expectations and social assumptions that has been going on in this century.

Curiously enough, The Group, less distinguished in its adherents at first than The Movement, was by its very nature more susceptible to the rapid evolutionary progress that was in the wind than the other publicized cliques and clusters of English poets. The reason seems to be that its emphasis was on the practical organization of discussions centered around poems that had been mimeographed and distributed to all possible participants before meetings took place. Invitations to participate were not hard to come by, a number of the participants were of a sufficiently high caliber both as poets and as critics, and the discussion was concrete and relevant. If there seems little question that the standards tended toward a certain mediocrity and that the schoolroom-air enhanced this tendency, nevertheless the dynamics of such a group tends toward its growing more and more open to the unfamiliar and the strikingly forceful as it develops. Moreover, figures like Ted Hughes and Peter Redgrove, the former associated with The Group at the beginning, though not for long, and the latter still a participant, could hardly be dominated by other people's predilections.

Quite apart from the War of the Anthologies, the Concretist movement has quietly progressed along lines quite alien to most assumptions in British or American poetry. It bears a certain relationship to the typographical manipulations of an older modernism — the European movements of Dadaism and Futurism, for instance, and the kind of visual designs set up by Cummings and others. But it is probably true that Concrete must so far be regarded as 'essentially a graphic medium,' which derives some of its international appeal from the fact that it so very easily crosses the barriers of language. The phrase 'graphic medium' was used by Michael Weaver in his informative essay 'Concrete and Kinetic: The Poem as Functional Object,' which appeared in the special undated number of the British magazine *Image* that was published in 1965 and subtitled 'Kinetic Art: Concrete Poetry.' This number of *Image,* together with the November 28, 1964 issue of the Cambridge University magazine *Granta,* contains a number of useful theoretical statements as well as examples of Concrete poems. Others have appeared in the *Times Literary Supplement,* which has been remarkably hospitable to this movement — perhaps a sign that, as *avant-garde* poetic movements go, this one has surely the best-mannered spokesmen and least offensive first impact on the consciousness. One's first impression, indeed, is of trivial though perhaps charming playfulness, or a type of harmless madness, compulsive, repetitive, and ultimately resulting, it may be, in the design of particularly amusing wallpaper for intellectuals. The publications of Finlay's Wild Hawthorn Press in Scotland all have most agreeable typographical design. As he himself describes their character (in his essay 'Communication and Structure in Concrete Poetry,' in the 'Concrete' issue of *Image*):

> Two features stand out immediately in any consideration of concrete poetry. It is concerned with a wide range of expressive techniques. Words are not simply arranged in lines and verses — they are fragmented, printed in varying colours and sizes of type, in short given an immense range of visual possibilities. But, on the other hand, it is essentially concerned with the conventional notation of the alphabet. It is entirely removed in origin from the indeterminate signs and forms that occur in abstract painting.

Here, for instance, is a poem, originally printed in red, from Finlay's book *Telegrams from My Windmill* (1964):

A

. . . blue boat
a brown sail

LITTLE POEM

a brown boat
a green sail

TO PUT

a green boat
a black sail

YOUR EYES

a black boat
a blue sail

TO SLEEP

a . . .

LITTLE . . .

I quote this piece first to suggest the whimsically imaginative charm of Finlay's basic poetic personality, which emerges even more fully in the non-Concretist poems of his volumes *The Dancers Inherit the Party* (1960) and *Glasgow Beasts, An a Burd* (1961). A more characteristic example of the typographical orientation of Concrete is the following poem, again from *Telegrams from My Windmill:*

```
tendressetendressetendressetendressetend
erdresstenderdresstenderdresstenderdress
tenderdresstenderdresstenderdresstenderd
ressetendressetendressetendressetendress
etenderdresstenderdresstenderdresstender
dressetendressetendressetendressetendres
setendressetendressetendressetendressete
nderdresstenderdresstenderdresstenderdre
ssetendressetendressetendressetendresset
enderdresstenderdresstenderdresstenderdr
essetendressetendressetendressetendresse
```

What I have called the 'compulsive, repetitive' character of this kind of poetry is perfectly obvious here. The words must be fitted into a pattern that will be perfectly regular in the sense that the same number of spaces are filled in each line. A kind of animated punning informs the verbal rectangle, based on the similarity of 'tendresse' and 'tender dress'; gently erotic texture results. Meanwhile, there are other half-accidental puns: 'tend,' 'her dress' ('er dress'), 'tendered' ('tenderd'), and perhaps 'russet' and 'undress' and 'underdress' and 'entendre.' The final result must please the eye and ear and be as close to monotony as possible without losing its insistent suggestiveness and sense that a field of force has been established. The poem is, as with Creeley's poetry, an effort to discover such a field while limiting oneself to minimal resources of language and structure. In the issue of *Granta* I have mentioned, a letter from Finlay to Weaver is quoted:

> . . . . What *reality* are the words to stand on? I could say so many things:
>
> The poem supreme, addressed to
> emptiness — this is the courage
>
> necessary. This is something
> quite different.
>
> ROBERT CREELEY
>
> — quite different from the *social* poem, of the person who has felt (known) nothing of the *sort* of experience one could indicate (the direction of) by talking of Neitzsche or Heidegger — the poem, of an order which is different from the sort of order known to those who feel society stretching to the *edge* of the world, as it were — who are safe in that *family,* and who don't know

> in their *body* that question about *form,* and who therefore feel language as a *home*-thing, which I don't, and never have. (But by *form* it is made familiar.) And yet, that there is an order, given, I don't doubt. I mean an order *there,* somewhere, and not an order we can *use* (to save us, as it were) but more, that could use us if we try. . . .

Finlay's language and syntax here are very close in their tumbling, nearly incoherent onrush to the style of Olsen's projectivist essay. Still, the quotation is useful for the depths it reveals beneath the geometrical surfaces of the poetry. There is a strongly felt resistance to the prevailing poetic methods, and by the same token to the imposition of normal sentence structure on individual words in poetry. The words must be allowed to determine their own small but intense and tightly bound systems of relationship. In his much more systematic essay in *Image,* Finlay writes that 'in the words of Pierre Garnier [the French Concretist poet], it is a matter of allowing the work "to take its own space." Or it may be a case of separating the letters of an individual word in order to disclose new decorative and semantic possibilities.' As for 'the relation between this overt use of space on the page and the structure of the poem,'

> The reader does not begin at the top left-hand corner and work his way steadily to the bottom right-hand corner. He is first of all aware of the skeleton of the poem — its formal arrangement. Then he isolates groups of words in no special order. His appreciation of the poem is the enlivening of a skeletal form with flesh and blood. Parallel to the reader's exploration of the actual space of the poem is his discovery of the 'semantic

> space' of the poem. . . . It is this possibility of different systems — corresponding or diverging but always interacting — that makes the structures of concrete poetry so fresh and enticing. . . . The unique feature of concrete poetry is that the sets of possibilities are sufficiently distinct in origin — though wedded in the final poem — for us to perceive the mysteries of structure at a conscious level.

Though Finlay is the best known Concretist in the British Isles, Dom Sylvester Houédard and others have played an important part in the movement, and the names of the French poet Garnier, the Austrian poet Ernst Jandl, and the Brazilian Pedro Xisto are, with those of other foreign poets, very well known to people interested in Concrete. The influence of this movement and of certain American tendencies has begun to touch the rest of British poetry. The work of Christopher Middleton (who, as a student of German literature, is a confessed admirer of Jandl's poetry) reflected this influence as far back as the poems collected in his *Torse 3,* published in 1963. The title of the book, in fact, is related both to Concrete theory and to Projectivist 'field' theory. It is taken from a definition in the *Shorter Oxford English Dictionary,* arranged as verse by the poet to make his epigraph to the volume:

> Torse³.
> [f.med.L.torsus,-um,
> for L. *tortus* twisted.]
> *Geom.* A developable surface;
> a surface generated
> by a moving straight line
> which at every instant is turning,

in some plane or other through it,
about some point or other
in its length.

This definition can at least be closely related, if not absolutely identified, with Finlay's conception of the structure and physical independence of concrete poems. A special kind of rigor — an imposed external discipline and objective dynamics that seem locked into Concrete writing — is helping to create new orientations toward the whole question of what constitutes poetic power. These orientations are partly in the modern experimental tradition, but partly they are related to hitherto neglected modern modes of scientific and philosophical thought, as well as of artistic practice generally. Weaver's article traces them to such sources as the 1938 edition of Moholy-Nagy's *The New Vision,* which predicted for poetry 'the move from "*mass to motion, from syntax and grammar to relations of single words.*" Size and weight — monumental metaphor heaped with symbolism — was no longer relevant.' Weaver gives serious attention as well to a germinal essay, Hans Arp's '*Konkrete Kunst,*' written at some time before 1946, which he believes led to 'the conception of the poem as constellation.'

> Of the words Arp used to describe the concrete work of art, two describe a state of solidification (*Verdichtung, Verhärtung*), while the others suggest the movement toward crystallisation, the process of fusion itself (*Gerinnens, Dickerwerdens, Zusammenwachsens*). Having found its true form in a kind of dynamic order, which appears to be at rest, the object is an equilibrium of invisible lines of force like a Takis magnetic sculpture.

As I have suggested at the beginning of the last chapter, the British poet and critic Donald Davie (under whom Weaver studied at Cambridge) has shown in his theorizing about Pound and about the Projectivists a certain influence of Concretist thought. The various threads come together in the poem 'Bolyai, the Geometer,' in Davie's collection *Events and Wisdoms* (1964). The poem itself is neither 'field' nor 'Concrete,' but it entertains the new perspectives and philosophizes about them:

> One sees the lately formless as most formal,
> The stanza most a unit when
> Open at all ends, all transition. . . .

The place of Donald Davie in the British poetic scene is an interesting one. His poetry, particularly the earlier work, strikes one at first as coldly intellectual and distant. His criticism responds to new currents, both British and international, without seeming to be deeply and significantly informed by them; though it is always intelligent and relevant, it tends to let go of issues before they are fully and sympathetically encompassed. Nevertheless, one grows to see that the 'defects' of detachment have enabled him to cultivate a valuable openness at the same time. Of the anthologies I have mentioned, for instance, Davie's work is represented in all but *Mavericks* (which omits on principle anyone included in *New Lines*) and *A Group Anthology*. This has happened, it seems to me, because the work is at once clear and witty, involved in the deeper issues of the age and of contemporary consciousness, and devoid of false attitudinizing. It has depths as well as surfaces, and survives contemplation. It provides one instance of the fact that British sensibility is beginning once more to take hold of the relevant considerations for a living poetry.

The new poetry is developing in its own way, incidentally, following the prescriptions neither of Conquest nor of Alvarez or any of the other editors and critics who have tried to guide it into special channels. The emergence of the Concrete movement, for example, was quite unpredictable, yet now it seems a natural enough response to the whole European urge to get back behind the mere articulateness, and domination by highly developed rhetoric, that had been brought to a kind of self-defeating perfection by writers like Auden and Empson. Their accomplishments had almost inevitably to be followed by the diluted achievements of the characteristic Movement and Group writers. The best new British work, with a few cherishable exceptions, involves a quiet assimilation of revolutionary tendencies. Thus, Davie has in *Events and Wisdoms* begun not only to ponder Concrete but to use the confessional mode in a perfectly natural way. 'Wide France' and 'Across the Way' are poems of family turbulence, and the sequence 'After an Accident' (about the effects of a terrible automobile smashup in which Davie was involved) is a serious effort to repossess a psychological state that was both traumatic and productive of painful private realizations. The stubbly thoughtfulness of most of Davie's other work holds one kind of spiritual independence, suggesting an intellectual honesty that refuses to preen itself on its virtues. But 'After an Accident' makes a leap into emotional clarification beyond what Davie had done so far.

Of the other writers in the British Isles who might conceivably be called in some sense confessional, the most obvious is Edwin Bronk but the most interesting are Peter Redgrove, who stands with Ted Hughes as the poet of greatest vividness and intensity now writing in England, and some of the Irish poets to be discussed in Chapter VI. Hughes's work, too, will be taken up in more detail later in the present chapter; he has ultimately the same motivations, probably, as those of the best of the confessional poets. His poetry, like theirs, is white-hot with a special kind of rage derived from his facing up to some interior horror that is inseparable from the world's condition as felt by Lowell and the others. In his strongest work, all this fierce recoil from self and society is transferred and actually hammered into the bestiary he presents — the sinister pike and the indefatigable otter, for instance. It is as though Lowell had built his poems entirely around the skunks of 'Skunk Hour,' say, and left the rest to our imagination. The savagery of the poems cannot be entirely accounted for by their manifest subjects. There is no question but that Hughes, now left a widower by the suicide of Sylvia Plath, wrote his poems within the framework of a reciprocity of emotion between the two poets of a unique order. He, Redgrove, and the Irish poets share certain confessional characteristics without really being a part of the movement. The springs and the precise character of Redgrove's poetry make it especially useful to consider him in the confessional context — this despite the fact that the literary movement he has been associated with, the 'Group' in England, generally represents diametrically different values.

Emotionally, Redgrove's poems usually combine fascination with the details of the natural world and the body and a revulsion against them. The speaker of his poems is extraordinarily responsive to those details, not only because of Redgrove's training in the natural sciences but because of his capacity for identifying with the organic life he cannot help feeling sympathetically:

> The fly is yellowed by the sun,
> Her plating heaves, her wings hum,
> Her eyes are cobbled like a road,
> Her job is done, her eggs are stowed
> No matter in what. The sun
> Yellows the hemlock she sits upon;
> Her death is near, her job is done.
> Paddling in pollen and the sun,
> She swings upon the white-flowered weed.
> As a last duty, yellow with seed,
> She falters round the flower-rim.
> Falters around the flower-rim.

Here there is none of the revulsion of which I have spoken; only a realization, common enough, of the inseparability of birth and death. The realization is objective enough to be relieved of sentimentality, but not so objective as to obliterate the pathos deliberately built up through the repetitions and through the slight personification of 'her job is done' and 'a last duty.' This poem, 'Ephemerid,' appeared in Redgrove's second book, *The Nature of Cold Weather and Other Poems* (1961). The simple but absolutely convincing description it presents may be compared with the closing stanza of 'Flies,' a piece in Redgrove's first volume, *The Collector* (1960): *

> Fine-grained eyes, hemispherical and dull,
> From lakes of sewage bordered by dusty hills
> You infect my meal with your self-interest

* *The Collector* is dated 1959, but a small insert informs us that it was not actually published until 1960.

Steadfast in the light with dabbing trunks,
Infect my tender mouth with what I kiss.
What refuse of whose loves is my career,
Whose diseases must I take upon my back,
What silent lips and nostrils are your food,
Whose film-eyed ending is my start of pain?

In 'Flies,' one sees more clearly than in the later poem the obsessive character of this poetic intelligence. 'Ephemerid' happens to pass as a good simple poem in an old tradition, as do a number of other things by Redgrove, but in another sense it too is obsessive. It is an invasion of his awareness by something outside himself, something fraught with the death-horror that 'Flies' exposes more explicitly. His disgust with the contamination of the self by the physical is sometimes as keen as Eliot's. In 'The Pregnant Father,' also included in the first volume, we have the following picture of the speaker and his wife returning from a walk:

Well, well, we start back; and the world turns round.
We leave soft footprints in the dust
While waves yawn and crack each others' backs
And that thrush snaps a worm short at the turf.
I feel my dung, and want to get back quick.
You feel your child, and want to muse your flowers.
I really want to weep. Where is our love
When you watch your belly like that with your tears?

The fifth line is an intrusion of some violence upon what is otherwise a touching if not too well resolved contemplation of a difficult moment in a marriage. Perhaps it is a not quite conscious intrusion; if so, it argues the obsession the more. 'Against Death,' the best poem in *The Collector,* gives it a further turn. It attempts a species of affirmation built up out of elements of frank dismay, and in this respect as in its anguished tone resembles confessional writing. The subject is the speaker's house — its dubious dependability, its functions, its implicit terrors. The relation of the domesticated modern sensibility to nature is ironically brought out at the start:

> We are glad to have birds in our roof
> Sealed off from rooms by white ceiling. . . .

And a little later:

> We keep no cats and dislike wet-mouthed dogs,
> And wind comes up the floorboards in a gale. . . .

And finally:

> And if there ever should be a corpse in the house
> Hard on its bedsprings in a room upstairs,
> Smelling of brass-polish, with sucked-in cheeks,
> Staring through eyelids at a scratching ceiling,
> Some firm'd hurry it outdoors and burn it quick —
> We'd expect no more to happen to ourselves
> Our children gradually foregoing grief of us
> As the hot bodies of the sparrows increase each summer.

The final referent of all of Redgrove's quick, tormented concreteness is probably the sense of private humiliation at the nastiness of physical existence, and of the psychological complications it is involved with, rather than simple death-horror itself — though doubtless the latter is always an aspect of the former. Only seldom, as in the fleeting fifth line of the stanza just quoted, does an explicit extension of the basic revulsion to some aspect of the social or economic structure occur. 'In Case of Atomic Attack' is another of the exceptions in *The Collector,* though here the horror of death and of the body's decay (accelerated, it is true) still holds the center of attention. 'In Company Time' is more subtly developed, in *At the White Monument* (1963). Exuberance finally triumphs in this poem, despite its preoccupation, once again, with death and the presumptuous undertaker. The role of father triumphs over that of employee; and when the protagonist reminds himself that though his new baby's 'boneless skull is pulsating to her teat' it was the father's 'grown-up' kissing of the mother that 'soaked her nightdress-front with milk,' the thought brings pleasure to him. But many of the poems are about the sourness of marriage and love. 'For No Good Reason,' in *The Nature of Cold Weather,* and 'Dismissal,' in *At the White Monument,* are among Redgrove's most beautiful lyric poems, and both have to do with the failure of a sexual relationship and the man's humiliation. 'Picking Mushrooms,' in the first of the three books, epitomizes all the qualities of this poet we have been looking at. The sheer detailed knowledge of mushrooms and the energetic, somewhat awed, rather dramatic poetic presentation of that knowledge takes us swiftly and humorously through a dialogue abruptly made shocking and morbid when the two speakers in the poem suddenly find a dead baby among the 'legs, angled breastplates, eliding from light, glimpsed' and the 'thin red wands, ragged with limbs' of the mushrooms. Here the obsessive and hysterical side of Redgrove's work stands out clearly, and as memorably as anything he has written. The voice might be mistaken, indeed, for Sylvia Plath's:

> What tiny ribs. A hairpin of a jaw.
> Soft in the leaves, shrunk to the bones,
> Itch of the wet and leaf-stench sent

The small ghost out for another body,
A monstrous sex which I would have nibbled
For my palate's sake, with red wine and pepper. . . .

Though poetically far less accomplished than Redgrove, Edwin Bronk has written lyric poetry of some interest, a fair amount of it confessional in character. His first books, *An Attempt at Exorcism* (1959) and *A Family Affair* (1960), have a few troubling close-ups of family griefs. Bronk's effort is not primarily to be touching, though. It is to explore what in the earlier volume he calls, in 'A Desperate Kinship,' the 'arbour of remorse' that the psyche has made:

My mother says a dead wasp still
may sting; that spiders I have slaughtered
will avenge, and all the puffed up toads
of Christendom may make my soul a
torment at its end.

My family garden's full of broken
bones, and burning bodies smoulder in
my weeds; the guilt that glistens here
I will atone; I sow the blight
that bites the tails of seeds. . . .

Accordingly, we have the evocations, in both books, of a too-early dead father ('Unlucky Jim'), of a mother whose life has been a bitter disappointment (the sonnets called 'To My Mother'), and of a wife of whose 'quiet despair' the speaker feels that he has been the careful artist over a period of ten years ('To My Wife'). A nostalgic bitterness marks these pieces, counterpart to the nostalgic melancholy for past visions of love and for childhood experience best represented by two pieces in the first book: the title poem and 'After Christmas.'

With Love from Judas (1963) represents a false maturing of these tendencies. The bitterness becomes rather cheap in the purely satiric pieces, such as 'Pop Venus' and 'Popsong for My Valentine,' which gibe at current mass-notions of ideal femininity and female beauty. To gain the feeling that his work is grounded in existential reality, Bronk has adapted the tone of Philip Larkin to his own themes. The speaker confesses to uncontrollable meanness of spirit and proclaims the misery of his private life. In the process, he subjects wife and children to the exposure of his feelings toward them without overcoming, through the total weight and affect of the poems, our sense of an unfortunate betrayal of those who are vulnerable, even if only fictitious. The first poem in the book, 'Here and Now,' sets the tone:

> I have chosen this way:
> the four walls of my nine-to-five,
> the two children who live on me,
> the grey view from an open window.
>
> I could leave the children to my
> unfaithful wife, go off with
> a lover, look at life from
> a window with a brighter view.
>
> But that's the worst illusion. . . .

The most striking of the poems are not necessarily the best ones. They are poems about the speaker's guilt at having been abusive to his children and about his certainty that, try though he will to make it up to them, he cannot help repeating his injustices.

Now that it's too late, I see the hard lines
I have scratched upon another person's God.
Nothing I can do will change a thing.
('A Proposal')

And they are poems, as he says, 'on the break-up of a marriage.' The most degrading is 'A Last Poem to My Wife,' for in it the speaker presents without sympathy and only with disgust the substance of the wife's religious faith as a dead foetus in her womb, with the further implication that this decaying foetus has prevented her conceiving fruitfully by him. This, the closing poem of the book, has been anticipated by 'An Ordered Sabbath,' in which the speaker describes himself attending church with his wife and children and then comments:

The excuse
I make for going is the children, and I wait
until they're out of hearing before I tell my wife

that my aftermath is like a pocket of green bile; she
eats her egg and bacon sadly. At one o'clock I'll take her
to the pub and roar in my own element; at three,
if the kids are out, I'll whip her into bed. . . .

'The Flavour of Spilt Milk' seeks to explain the couple's unhappiness by their prolonged adolescence. The poems as a whole are out for confession without corresponding aesthetic energy that would create transcendence of any sort. In Bronk, the better poems have at least a minimal indirection — as in 'The Camera Does Not Lie,' which introduces the subject of divorce, a failed marriage, through an imagery of photography that holds us off the scent for a moment. Similarly, 'An Attempt at Adultery' beautifully presents an experience of sexual failure through incidental impressions before getting to the heart of the trouble. But on the whole, the unevenness of Bronk's work illustrates both the revitalizing effect of the confessional perspective on an otherwise usually tepid artistry and the ease with which the perspective can be spuriously exploited to make one's work interesting at the expense of artistic integrity.

In Tony Connor's *Lodgers* (1965) we find another instance of the quiet working of this influence. Connor's writing has naturalness and ease of formal movement here far beyond his first book, *With Love Somehow* (1962). The improvement seems directly related to the release of writing about his own embittered life, first as the child of a broken home and then as a husband and father in an apparently difficult marriage. A more flexible stylist and exuberant spirit than most of his countrymen, he nevertheless does not get through as effectively as, say, the more rigid Davie except in the elegiac half-dream-poem 'Beyond Hindley' and in the brilliantly executed 'The Small Hours in the Kitchen,' which brings him close to the terrifying wellsprings of his own creative impulse.

Recent books by John Wain, Roy Fuller, Paul West, Bernard Spencer, and C. A. Trypanis are more characteristic than the work I have just been discussing of the body of relatively accomplished British poetry considered as a whole. The weakness of Wain's latest book, *Wildtrack* (1965), is precisely that it so seldom relies on his personal, idiosyncratic voice of knowledge. It is conceived as a sustained sequence that seeks out the 'crucial mystery' of man by way of accurate identification of the subjective ego. (The language and bearing of this purpose are contained in a quotation from Joseph Campbell's *The Hero with a Thousand Faces,* placed at the head of the poem.) Yet

Wain writes in a truly lyrical and inward voice only at very few points, particularly in the mystically visionary sections called 'The Day-Self Contemplates the Defeat of Time' and 'The Night-Self Sees All Women in One Woman.' These sections, together with a remarkable adaptation of Alexander Blok's 'The Twelve,' are interesting and powerful — as good as anything Wain has ever done. The Blok passage dwindles into tendentious political commentary, just as a good deal of the rest of the poem becomes an awkward machinery for the thematic contrasting of mass-man (creature of political, technological, and economic manipulation — the 'Day-Self') and subjective man (the 'Night-Self'). This machinery is vaguely reminiscent of Hardy's *The Dynasts;* it involves Wain in some historic portraiture, especially some touching eighteenth-century close-ups. *Wildtrack* is nevertheless a doughty effort to break through the oppressive British thing of mere articulateness.

Roy Fuller's *Buff* (1965) and Paul West's *The Snow Leopard* (1964) barely overcome that condition, accomplished as both writers can be. Fuller's sequence 'To X' is the account of a furtive love-affair that the poet, at an advanced age, has found himself unexpectedly launched upon. In verse and diction after the manner of Empson, it leaves no room for anything but a minimal sad clowning. Like much of Fuller's work, it is a half-shocker for the fashionably disillusioned. The wit, the light play of imagination, the resourcefulness of language of this writer are a half-pleasure in poems like 'Bagatelles' and 'The Zouave,' which yet leave the taste of the already often experienced, of attitudes struck rather than discovered. One hears voices — sometimes the poet's own, for a moment, but very likely Auden's as well (especially in the sonnet sequence 'The Historian') or Yeats's or Stevens's; and most of all, the voices of a generation not lost but forever self-echoing. Even a truly fine piece like 'Favouring the Creatures' adds up to very old reckonings and insights indeed.

West, too, though by no means as deft a craftsman, plays winningly with the *déjà vu;* one almost doesn't notice his slight tendency to chase some elusive theme completely out of sight, to un-express the expressible, as it were, reversing a dictum of Eliot's. His feeling for the past and for the unnoticed or unstated is, like Fuller's, delicately colored by a sense of lost historical and political possibilities, and of individual lives gone awry. In these motifs Fuller and West are joined by Bernard Spencer (*With Luck Lasting,* 1965) and C. A. Trypanis (*Pompeian Dog,* 1964) both of whom write more concretely and with a more immediate evocativeness. Landscapes, memories of old loves, re-creation of notes from vanished civilizations — how winningly these poets and others like them conjure these things up, and how hard it will be for English poets to break the spell of the tradition they represent!

Added to its burden of traditionalism, British poetry often suffers as well from its chattiness, as though it were intended primarily as material for those columns of personal comment that one reads for their intelligently conversational character in English weeklies. 'Most of life,' writes E. M. Forster, 'is so dull that there is nothing to be said about it, and the books and talk that would describe it as interesting are obliged to exaggerate, in the hope of justifying their own existence.' In the work of such poets as Anthony Thwaite and the Australian-born Peter Porter, fastening as they do on the themes of life's dullness and injustice, we see how even sensitive spirits and ironically self-critical ones lose themselves in the effort to say interesting things about the well-known or the commonplace. They force the language without discovering a sufficient form to make a distinguished poem very often. One can only hope that, despite the pressure on well-published young writers to continue to 'produce' at a certain rate, they will find the strength to try more difficult but meaningful directions.

A series of books by D. J. Enright shows one kind of partial solution to the characteristic problem of mere articulateness. Enright's form is usually very flat and conversational, approaching in a way the 'minimal' style of Robert Creeley, and though actually the poetry is intellectually oriented the statement is kept as simple as possible. He sometimes sounds a more rational Lawrence, or a plainer Empson. A tremendous identification with the betrayed innocents of the earth marks his writing and, together with his tart self-knowledge, accounts for the basically sympathetic speaking character he presents. Enright's subject matter gives him a great advantage, for he has lived and taught literature in various foreign parts, particularly in Asia, and the hard-bitten realism of what he reports is intrinsically of the greatest interest. In his most telling collection, *Addictions* (1962), the bitterness of his encounters with official repression in a 'new' nation explicitly enters a number of the poems. His disillusionment — that of the Western radical with the developing, altered world which he himself has helped create — is all the more convincing because Enright, despite his own unfortunate experience, does not allow himself to condemn humanitarianism or social progress. It is, rather, the impersonality, the inevitable philistine indifference of political process to the ordinary person, and at the same time certain doubts about his own motives, that disturb him. An unusual sequence of poems (for Enright) in this same volume concerns a love-affair that has gone wrong in very much the same sense as modern history has gone wrong. Somehow, things went awry; the dreamt-of came to pass and yet was not what it should have been. In his highly candid and precise speech and his amateurish free-verse, he involves us, wearies us, stamps his personality on our sympathies.

Within the context of his awareness of tradition and of the social and journalistic roles of poetry in his country, the British poet need only make slight shifts of formal or idiomatic nuance to gain effects that would seem to require greater violence or inventiveness of an American. That is, he works alongside everpresent ghosts of genius, who require of him only that he learn from their richness and either add nothing else but his own voice and experience to the line of continuity that they provide or avoid competition altogether. Thus, the nuance that a poet like Michael Hamburger can provide — a trembling sense of instability that ultimately derives from his family's experience as refugees from Germany — within a modest mastery of the lyric tradition counts in a manner that would be less likely in the United States. The quiet perfection of a rightly managed poetry of sensitive, witty observation of the external world — a finely articulated impressionism centered in the daily experience of Scottish urban and rural life — achieved by the Edinburgh poet Norman MacCaig is another instance of an important British poetic value that Americans are likely to overlook. Yet the very recent experimentation by MacCaig with looser and more open forms underlines the new orientation that is slowly emerging in British poetry.

2. TED HUGHES

The most striking single figure to emerge among the British poets since the last war is undoubtedly Ted Hughes. The total volume of his serious published work remains slight. It is to be found in scattered periodical publications and in two books, *The Hawk in the Rain* (1957) and *Lupercal* (1960). Even in these books, the total number of poems that stand out from the rest through the extraordinarily fierce power and concentration that one thinks of as the marks of Hughes's special genius is rather small. In the first book, published when he was twenty-seven, this unique forcefulness is more marginal or potential, usually, than actually present. That is, there are moments — a single stanza or phrase, perhaps — when the smoldering fire blazes forth savagely. But only in one of the poems, 'The Thought-Fox,' does it dominate the whole poem and give it a consistent, passionately vivid life throughout. Uncharacteristically, the poem embodies an abstraction, suggested by the title: a thought coming to life on the printed page, like a wild beast invading the speaker's mind. The process is described in exquisite gradations, from the first moment when

> I imagine this midnight moment's forest:
> Something else is alive
> Beside the clock's loneliness
> And this blank page where my fingers move.

After an interval, the living metaphor moves into the poem:

> Cold, delicately as the dark snow,
> A fox's nose touches twig, leaf;
> Two eyes serve a movement. . . .

The movement is completed in the last stanza:

> Till, with a sudden sharp hot stink of fox
> It enters the dark hole of the head.
> The wind is starless still; the clock ticks,
> The page is printed.

Something like the effect in this poem of the physical realization of a meaning, quick with its own rank presence, occurs in all the best work of Hughes. One other poem, 'Wind,' comes close to it in *The Hawk in the Rain.* But this poem is more representative of Hughes in the sense that it presents literal reality (though through the distortion of metaphor) rather than an abstraction made tangible. Nevertheless, it takes on symbolic meaning through the very accuracy and intensity of its literal presentation. The opening stanza will illustrate:

> This house has been far out at sea all night,
> The woods crashing through darkness, the booming hills,
> Winds stampeding the fields under the window
> Floundering black astride and blinding wet. . . .

In both these poems, we have examples of the authority that stamps this poet's work. The stage of the imagination is set with such sureness that one does not quarrel with its rightness. The 'thought-fox' is alive in its own way; the reader has no more choice than the protagonist as to whether or not he will make room for it. The conception of the house as a ship on a wildly treacherous sea is equally uncontestable, given the initial figure that launches the poem.

Even in poems that are not completely successful, such as the deliberately weird piece of buffoonery called 'Vampire' or the half pitying, half contemptuous 'Secretary,' the authority of the conception is compelling. The dazzling gate-crasher at the party described in the former poem, who is really somehow absorbing his hosts' blood for the sake of his 'real' body, a 'fusty carcass' that becomes a 'grinning sack . . . bursting with your blood,' is a small triumph of Hughes's exuberantly horrid imagination. An ultimate terror and fascination at the gross brutality of nature, and of man in his more unreflective animal aspect and in the savagery of his wars, makes itself felt in this poet as it did in the writing of his wife, Sylvia Plath. 'Secretary' is the portrait of a woman who lives her frightened days among the men in her office 'like a starling under the bellies of bulls' until, at the end of the day, she 'scuttles down the gauntlet of lust / Like a clockwork mouse.' Four of the poems in the book touch on the theme of war; one of them, 'Bayonet Charge,' imagines the frenzy and terror as vividly as Stephen Crane did in *The Red Badge of Courage.* (Like Crane, Hughes was too young to have fought in the war but was deeply affected by it.) *

The title poem of *The Hawk in the Rain,* carrying echoes of Hopkins and Dylan Thomas, places the speaker, a man slogging through the sucking, clinging mud in a heavy rain, in a curiously interdependent polar relationship with a hawk in the distant sky that 'effortlessly at height hangs his still eye.' The speaker 'strains toward the master-/ Fulcrum of violence where the hawk hangs still'; yet the

* In many ways Hughes seems the legitimate heir to the young British poets of World War I, so many of whom were killed in battle. His sensibility exists in some sort of continuum with theirs, but far beyond the Georgian context. His introduction to the *Selected Poems* (1964) of Keith Douglas (killed in World War II) underlines this affinity.

hawk may one day view the earth from a victim's standpoint and feel 'the ponderous shires crash on him.' The poem attempts too much, but reflects better than any other in the book the obsession of the poet with one aspect of nature — the power and the gift of animals to make the kill, and behind that the intransigent force of being itself that is so indifferent to suffering and weakness. The symbolic application to man is fairly clear. Hughes picks up cues from Lawrence and Thomas, including the latter writer's artistic creed: 'Man be my metaphor.' More than either Lawrence or Thomas, he carries them to unsentimental limits in his best poems.

The second volume, *Lupercal,* includes a half-dozen or more poems that fulfill the first book's promise superbly. No poet of the past has quite managed to 'internalize' the murderousness of nature through such brilliantly objective means, and with such economy, as Hughes in poems like 'Esther's Tomcat,' 'Hawk Roosting,' 'To Paint a Waterlily,' 'View of a Pig,' 'An Otter,' 'Thrushes,' and 'Pike.' Like Lowell, he has the gift of presenting image and thought in a context of hurtling action; there is a strong narrative and dramatic element in all his projections, and the pacing is of the varied, shifting kind employed by a skilled narrator impatient of any description or comment that is in any way inert.

> A tomcat sprang at a mounted knight,
> Locked round his neck like a trap of hooks
> While the knight rode fighting its clawing and bite.
> After hundreds of years the stain's there
>
> On the stone where he fell, dead of the tom. . . .

Or the hawk, characterizing itself:

I kill where I please because it is all mine.
There is no sophistry in my body:
My manners are tearing off heads. . . .

Or the poet contemplating a dead pig:

Once I ran at a fair in the noise
To catch a greased piglet
That was faster and nimbler than a cat,
Its squeal was the rending of metal.

Pigs must have hot blood, they feel like ovens.
Their bite is worse than a horse's —
They chop a half-moon clean out.
They eat cinders, dead cats.

Distinctions and admirations such
As this one was long finished with.
I stared at it a long time. They were going to scald it,
Scald it and scour it like a doorstep.

A passage like the one just quoted would have been less likely to appear before the last war. Its bloodymindedness is a reflex of recent history, the experience of the Blitz, the Bomb, and Auschwitz — an expression of them, a recoiling from them, an approach to experience by way of their implications. Hughes resembles Sylvia Plath closely in such a passage. His Nature is Nazi, not Wordsworthian. Even the 'attent sleek thrushes on the lawn' are terrifying,' he says.

More coiled steel than living — a poised
Dark deadly eye, those delicate legs
Triggered to stirrings beyond sense — with a start, a bounce, a
stab
Overtake the instant and drag out some writhing thing. . . .

Is it their single-mind-sized skulls, or a trained
Body, or genius, or a nestful of brats
Gives their days this bullet and automatic
Purpose? Mozart's brain had it, and the shark's mouth
That hungers down the blood-smell even to a leak of its own
Side and devouring of itself. . . .

It would be false to say that this fierce turn of mind is all there is to Hughes. This very poem, 'Thrushes,' is as a matter of fact unusually contemplative for him. Despite the allusion comparing Mozart's brain to the murderously triggered thrush, which would suggest that the great artist's sureness of method and insight is a more sophisticated functioning of the same process as is involved in the kill, the poem ends by saying that 'with man it is otherwise.' Time and waste, depths of distraction, and the essential distinction between man himself and his acts are, he tells us, characteristic of human effort. So we must distinguish between the implications of Hughes's most telling poetic method (the comparison of Mozart with the thrush and the shark gives away the feeling about existence with which he must deal as an artist) and his thought outside the context of that method.

Despite this necessary consideration, which only reminds us that Hughes is, after all, humanly free to dissociate himself from the vision of terror whose literal acceptance would constitute a form of madness, the bias of the poetry lies in another direction. In such magnificent poems as 'An Otter' and 'Pike'—poems that with 'November' and possibly the mysterious poem 'Lupercalia' approach the full articulation of great art—it is sheer bitter endurance and the devouring ferocity lurking in every depth and crevice of life that obsess him. His empathy with the animals he contemplates is so thorough and so concretely specific that the effect is of magical incantation, a conjuring up of another possible kind of self. Both otter and pike, though they *can* be caught and killed by man, are given supernatural attributions by the language that Hughes sometimes employs in describing them, and by his awestruck feeling of the mystery of their existential reality, so different from our own though constantly suggestive of the human. 'Neither fish nor beast is the otter,' who carries 'the legend of himself' wherever he goes and seeks 'some world lost when first he dived.' He is 'like a king in hiding'—a note Lawrence would have recognized, as he would have seen in Hughes a kindred seeker for the deepest identity of the submerged physical self. The pike, 'killers from the egg, the malevolent aged grin,' have

> A life subdued to its instrument;
> The gills kneading quietly, and the pectorals.
>
> Three we kept behind glass,
> Jungled in weed: three inches, four,
> And four and a half: fed fry to them—
> Suddenly there were two. Finally one
>
> With a sag belly and the grin it was born with. . . .

'Pike' is Hughes's supreme construct, a series of descriptions, anecdotes, impressions building up the single theme. The closing passage focuses, in a single anecdote that might well be considered a twentieth-century recasting of Wordsworthian motifs, the whole sense that one gets from Hughes of man confronting the final implications of his place in history and in nature:

> A pond I fished, fifty yards across,
> Whose lilies and muscular tench

Had outlasted every visible stone
Of the monastery that planted them —

Stilled legendary depth:
It was as deep as England. It held
Pike too immense to stir, so immense and old
That past nightfall I dared not cast

But silently cast and fished
With the hair frozen on my head
For what might move, for what eye might move.
The still splashes on the dark pond,

Owls hushing the floating woods
Frail on my ear against the dream
Darkness beneath night's darkness had freed,
That rose slowly towards me, watching.

'November' and 'Lupercalia' give us other, though related, views of this young poet that should be noticed. In 'November' our attention is directed, not to the animal world but to the human in a degraded form. Its subject is a tramp observed sleeping in the rain — 'I took him for dead' — in a farmland ditch. The close-up view the poem gives us is as accurate and detailed as those of the beast-poems; indeed, the tramp is but one of a myriad beings watersoaked in the woodland countryside: 'weasels, a gang of cats, crows,' a hare that 'crouched with clenched teeth,' and such lesser objects as 'the buried stones, taking the weight of winter,' 'the bare thorns,' 'the rotting grass.' The poet admires the sleeping tramp's 'strong trust,' lying there with his face covered by his beard, 'in the drilling rain' and the 'welding cold.'

'November' recalls at least one poem, 'The Hawk in the Rain,' in the earlier book; and two others, 'Things Present' and 'Everyman's Odyssey,' in *Lupercal.* All these poems have in common the figure of the beggar or of a rain-beaten, bedraggled speaker hammered into nonentity by the elements. 'I drown in the drumming ploughland,' says the speaker in 'The Hawk in the Rain,' who describes himself also as a 'bloodily grabbed dazed last-moment-counting / Morsel in the earth's mouth.' 'Things Present,' the opening poem of *Lupercal,* projects an image of the speaking self as 'a bare-backed tramp' in a 'ditch without fire / Cat or bread.' The next poem, 'Everyman's Odyssey,' sees the Homeric tale of the despised beggar who turned out to be the evil-destroying Odysseus as an embodiment of the common dream. Underlying the recurrent beggar figure in these poems is a humiliated sense of human loss, of a falling off from a previous exalted state, that justifies the hostile, death-wielding tone of the books. In the rather difficult poem 'Lupercalia' itself, we have a series of powerful images of the 'declined blood' of man and beast, then a glimpse of something beyond brute grossness in the images of dancing fauns, and a prayer for transformation out of the 'frozen' spiritual state of the speaker.

The poems of *Lupercal* seemed a fulfillment of Hughes's powers in the directions pointed by his earlier book. Since then, relatively little serious poetry by him has appeared, although he has published children's books and has done a good deal of writing for the Third Programme of the BBC, a certain amount of it poetic drama or work including long sections of poetry. Nevertheless, a new volume of extraordinary power is in the making. At this writing, his most interesting poem to appear fairly recently is 'Cadenza,' published in the April–May, 1965, issue of *Agenda* (subtitled *English Poetry Now: An Anthology of New Poems*). Tremendous energy is concentrated into the buoyant, beating music of this poem's two-line stanzas. The rhythm carries the central imagery of death-horror in a movement at once inexorable and paradoxically soaring toward the final explosion. The poem is a series of impressions supposedly evoked by the violin-music to which the title refers. It has precisely the kind of dynamics that Sylvia Plath at her best achieved, especially in her poem 'Ariel.' It is hard to read 'Cadenza' without thinking of it as a lament for her:

> The full, bared throat of a woman walking water,
> The loaded estuary of the dead,
>
> And I am the cargo
> Of a coffin attended by swallows,
>
> And I am the water
> Bearing the coffin that will not be silent. . . .

Other recent poems by Hughes (seen in magazines, in BBC scripts, and in manuscript) are in the same horror-fraught tone. They are powerful poems, though not always as subtle as this one in their 'scoring,' and are often more complex in their structure than the pieces in *Lupercal.* Their method lies somewhere between the forceful directness of the earlier work and the symbolic, Plath-like escalation of 'Cadenza.'

3. PHILIP LARKIN

Among English poets who have come to attention since 1945, Philip Larkin is the one whose reputation most closely rivals that of Hughes. Eight years older than Hughes, he was a student at Oxford during the war — a subject to which his poetry does not allude at all though his two excellent novels, *Jill* (1944) and *A Girl in Winter* (1957), do present young people in wartime and illuminate the particular attitude of weary, tolerant irony in most of the poems. There is little in Larkin to resemble the large risks that Hughes takes, neither the bare confrontations with hostile nature nor the attempt at a clean, hard language and rhythm that will liberate the poem from its maker. Hughes's essential insight, expressed in 'Thrushes,' that art must either be so swift a reflex of personality that it strikes unerringly for the mark as if purely instinctual ('Mozart's brain had it') or involve a long process of dissociation from the artist's private motives is stated more simply in the first line of 'Cadenza.' 'The violinist's shadow,' we are told, 'vanishes' when the musical structure comes into its own. Though a few poems at least in his first important book, *The Less Deceived* (1955),* approach this ideal, Larkin rarely gives himself to the process wholly.

A fundamental lugubriousness marks, and mars, much of Larkin's writing despite its colloquial ease and half-confessional naturalness. It is related to the question-begging assumption, only incompletely saved from dreariness by his witty effects, that most life is nothing much. Childhood — his own, at least — was 'a forgotten boredom.' It is silly to expect much happiness from love. As for his early home life and family, 'Nothing, like something, happens anywhere.' In 'Send No Money,' a poem in Larkin's only new collection, *The Whitsun Weddings* (1964), he describes himself as one who chose to observe what hap-

* This was Larkin's second book of poems. His first, a promising but highly derivative collection, was *The North Ship* (1945), reissued in 1966 with a witty, informative introduction by the poet.

pened to life rather than to 'have a bash' at it himself as 'all the other lads . . . were itching' to do. The result:

> Half life is over now,
> And I meet full face on dark mornings
> The bestial visor, bent in
> By the blows of what happened to happen.
> What does it prove? Sod all.
> In this way I spent youth,
> Tracing the trite untransferable
> Truss-advertisement, truth.

The language is admirable, yet the poem suffers from the obvious fact that its mood is anchored in no justifying referent. The poem is a voice without a body; there is no dive into the specifics of observation and experience that would give it a body, however fantastic or removed from ordinary life the images chosen. Only a very few of Larkin's pieces, most of them in *The Less Deceived,* do embody the double process of which Hughes speaks, whereby poems come fully into their own and the poet's direct presence 'vanishes.' 'No Road' is an excellent example of such a success; it is a simple poem about the difficult determination to let a close relationship come to an end. The basic image of letting 'the road' between the two people who have agreed to grow away from each other 'fall to disuse' dominates the poem. The actual moment of poetic awareness is one in which the road is still only a little changed: 'Leaves drift unswept, perhaps; grass creeps unmown' — and the determination to let the process continue is both the triumph and the 'ailment' of the speaker.

'No Road' calls for less attention to itself than do such characteristically wittier poems as 'Poetry of Departures,'

'Toads,' and 'Church-Going.' The first of these perfectly catches the worldly and hilariously self-ironic comic sense of the younger generations in England, their gift for satirical mimicry that has come across so brilliantly in British films and in Kingsley Amis's *Lucky Jim*. Kingsley Amis, in fact, is the great mimic of Larkin's generation. His feats at Oxford are admiringly described by Larkin in his introduction to the 1964 edition of *Jill*. Anyone who reads that introduction and knows Amis's novels — and better yet, has heard him going through his marvelous repertory of imitations of machinery and of the clichés of film drama — will recognize the Amis touch, and the whole cultural ambience that goes with it, in the first and third stanzas of 'Poetry of Departures':

> Sometimes you hear, fifth-hand,
> As epitaph:
> *He chucked up everything*
> *And just cleared off,*
> And always the voice will sound
> Certain you approve
> This audacious, purifying,
> Elemental move. . . .
>
> *He walked out on the whole crowd*
> Leaves me flushed and stirred,
> Like *Then she undid her dress*
> Or *Take that you bastard;*
> Surely I can, if he did?
> And that helps me stay
> Sober and industrious.
> But I'd go today. . . .

'Poetry of Departures,' though, makes a wistful, self-mocking joke about the dream of freedom out of these echoes from the melodrama of everyday speech. Glad to have been able to delight the reader with these effects, it ends with a trite reversal of viewpoint. 'Toads' is much tougherminded — a complaint against 'the toad *work*' that 'squats' on a man's life unless he is willing to relinquish his bourgeois comforts and security. The speaker dreams of liberation, as in 'Poetry of Departures,' and the language of the dream crackles with the articulate, racy idiom of contemporary England:

> Lots of folk live up lanes
>   With fires in a bucket,
> Eat windfalls and tinned sardines —
>   They seem to like it.
>
> Their nippers have got bare feet,
>   Their unspeakable wives
> Are skinny as whippets — and yet
>   No one actually *starves.*
>
> Ah, were I courageous enough
>   To shout *Stuff your pension!*
> But I know, all too well, that's the stuff
>   That dreams are made on. . . .

Instead of the slightly shabby turnabout of 'Poetry of Departures' (which argues that escape could only end in selling out again, for the sake of a new if unconventional set of creature comforts), 'Toads' deepens its initial insights toward the end by a reinforcing image of the speaker's inward condition. He is inhibited by a thwarting caution, which prevents him from becoming either a carefree romantic or a swashbuckling operator. Though what he is saying about *himself* is very unlike what Lawrence would say here, both the psychological set of the thought and tone and the colloquial rhythm do recall Lawrence's speaking personality and his uncompromising pursuit of his own meanings:

> For something sufficiently toad-like
> Squats in me, too;
> Its hunkers are heavy as hard luck,
> And cold as snow. . . .

Caught between the two 'toads,' he can only acknowledge his own ineffectiveness and let his images carry the connotations of self-disgust:

> I don't say, one bodies the other
> One's spiritual truth;
> But I do say it's hard to lose either,
> When you have both.

This is a level of thought that convinces even while one resists the cringing view of possibility it insists on. 'Heroic self-demeaning' might be the appropriate phrase here; one accepts the self-characterization of the speaker though not the implication of universal spokesmanship. The poem 'Deceptions' (a phrase of which gives *The Less Deceived* its title) presents a similar problem. It is based on a quotation from Mayhew's *London Labour and the London Poor,* in which a woman tells of having been drugged and raped, and of how the next morning she was 'horrified to discover that I had been ruined, and for some days I was inconsolable, and cried like a child to be killed or sent back to my aunt.' Larkin's poem, a sort of elongated sonnet in two stanzas of nine and eight lines respectively, beautifully evokes that grief-wracked morning in the first stanza, and then comments:

Slums, years, have buried you. I would not dare
Console you if I could. What can be said,
Except that suffering is exact, but where
Desire takes charge, readings will grow erratic?
For you would hardly care
That you were less deceived, out on that bed,
Than he was, stumbling up the breathless stair
To burst into fulfilment's desolate attic.

The thought carries a certain smart sense, but is ultimately shallow. The shift of attention from the woman's vividly remembered suffering to her ravisher's hypothetical frustrated romanticism is neither realistic nor symbolically right. For no visible reason, the man is supposed to have been a person like the speaker in Larkin's poems. We are to suppose that, sick with desire for experience beyond the power of ordinary contemporary existence to afford, he was nevertheless incapable of coming through into fulfilment on any terms. The image of 'fulfilment's desolate attic' does not grow out of what is given in this poem but out of the private assumptions of the poet. Touching as the first part of the poem is, the ending is as contrived and obtrusive as the rhyming of 'erratic' and 'attic.' Another poem, 'Dry-Point,' which does not specify its subject so clearly, creates its symbolic structure around a similar emotional and conceptual complex — the failure of ideals and expectations by which, nevertheless, we are trapped — more effectively. The overriding image appears to be sexual:

Endlessly, time-honoured irritant,
A bubble is restively forming at your tip.
Burst it as fast as we can —
It will grow again, until we begin dying.

Silently it inflates, till we're enclosed
And forced to start the struggle to get out:
Bestial, intent, real.
The wet spark comes, the bright blown walls collapse. . . .

The slight ambiguity, and the fact that from the start of these opening stanzas an inward state of the poet's consciousness is projected within the sexual figures, help establish the authority of whatever 'truth' the poem assumes. The third stanza is all aftermath and letdown: 'sad scapes,' 'ashen hills,' 'shrunken lakes.' Finally, the closing stanza gives us an image very much like 'fulfilment's desolate attic,' but one far less vulnerable to objection. The images of the poem have all along been private ones with connotations that can be followed through but cannot be either assented to or quarreled with. They are not based on explicit experience whose interpretation is debatable by all interested parties.

> And how remote that bare and sunscrubbed room,
> Intensely far, that padlocked cube of light
> We neither define nor prove,
> Where you, we dream, obtain no right of entry.

All the poems so far discussed, except for 'Send No Money,' are in *The Less Deceived.* The latest collection, *The Whitsun Weddings,* does not match the best earlier pieces unless perhaps in the opening poem, 'Here.' This is a poem unusual, for Larkin, in its swift movement that carries us from more industrial regions along the highway into the city of Hull, gives us close-ups of the city's inhabitants and sights, and then takes us out beyond the 'mortgaged half-built edges' past wheat fields and 'isolate villages' toward the beach and the North Sea. The movement seems to owe something to Stephen Spender's 'The

Express' in its fast-changing orientation by reference to landscape and in its use of participial phrases to underline the effect of speeding through that landscape:

> Swerving east, from rich industrial shadows
> And traffic all night north; swerving through fields
> Too thin and thistled to be called meadows. . . .

or:

> Gathers to the surprise of a large town:
> Here domes and statues, spires and cranes cluster
> Beside grain-scattered streets, barge-crowded water. . . .

and:

> Luminously-peopled air ascends;
> And past the poppies bluish neutral distance
> Ends the land suddenly beyond a beach. . . .

Despite the derivative echoes of Spender (and, curiously and unexpectedly, of William Carlos Williams in some of the incidental phrasing), the poem is brilliantly active in its evocation of Hull, where Larkin lives and pursues his career of university librarian. It was not surprising that a television interview with Larkin began with his voice reading this poem while the camera swept over the panorama described:

> A cut-price crowd, urban yet simple, dwelling
> Where only salesmen and relations come
> Within a terminate and fishy-smelling
> Pastoral of ships up streets, the slave museum. . . .

In 'Here,' Larkin almost loses himself in the excitement of sense-awareness as Williams might have done. The poem, though, is less spontaneous in feeling than it should be, because it is hag-ridden by a rather heavily regular pattern of rhymes in each of its eight-line stanzas. Larkin varies the pattern with a number of half-rhymes and with a criss-cross arrangement in alternating stanzas: *aba′bcdd′c, eff′eghgh, ijij′kllk, mnnm′opop*. Despite the two kinds of variation, the rhyming calls too much attention to itself in the course of each long stanza, though the onward movement and the vivid, accurate details are organically so alive that they survive this dragging effect. The poem runs in a beautiful curve from 'the piled gold clouds, the shining gull-marked mud' that accompany the Humber's 'slow presence' in rural regions to the busy commerce of the city —

> Cheap suits, red kitchen-ware, sharp shoes, iced lollies,
> Electric mixers, toasters, washers, driers —

and then towards the sea, where 'silence stands / Like heat' and

> . . . past the poppies bluish neutral distance
> Ends the land suddenly beyond a beach
> Of shapes and shingle. Here is unfenced existence:
> Facing the sun, untalkative, out of reach.

Only at the very end, in the oddly futile suggestion of a goal forever unattainable that renders the whole intense sequence of effects up to this moment peculiarly pointless, are we recalled to the mood of 'fulfilment's desolate attic' and of 'that padlocked cube of light.' It is as though Larkin had suddenly remembered his gloomy tenets and snapped himself out of his delighted absorption in reality, both at its loveliest and at its commercialized worst, by an act of rote insistence.

'Here' is easily the best of these newer poems, and the

one that succeeds most in downing its own lugubriousness. 'Toads Revisited' is interesting too, however, as a mild recantation of the toughminded thesis of the earlier 'Toads.' In the new poem, Larkin looks with a disheartened eye at the world of those whom the world does excuse from 'the toad work,' mainly because they are 'stupid or weak,' and decides that he is better off than they after all —

> No, give me my in-tray,
> My loaf-haired secretary,
> My shall-I-keep-the-call-in-Sir:
> What else can I answer,
>
> When the lights come on at four
> At the end of another year?
> Give me your arm, old toad;
> Help me down Cemetery Road.

His catalogue of the refugees from work — 'palsied old step-takers,' 'hare-eyed clerks with the jitters,' convalescents 'still vague from accidents,' and the like — is clever and full of a kind of dismay though of course deliberately oversimplified. Though the poem in a sense repents of the earlier complaint against the monstrousness of a life dominated by work, it actually carries the same meaning: the uselessness of trying to break out of the particular set of conditions of a very specialized kind of bourgeois professional life. The charm of the ending lies in its humorous surrender to the 'inevitable' while mustering up the morale to accept without bitterness, *faute de mieux,* a way of life alien to human nature. 'Toads Revisited' is saturated with a kind of nostalgia for an old, now forsaken romantic dream of freedom. And indeed, behind most of

Larkin's acceptance of failure of nerve in one form or another this nostalgia does lurk. His poem 'MCMXIV' is a rather lovely example — the old world of 1914 is evoked, so appealing ('moustached archaic faces,' 'dark-clothed children at play,' 'the pubs / Wide open all day'), so class-ridden at the same time ('the differently-dressed servants' in their 'tiny rooms in huge houses'), and so unaware:

> Never such innocence,
> Never before or since,
> As changed itself to past
> Without a word. . . .

4. CHARLES TOMLINSON

While Hughes and Larkin are the best known of the relatively younger British poets in England, Charles Tomlinson is probably better known than either of them in the United States. He is well enough respected in England, but Americans have recognized more sharply just what, formally, he was up to. Tomlinson is one of the few British poets to go to school with the French Symbolists and with the American masters of the generation of Pound, Stevens, Eliot, Williams, and Marianne Moore. His first book to be published in the United States, *Seeing Is Believing* (1958), gave clear evidence of this study. The sequence 'Antecedents: A Homage and a Valediction' echoes its French and American sources subtly and wittily. Sometimes grave, sometimes parodying or self-ironic, it indicates what Tomlinson loves in the tradition and what he is perhaps willing to bid farewell to — 'How long / Can a sun go on setting?' But it also indicates his post-Imagist bearings and insistence on an aesthetic viewpoint close to Pound's:

> . . . There are
> In lucidity itself
> Its crystal abysses
> Perspective within perspective. . . .
> . . . snow-prints
> Wanting a direction; perhaps
> At the most, as a constellation
> The cut stone
> Reassembled on dark.

The passage is of a piece with the prose-note at the end of the book that says:

> . . . Writing of his own work in the *Poems in Folio* series, Tomlinson has commented: 'The hardness of crystals, the facets of cut glass; but also the shifting of light, the energizing weather which is a result of the combination of sun and frost — these are the images for a certain mental climate, components for the moral landscape of my poetry in general.'

Among the more impressive of the poems in *Seeing Is Believing,* the ones that fit the programme implied in these quotations are very likely the best known. These include 'The Atlantic,' a poem of the most accurate observation of the movement of a wave breaking on a shore, which is marked not only by its kinetic precision but by its close adherence to its theme through all the stages of the wave's movement and its retreat. They include as well 'Paring the Apple' and 'Farewell to Van Gogh,' both poems that combine exquisitely noted detail with the exact kind of movement appropriate to its unfolding. The former poem is delicately sculptural in its feeling for the kind of artistic process that results in simultaneous discovery of motif and organic form. The latter poem is a 'quarrel' with Van Gogh over the painter's 'violence,' 'rhetoric,' and 'instructive frenzy.' For all these qualities the speaker is grateful, yet at the end he argues, in his concretely evocative post-imagistic manner, that the frenzy is not really warranted:

> . . . The world does not end tonight
> And the fruit that we shall pick tomorrow
> Await us, weighing the unstripped bough.

Another side of Tomlinson revealed in *Seeing Is Believing* in his strong feeling for the English past. He shares this feeling with many other English writers, including Larkin. However, poems like 'On the Hall at Stowey' and 'The Ruin' are not wry in the Larkin manner. Rather, they subordinate the speaker's personality to the search for empathy with their subjects. The stone hall at Stowey, at least five centuries old and fallen into half-decay, is come upon toward dusk by the poet on a walking tour. Its relation to landscape and atmosphere is naturally and seriously conveyed because the poet approaches it, over an 'aimless track' rutted by red marl, in a mood of discovery and readiness for perception of what is there on its own terms:

> A house. The wall-stones, brown.
> The doubtful light, more of a mist than light
> Floating at hedge-height through the sodden fields
> Had yielded, or a final glare
> Burst there, rather, to concentrate
> Sharp saffron, as the ebbing year —

Or so it seemed, for the dye deepened — poured
All of its yellow strength through the way I went. . . .

The mood, the readiness for perception, requires a certain restraint of personality, characteristic of Tomlinson, so that the eye (and indeed the whole complex of sensuous receptivity engaged by the ambience of the moment) may be as responsive as possible. Compare this passage with the beginning of Larkin's 'Church Going' and it will be clear what Larkin has lost through exploiting similar materials primarily to project a picture of himself:

Once I am sure there's nothing going on
I step inside, letting the door thud shut.
Another church: matting, seats, and stone,
And little books; sprawlings of flowers, cut
For Sunday, brownish now; some brass and stuff
Up at the holy end; the small neat organ;
And a tense, musty, unignorable silence,
Brewed God knows how long. Hatless, I take off
My cycle-clips in awkward reverence,

Move forward, run my hand around the font.
From where I stand, the roof looks almost new —
Cleaned, or restored? Someone would know: I don't.
Mounting the lectern, I peruse a few
Hectoring large-scale verses, and pronounce
'Here endeth' much more loudly than I'd meant.
The echoes snigger briefly. Back at the door
I sign the book, donate an Irish sixpence,
Reflect the place was not worth stopping for. . . .

It is true that in succeeding stanzas Larkin gradually works his poem around to a contradiction of the last line just quoted. The church is after all important. 'A serious house on serious earth it is,' and 'someone' is always discovering through such houses 'a hunger in himself to be more serious.' Nevertheless, Tomlinson holds the advantage of making his poem a discovery of a concrete phenomenon with an organic relationship not only to the immediate surroundings but to the modern world and to the past as well. Whereas Larkin's ending is ultimately a merely piously self-defensive intellectual rearguard action, Tomlinson's grows directly out of the deep apperception of a reality that his whole poem has recovered by a kind of surrender to it:

Within, wet from the failing roof,
    Walls greened. Each hearth refitted
For a suburban whim, each room
    Denied what it was, diminished thus
To a barbarous mean, had comforted (but for a time)
    Its latest tenant. Angered, I turned to my path
Through the inhuman light, light that a fish might swim
    Stained by the grayness of the smoking fields.

Five centuries. And we? What we had not
    Made ugly, we had laid waste. . . .

Tomlinson's two more recent volumes, *A Peopled Landscape* (1963) and *American Scenes* (1966), reflect a continuing relationship with the formal discoveries of American poetry and also with literal American experience. Since the appearance of *Seeing Is Believing,* he has taught at the University of New Mexico for a year and made other American visits. Although many other British poets have had similar American sojourns, Tomlinson is almost unique in the way these experiences have taken with him. Without surrendering either his British consciousness or the special characteristics of his earlier style — the restraint, precision, fine 'sculptural' eye, and feeling for the literal realities of place and atmosphere — he has come rather strongly under the influence of Williams and of the Black Mountain poets. 'Return to Hinton,' in the 1963 volume, is an interesting and clear example of the way the American influence has acted on him. This is a poem 'written,' we are told, 'on the author's return to Hinton Blewett from the United States.' Looking again at the Somerset village where he once lived, he writes (in the three-ply line developed by Williams, and in the vein of Williams's unprovincial localism) with love of the fading rural world, simple and stoical, and of its 'farm-bred certainties' that 'I do not hold.'

> Death's
>   not the enemy
>   of you nor of your kind:
> a surer death
>   creeps after me
>   out of that generous
> rich and nervous land
>   where, buried by
>   the soft oppression of prosperity
> locality's mere grist. . . .

In the same volume and in *American Scenes,* many of the poems have a new flexibility of statement which seems related to greater freedom in purely personal and emotional statement. 'The Farmer's Wife' moves from the kind of observation of an entire scene and its atmosphere projected in 'The Hall of Stowey' to a touching insight into the effect of childlessness on an otherwise deeply contented woman. 'The Picture of J. T. in a Prospect of

Stone' (on the poet's little daughter, and in the spirit if not quite the manner of Marvell's 'The Picture of Little T. C. in a Prospect of Flowers') and 'Up at La Serra' are especially telling further instances of the extension of resources gained by Tomlinson's later methods. Private tenderness, a delicately restrained concern, and the feeling of the uncontrollable pressures of the world are all involved in the fragile-seeming yet sinewy structure of the former poem. 'Up at La Serra' gains spontaneity and an ease in relating a series of impressions to one another in what seems a context of improvisation and surprisingly discovered associations. The subject is the mixture of tradition, revolutionary attitudes, closeness to the earth and to the sea, and urban influence in an Italian seaside town.

In addition to these advances in representative poems of *A Peopled Landscape,* Tomlinson gives his humor and his capacity for intense statement more play than before in *American Scenes.* The humor is fairly broad, for instance, in 'Chief Standing Water, or My Night on the Reservation.' It is gently bemused and humane in 'Las Trampas U. S. A.' And it is subtly involved with the elegiac in 'Arroyo Seco.' Tomlinson never 'lets go' entirely. He never gives the game away or even takes the risk of doing so as Lowell does, or uses the language of objective observation with such concentration that it gains major power and violence as Hughes's work does. But the intensity of his work at its best does approach passion. 'A Death in the Desert,' about an old Hopi dollmaker; 'The Fox,' an awe-thrilled poem about a dead fox in the snow; and 'The Cavern,' about the mysteries of the earth's interior — all these poems and a number of others approach a new kind of personal commitment beyond the barriers of the early 'coolness.'

Pulse of the water-drop,
veils and scales, fins
and flakes of the forming
leprous rock,
how should these
inhuman, turn
human with such chill affinities?

Hard to the hand,
these mosses not of moss,
but nostrils, pits
of eyes, faces
in flight and prints
of feet where no feet ever were,
elude the mind's
hollow that would contain
this canyon within a mountain. . . .
('The Cavern')

5. THOM GUNN

Another American-involved British poet is Thom Gunn, who has for a number of years taught at the University of California in Berkeley. In his first book, *The Sense of Movement* (1957), Gunn showed a fascinated interest in the world of the tough, leather-jacketed young motorcyclists and their slightly sinister, apparently pointless activity:

On motorcycles, up the road, they come:
Small, black, as flies hanging in heat, the Boys,
Until the distance throws them forth, their hum
Bulges to thunder held by calf and thigh.

In goggles, donned impersonality,
In gleaming jackets trophied with the dust,
They strap in doubt—by hiding it, robust—
And almost hear a meaning in their noise.

Exact conclusion of their hardiness
Has no shape yet, but from known whereabouts
They ride, direction where the tires press. . . .

Where Tomlinson is concerned with the precise ambience and impact of a given scene or personality, and with its proper idiom (rhythmically as well as in phrasing), and relates these concerns to his passion for the integrity of cultural heritage and of natural materials, Gunn turns his similar talents in other directions. He is attracted to the life of action, as a theme and as a way of meeting the world. And beyond that, as in the poem 'On the Move' just quoted, whose epigraph is *'Man, you gotta Go,'* he is something of a 'metaphysical' poet. 'On the Move' begins by observing that there is 'hidden purpose' in the sudden movements of birds—'the blue jay scuffling in the bushes,' a 'gust of birds' that 'spurts across the field,' 'the wheeling swallows.' We can discover their meaning, but to gain 'their instinct, or their poise, or both' in human affairs is to move 'with an uncertain violence,' under 'dust thrown by a baffied sense,' amid 'the dull thunder of approximate words.' Then come the motorcyclists of the quoted passage, as if to embody the abstract thought behind these images. After the close-up of 'The Boys,' Gunn devotes the second half of his poem to contemplation of the human significance of their kind of concentrated action:

It is a part solution, after all.
One is not necessarily discord

On earth; or damned because, half animal,
One lacks direct instinct, because one wakes
Afloat on movement that divides and breaks.
One joins the movement in a valueless world,
Choosing it, till, both hurler and the hurled,
One moves as well, always toward, toward. . . .

'On the Move' is the opening poem of *The Sense of Movement.* It is followed by an allegorical poem, 'The Nature of an Action,' which turns the issue of 'movement' inward much as Herbert does with the issue of free will in 'The Collar.' The speaker describes his passage from the habits of passivity and introspection under the domination of the overwhelming power of tradition to a more active state, 'directed by the compass of my heart.' Painfully he moves through a short, narrow corridor, from the room of the past to the room of the future. The passage takes twenty years, full of doubt about his existence or the existence of anything else, until he finds the proper 'handle in the mind'—his will—to open the second door. The furnishings inside are the same as in the first; the only difference lies in the changed character of his presence among the room's

. . . heavy-footed chairs,
A glass bell loaded with wax grapes and pears,

A polished table, holding down the look
Of bracket, mantelpiece, and marbled book. . . .

A youthful preciosity and intellectual self-consciousness marks the greater number of Gunn's poems in this early book. The two opening poems break into the clear, however, as do a few others. 'Human Condition' is another metaphysical contemplation, this time on the imprisoned state of that 'pinpoint of consciousness,' the individual self. 'The Unsettled Motorcyclist's Vision of His Death' is a vivid 'vision' indeed, of the risk of 'being what I please.' It is an assertion, as well, that even the very concretely imagined death of the symbolic motorcyclists (sinking into marshland out of a stubborn refusal to yield to circumstances) is merely a confrontation of volitionless nature by man's invincible will. 'Lines for a Book' is written in Audenesque, half-ironic praise of the 'toughs' of history as opposed to the men of mere sensibility ('I praise the overdogs from Alexander / To those who would not play with Stephen Spender'). 'Market at Turk,' a sympathetic close-up of a hoodlumish San Franciscan, celebrates the young ruffian's poised readiness — purposeless yet oriented toward some undefined and dangerous violence. 'In Praise of Cities' is a 'love song' on the changeableness, the surprises, the tantalizing promise and hardness of the great cities in the image of an infinitely varied woman. Amid the echoes of Yeats, Auden, Crane, and other masters, these poems show signs of a power of concentration and of an ability brutally to suppress self-indulgence and sentimentality, in the interest of testing forbidden sympathies and of pursuing realities outside the over-protected and over-civilized private self.

To a certain degree the promise was fulfilled in Gunn's second book, *My Sad Captains* (1961), but really in only two poems, 'In Santa Maria del Popolo' and the title poem. The former is Gunn's most successful poem, in combined sublety, power, and intricate yet subdued patterning. The poem contemplates a painting by Caravaggio 'on one wall of this recess.' It is a painting of Saul fallen from his horse and 'becoming Paul,' and one must wait until evening when the sun becomes 'conveniently oblique' to see it fully. At first, while waiting,

> I see how shadow in the painting brims
> With a real shadow, drowning all shapes out
> But a dim horse's haunch and various limbs,
> Until the very subject is in doubt.

Then the whole scene emerges — 'the act, beneath the horse,' of transformation, with an 'indifferent groom' present and Saul sprawling, 'foreshortened from the head, with hidden face,' among a 'cacophony of dusty forms' and making a mysterious 'wide gesture of the lifting arms' during his convulsive fit. Content with the external details, the possibly symbolic gesture, the sense of 'candor and secrecy inside the skin' that he was able to convey, the painter leaves the scene a mystery. Gunn remembers other paintings of Caravaggio's — the hard city types in them — and the artist's murder ('for money, by one such picked off the streets'). Turning, 'hardly enlightened,' from the chapel to the church's dim interior, he sees the people praying:

> Mostly old women: each head closeted
> In tiny fists holds comfort as it can.
> Their poor arms are too tired for more than this
> — For the large gesture of solitary man,
> Resisting, by embracing, nothingness.

So Gunn in this poem closes in on a multiple and sympathetic view of the human condition. He discovers his driving motif in the movement from the darkness within the painting to the darkness of meanings revealed by the painting itself when it comes into full view, and then to the vulnerability of the worshipers in their dark setting and in the poor comfort of their prayers and their physical attitudes; and so the final pair of lines, abstract as they are, becomes the largest statement of what the human gesture in the face of 'nothingness' creates or means. The poem 'My Sad Captains' reaches through to a comparable insight, but in quite different terms. The 'sad captains' are a few friends and a few historical figures who have come to be spiritual models to the poet:

> . . . They were men
> who, I thought, lived only to
> renew the wasteful force they
> spent with each hot convulsion. . . .

But now

> they withdraw to an orbit
> and turn with disinterested
> hard energy, like the stars.

Gunn's preoccupation with existential emptiness on the one hand, and with the assertion of meaning through sheer will or willful action on the other, brings him in 'My Sad Captains' to the same essential confrontation as does 'In Santa Maria del Popolo,' but without the merciful buffer of anything like the Caravaggio painting. The 'message,' in the spirit perhaps of Williams's 'El Hombre,' is a desolate courage that stakes everything on pure energy. As in the earlier volume, the poems that stand out — in particular, these two — are so sharply differentiated from the rest that the latter for the most part seem mere exercises by comparison. At any rate, the lesser pieces are on 'set' themes — the difficulty of reaching past lust to love, the 'compact innocence, child-like and clear,' that made the Nazi stormtrooper the peculiarly unshakable monster he was, the fate of a middle-aged rake, and so on. Derivative notes, especially from Auden but also at times from Edwin Muir and others, constantly interfere with Gunn's own voice in poems like 'The Byrnies' and 'Modes of Pleasure' that are otherwise imaginative and psychologically stirring.

6. CHRISTOPHER MIDDLETON AND GEORGE MACBETH

One might almost argue from the work of the British poets we have reviewed with special attention that their finest poetry is intimately involved with specific scenes and places. Their absorption of intricate detail into the speaking psyche reveals empathy of an extraordinarily responsive and receptive order. Hughes's ability in this respect is by far the greatest, and Gunn's the most uneven. But there are British poets whose work draws on other resources. Christopher Middleton is one of these. His poems strike one at once as the expression of a sophisticatedly elusive personality. He too responds actively and sensuously to the impact of literal scenes, but the source of his art is usually something else, a dance of the mind among perceptions and eccentric associations.

He *can* be as much a localist as the other poets, as the poem 'At Porthcotan' in his first book, *Torse 3* (1962), shows. It is about the death of a bird, a sick shag he found 'in a small pool the sea had left,' and apart from a certain deftness and wit that leaven the mood rather than sharpening it as Hughes would do, it might be by Hughes. But most of the poems in the same book take their pitch and movement from the lyrical key and the level of fantasy established at the beginning, and then from a process of rapidly shifting association along the way. 'The Dress,' for instance, begins with an odd turn of syntax, and also as a romantic song:

> Her blue dress lightly
> Is all my care. . . .

The odd tone mingles with the music all the way through, the poem seeming to build up a nearly eccentric vision of an ideal woman and then turning her purely ethereal just before the end, which comes with a shock of gross physical directness:

> For she must come
> Unseen, without wanting:
>
> Then I shall lightly
> With all my care
> Have my hand under
> Her blue dress when she is there.

Middleton's range is that of an informed modern mind, with titles as far apart in specific theme as 'German Ex-PW's (Russia) at Münsterlager, 1948' and 'Antiphon, After Laforgue's *Stérilités*.' He can be as simple as in 'The Thousand Things,' which is mainly an impression of the atmosphere surrounding the burning of dry vine leaves in the angle of a wall —

> . . . Dry vine leaves
> and a few dead flies on fire
> and a Spanish toffee spat
> into an angle of the wall
> make a smell that calls to mind
> the thousand things. . . .

A naked child jumps over the threshold,
waving a green spray of leaves of vine.

The small but surprising leap at the end of this poem is an instance of Middleton's lively, engaging resourcefulness of technique. His second book, *Nonsequences: Selfpoems* (1965), makes fuller use of this resourcefulness, though seldom just to charm or amuse the reader, even in the fashion of 'The Thousand Things.' A political dimension enters a number of the new pieces, not in any directly polemical sense but as part of their fabric of historical and cultural assumption. The shared ironies and bitterness of a half-century of modern experience of the fate of revolutionary idealism enter naturally into a poem like 'January 1919.'

What if I know, Liebknecht, who shot you dead.
Tiergarten trees unroll
staggering shadow, in spite of it all.
I am among the leaves; the inevitable
voices
have left nothing to say, the holed head
bleeding across a heap of progressive magazines;
torn from your face,
trees that turned around,
we do not sanctify the land with our wandering.
Look upon our children, they are mutilated.

In a poem like 'The Ancestors,' Middleton's resourcefulness is turned to the pursuit of the actual sense of most moderns for the past — their elusive guilt toward 'the ancestors' because they are the ones who are living and because of their greater prosperity in any case. The guilt allows the dead to drive us out of our comfortable self-possession —

When they come, we begin to go;
it's the ancestors,
they walk into the warm rooms. . . .

Lightness of movement, sureness of ear, a serious intelligence, unpredictability of form and association — a most unusual combination in British poetry — mark Middleton as the most varied and original of the younger English poets, if not the most powerful. The only other poet to match him in highspiritedness, if not in over-all accomplishment, is George MacBeth, whose two chief publications, so far, are *The Broken Places* (1963) and *A Doomsday Book* (1965). MacBeth is an extraordinary phenomenon, but his real 'presence' as a poet rather than a performer has yet to be demonstrated — he is the Unidentified Flying Object of British verse. He has written, for instance, a poem called 'Scissor-Man' in which, according to his note, 'a jealous pair of scissors complains about the racial prejudice which has prevented it from obtaining its rights in the way of housing, and which still interferes with its love-affairs.' The poem begins:

I am dangerous
   in a crisis
with sharp legs and a screw

   in my genitals. I slice
bacon-rind for a living. At nights I
   lie dried

under the draining-board, dreaming
   of Nutcrackers
and the Carrot-grater. If I should

   catch him rubbing
those tin nipples of hers. . . .

Another poem, 'The Son,' is described thus: 'A mortuary attendant rapes the body of a dead woman. He associates her with his mother, who died of a liver disease. He believes in a concrete form of resurrection by the power of love.' * This account, like some of the others that MacBeth gives of his poem, reads like a parody of those furnished by Robert Lowell for the poems in *The Mills of the Kavanaughs*. 'The Son' itself, despite its notes of buffoonery (again perhaps parodying Lowell's way of building into full tragic realization through sheer speed and intensity and the furious accumulation of images), is the work of a poet of virtuosity and forceful, clean-edged articulateness:

I thought of the clotted mercury in
The broken thermometer of

Her body. It rose again in
My head to a silver column, a sword
Of blood in the sun. . . .

MacBeth's mixture of grotesque humour and grisly seriousness with a buoyantly active style is a welcome addition in British poetry and cannot but have a liberating effect. His dead-serious poems, on themes involving the horror of war, the meaning of Eichmann, private suffering — all, once more, suggesting a Lowell influence at a certain remove — gain in sheer intelligent effervescence from his capacity for comic fantasy but by the same token lack a final conviction. Mind, sensibility, phrasing are pyrotechnically exploited; but the bright contriving that makes

* The notes by MacBeth quoted here were written for *Penguin Modern Poets 6* (1964), pp. 119–21. The poems quoted are from *The Broken Places*.

MacBeth's buffoonery so welcome also makes his more serious writing seem hollow, as though its conception were not truly his — not yet, at any rate. At this writing, he is thirty-three years old, one of the youngest and most prolific poets of some distinction in England, and very much in the midst of a rapid development.

VI
Contemporary Irish Poetry

1. ISSUES OF IRISH POETRY; AUSTIN CLARKE AND DENIS DEVLIN

Though Americans and Englishmen both have been too little aware of them, Irish poets still walk the earth and write. Poetry did not cease in Ireland when Yeats died in 1939. Austin Clarke, who grew up in the great man's shadow, has come into his own during the past decade. Patrick Kavanagh, who began as the lyrical, impressionistic, realistic singer of rural Ireland, has grown through various stages culminating in *Come Dance with Kitty Stobling* (1960) and the *Collected Poems* (1964). The poet-diplomat Denis Devlin's *Selected Poems,* edited by Allen Tate and Robert Penn Warren, appeared in 1963, four years after his death. His *Collected Poems,* edited by Brian Coffey, were published as a special issue of the *University Review* the same year and in book form a year later.

Mr. Clarke, now the dean of active Irish poets, was born in 1896. Mr. Kavanagh was born in 1905, and Denis Devlin in 1908. A younger generation is making itself felt as well. Thomas Kinsella, born in 1928, has won some attention as a translator from the Gaelic, but much more as poet in his own right. His tone and idiom are indicative of the new tendency in Irish poetry, for they are in harmony both with the general development of verse in English since the 1930's and at the same time distinctly local and personal. Two other poets still in their thirties, John Montague and Richard Murphy, are similarly coming into their own. Together with Clarke and Kinsella, they are substantially represented in Robin Skelton's useful anthology *Six Irish Poets* (1962), and all have published interesting work since then.* These younger men share with their elders a savage and nostalgic wryness at Ireland's and the world's present state, a wryness that inevitably has its purely personal source and dimension as well as its public ones. The mood is often reflected in the titles of their books — in those of Kinsella's *Downstream* and *Wormwood,* for example, or Murphy's *The Last Galway Hooker,* or Montague's *Poisoned Lands* and *All Legendary Obstacles.*

A shrewd observer might perhaps have gauged this shift of direction in Lennox Robinson and Donagh MacDonagh's *The Oxford Book of Irish Verse,* published in 1958. Here among the dazzling constellations of four centuries we find some of these same figures, together with others who, after promising beginnings, have not so far followed through. Scattered as it was in the modern section, however, and engulfed by poems in a heroic or creamily lyric tradition, their work with its astringencies was easy to miss.

* Kinsella, Montague, and Murphy hardly exhaust the list of interesting younger writers, which includes Richard Weber, Richard Kell, Desmond O'Grady, Pearse Hutchinson, James Liddy, Michael Harnett, and others. However, these three poets have so far made the deepest mark.

Moreover, that very work is itself, often, a bridge between the older traditions and the newer modes. Thus, in the Oxford anthology we find Clarke's early 'Pilgrimage' and 'The Planter's Daughter,' both poems of the 'magical' Celtic variety, side by side with his 'Celebrations' and 'Marriage' — harshly specific criticisms of the Church and State.

Contemporary Irish poets still walk that bridge, though they tend more and more to find their home on the near side of it, in the literal modern world with its peculiarly urban, internationalized sensibility. With the considerable help of the brilliant Dublin publisher Liam Miller and his Dolmen Press, a new appreciation has arisen of the double presence in Irish literature of a vividly exotic and meaningful past and of the pressures of the modern. What looked at one time to be an isolated thrust by Yeats toward realization of this double presence has clearly become part of the whole body of accomplished Irish writing today. By far the most significant publication of modern Irish poetry, certainly, has been that of the Dolmen Press. Miller has made it a primary concern to provide a proper, dependable program of publication for the books of Clarke. At the same time, he has published Kinsella, Montague, and a number of other younger figures as well, has associated himself with various new literary magazines (including *Poetry Ireland* and the now defunct but germinative *Arena*), and undertaken to print a wide variety of books that are of special Irish interest without sinking into a merely provincial outlook. Through his links with other presses abroad, he has helped bring Irish writers to foreign attention while maintaining a function comparable with that of the Yeats family's Cuala Press at home.

A recent pamphlet conceived and edited by Miller,

together with John Montague, and published by Dolmen Press — *A Tribute to Austin Clarke on His Seventieth Birthday* (*1966*) — includes a contribution by Montague that points to the combination in Clarke's work of the best of the old and the new. It points also to Clarke's fine sense of the actualities of Ireland that underlies his poetry generally.

> There are certain things I particularly admire in Austin Clarke. The first is the way, like the painter Patrick Collins, he has made the Irish landscape the background of his work: those changing veils of rain and mist could not be anywhere else, yet they are not painted to attract visitors, but because they are part of the permanent furniture of our lives, like the rocks and thorns beneath.

Even more admirable, I think, is the way that Clarke puts The Irish people, in their day-to-day lives, in the foreground of his work against this 'permanent furniture.' It is the quotidian reality, impersonal and personal, in detail, that gives one the sense of literal accuracy, deceptively homespun and penetrating at once, in Clarke's work. Montague gets at this quality further on, when he says that Clarke 'confronts the problems of his own time and place' with his archaic but adaptable techniques. 'He is the last representative,' we are told, 'of the intellectual idealism of the national movement' — a fact that 'makes his comment all the more savagely appropriate' — and because of him 'one is no longer afraid of those aspects of our life which had become stage-Irish properties.' The reason must be precisely the memory of the past in his work, and the deep grasp of permanent Irish character and experience, combined with his confrontation of demeaning daily reality.

The other side of Clarke that Montague points to is the

deep assimilation of the Gaelic tradition. In his autobiography (*Twice Round the Black Church*), as Montague says, Clarke 'tells us how that wonderful trio of scholars, Douglas Hyde, Sigerson and Stephen MacKenna, incarnated' that tradition for him when he was still a student at University College, Dublin. 'The influence of Irish versification, the influence of the Irish way of speech, the influence of Irish music are what MacDonagh specified in *Literature in Ireland,* that delicately persuasive study. . . . In one aspect of his work Austin Clarke is the fulfillment of MacDonagh's dream of a separate Irish mode; the first completely Irish poet to write in English.' * The

* The MacDonagh here referred to is Thomas MacDonagh, the father of Donagh MacDonagh and one of the martyrs of the Easter Rebellion to whom Yeats alludes in his poem 'Easter 1916.' The book is *Literature in Ireland: Studies Irish and Anglo-Irish* (Dublin: The Talbot Press, n.d.).

It is interesting to note that the year 1966, when *A Tribute to Austin Clarke on His Seventieth Birthday* appeared, was also, of course, the fiftieth anniversary of the Easter Rising. The anniversary was honored in many ways, including the opening of the new Abbey Theatre in Dublin. A nine-poem sequence by John Montague was to be published as well, under the title of *Patriotic Suite.* At the time that the present book was being written, I had seen the proofs of this sequence of short poems, but the pamphlet in which they were to appear had not yet been published. An interesting point is raised on the jacket of *Patriotic Suite,* presumably by Montague himself: 'The poets have been strangely silent during the 1916 Commemoration. Is it because, as Lenin said, the Irish Revolution was premature, and bound to turn bourgeois?' The sequence itself is followed by two quotations. The first is by Edmund Spenser: 'They say it is the Fatal Destiny of that land that no purposes whatever which are meant for her good will prevail.' The second is by Friedrich Engels: 'The real aims of a Revolution, those which are not illusion, are always to be realized after that Revolution.'

The sequence as a whole markedly shows the influence of Clarke in style and attitude, though Montague's individual touch makes itself felt as well. The poems touch lyrically and nostalgically on the idealism and the unrealized dream behind the Irish Revolution, but their dominant note is suggested by the prose passages I have already quoted and by such passages of actual poetry as the following:

statement may be an exaggeration, but Clarke does lead a parade of poets who find ways of being at once deeply traditional, in his sense, and authoritatively modern.

One of the most interesting aspects of his modern side is that Clarke's most recent book, a single narrative poem called *Mnemosyne Lay in Dust* * (1966), approaches the spirit of confessional poetry as closely as any work that has yet appeared in the British Isles. Though written in the

---

All revolutions are interior
The displacement of spirit
By the arrival of fact.
('Revolution')

Already a shocked Belfast beholds
A black-veiled Queen enter the Vatican.
Through Washington and Canterbury
All roads lead to Rome.
Granted a saint, we might shepherd
Another Dark Ages home.
('Annus Mirabilis, 1961')

The gloomy images of a provincial catholicism

(in a thousand schoolrooms
children work quietly while
Christ bleeds on the wall)

wound in a native music
curlew echoing tin whistle
to eye-swimming melancholy
is that our offering?
('1966 and All That')

On this same subject, of the attitude of the poets toward recent Irish history, see the discussion in Section 3, below, of Thomas Kinsella's 'A Country Walk.'

* First published in the United States, under the title 'The Loss of Memory,' in *Quarterly Review of Literature,* Vol. XIV (Numbers 1–2, 1966), pp. 116–40.

third person, this book has an autobiographical ring to it. It has to do with the hysterical breakdown and amnesia, hospitalization, and recovery of one 'Maurice Devane,' Clarke's relatively youthful protagonist. Formally, it represents a culmination of Clarke's entire development. After his early period of romantic work, he has for years cultivated an astringently compressed style employing certain rhyming and alliterative devices that appear eccentric in English but that are precisely that 'influence of Irish versification' to which Montague refers. The remarkable turn, achieved in old age, that *Mnemosyne Lay in Dust* represents is clearly the result of a fusion of resolutions, artistic and psychological.

Clarke may have been influenced by the confessional movement, as well as by the painful but eventually triumphant private experience he describes in the poem, but this late re-flowering of his art seems firmly rooted in his own earlier practice. He can be uncomfortably plain in his simple, unsqueamish factual presentation, as in Section VI of the sequence, which deals with a fit of depression that led to Maurice's being put for a while in a padded cell. I shall quote the first and last stanzas of this section, to suggest the range of emotion and tone that Clarke can quickly encompass, as well as certain resemblances, but never derivative ones, to Lowell and Berryman:

> One night he heard heart-breaking sound.
> It was a sigh unworlding its sorrow.
> Another followed. Slowly he counted
> Four different sighs, one after another.
> 'My mother,' he anguished, 'and my sisters
> Have passed away. I am alone, now,

Lost in myself in a mysterious
Darkness, the victim in a story.'
Far whistle of a train, the voice of steam.
Evil was peering through the peep-hole.

And:

Early next morning, he awakened,
Saw only greyness shining down
From a skylight on the grey walls
Of leather, knew, in anguish, his bowels
Had opened. He turned, shivering, all shent.
Wrapping himself in the filthied blankets,
Fearful of dire punishment,
He waited there until a blankness
Enveloped him . . . When he raised his head up,
Noon-light was gentle in the bedroom.

Revelations concerning his own self, which he is struggling to re-create, mingle in this poem with the sights and smells of Dublin, inside and outside the hospital, and with a vivid sense of both the literal nature and the strangeness of the other human beings whom Maurice observes from his vantage point. The poem is the full-bodied realization of a world, yet it never loses its subjectivity. The visions that come to Maurice in his traumatized state and the lyrical interpretations of his experience, sometimes (as in Section III) fearful and depressed, sometimes (as in VIII) tragically and prophetically buoyant as Yeats was in, say, 'Lapis Lazuli,' exalt the poem into self-transcendence.

Though Clarke began his career under the influence of the Celtic renaissance, he always combined romanticism with harsh wit and realism. His major books between the *Collected Poems* of 1935, now long out of print, and

Mnemosyne Lay in Dust are, like the latter, the work of his old age. *Later Poems* (1961) and *Flight to Africa* (1963) contain a good deal of satire of an unusual sort. It is the self-flagellant satire of a man of strong and compassionate feeling, and this is the root of Clarke's late confessional tendency. His identification with Ireland is as complete and unself-conscious as with his own family, and the criticisms he directs against her have the domestic authenticity, so to speak, of a man complaining of wife or mother.

Even in certain early poems, such as 'Repentance' and 'Celibacy,' reprinted in the *Later Poems,* the lyrical assimilation of national preoccupations and problems is striking. Clarke's interesting note on the latter poem, by the way, observes: 'The Confession poem was a recognized literary form in Gaelic and lasted until the eighteenth century.' Clarke obviously refers to a movement much older than the one touched off by Lowell, but the motivation is the same in certain ways, as his poems of the last decade have made clearer. Among these are 'Ancient Lights,' on the woes of self-liberation from Catholic conscience; 'The Envy of Poor Lovers,' which manages to present the frustrations of young lovers in a sociological and religious context of explanation and complaint without being tendentious; and 'Usufruct' in *Too Great a Vine* (1957), about Clarke's own home, Templeogue, the ultimate ownership of which was signed over to the Church by his pious mother. This deeding away of Templeogue seems intimately connected with his bitterness against the worldly concerns and display of the Church in various other poems, such as 'Intercessors' and 'Irish-American Dignitary.' But *Mnemosyne Lay in Dust* transcends that special bitterness. Its treatment of the poet's temporary condition is saturated with the very taste and smell of Dublin. Its vision, and the picture of recovery at the end, have a greater intensity than any other recent work in Ireland possesses. Such shorter recent pieces as 'Street Game' and 'A Simple Tale' and 'Martha Blake at Fifty-One' approach its pained feeling for the human condition. The little Protestant orphans mocked by Catholic children ('Feckin' bastards!') as they are marched through the streets, the committing of a poor man's children to an 'industrial school,' the neglect and insult to a pious, gravely ill woman of the people — such are the themes of these poems. Clarke's striking gift for picking up literally the degrading atmosphere of existence for so many of the Irish poor is in part the reflex of his own experience as a person of pride and sensitivity whom circumstance brought close to their condition. In the longer poem the humiliation of that daily life is absorbed into a larger social and psychological awareness that gives ample room for the right balance to be struck among his lyrical imagination, his homely realism, and his bitter inwardness.

Denis Devlin lacked Austin Clarke's great ability to present himself and his thought simply and unaffectedly, even when he moves among ambiguities. There is nothing in Devlin's ratiocinative poetry to match the way, in a poem like 'Repentance,' Clarke presents the subtle conflicts and counterbalancings of a spirit like his own caught between love of an ancient faith and love of openness to life's possibilities at every level:

> Could I unbutton mad thought, quick-save
> My skin, if I were caught at last
> Without my soul and dragged to torment . . . ?

Devlin moved habitually among ambiguities in his writing, except in the uniquely (for him) direct and vivid

'Ballad of Mistress Death' and 'The Tomb of Michael Collins' and in stray pieces like 'Anteroom: Geneva' or 'Pays Conquis,' in which he emerges from behind his extraordinary verbal fortifications. He set up the fortifications, apparently, to protect if not quite conceal a personality and religious nature deeply at odds with itself. Even 'The Tomb of Michael Collins,' an uninhibitedly emotional threnody, gives the impression of a need to resist final commitment. The Michael Collins poem mourns and celebrates a national hero, yet it implies, though far more discreetly and tangentially than do several of Yeats's pieces, a revulsion against uncompromising nationalist ardor. The most lyrically pure stanza brings out this revulsion but clouds it with the word 'angels':

> And sad, Oh sad, that glen with one thin stream
> He met his death in; and a farmer told me
> There was but one small bird to shoot; it sang
> 'Better Beast and know your end, and die
> Than Man with murderous angels in his head.'

In 'Lough Derg,' the poet's contemplation of his own sophisticated religiosity in the light of the naïve devotion of most of his countrymen involves considerations similar to those of Clarke's 'Repentance' but is far more complex. As Devlin handles the problem, it becomes a subject with every sort of intellectual repercussion. The poem expresses the workings of a fine mind seeking an acceptable balance among its own motives. Devlin, though hardly as dynamic as Hart Crane, approaches him in his continuing effort at self-identification.

> All is simple and symbol in their world,
> The incomprehended rendered fabulous.
> Sin teases life whose natural fruits withheld

Sour the deprived nor bloom for timely loss:
Clan Jansen! less what magnanimity leavens
Man's wept-out, fitful, magniloquent heavens

Where prayer was praise, O Lord! the Temple trumpets
Cascaded down Thy sunny pavilions of air,
The scroll-tongued priests, the galvanic strumpets,
All clash and stridency gloomed upon Thy stair;
The pharisees, the exalted boy their power
Sensually psalmed in Thee, their coming hour!

The interesting poem 'From Government Buildings' does not resolve itself adequately and has various derivative notes, yet is striking in incidental effects and in its attempt to place the speaker within several worlds at once. There is the bureaucratic world suggested by the title — the world of both 'the badgered great' and 'the little': all officials who, 'smiling, sour the milk of charity.' There is the world of simple nature, whether in Rome where at evening 'swallows traced eggshapes on the vellum sky' or in Dublin where 'the wind was warm with blue rain.' There is the modern political world of the 'famous exile,' the deportations, 'the bombed cathedral.' (The poem appeared in Devlin's 1946 volume *Lough Derg and Other Poems,* and provides a faint echo, as it were, of the whole political history of the decade or more preceding the book's appearance.) There is the world of the 'painted saints' and of the poet's inability to be part of its mystical regime, and there is also the more intellectually repossessed world of myth and religious allegory:

When the culture-heroes explored the nether world
It was voiceless beasts on the move made Death terrible.

These lines, at the end of the fourth stanza, prepare us through their vision of terror for the almost morbid refusal of commitment in the fifth stanza, the center of the poem. The 'you' the speaker addresses throughout the poem seems to be his inner, frightened, cowering self that would remain free despite the pressures of social and natural reality on it. In modern psychological jargon, it refuses to allow itself to 'internalize' a world in which the speaker's room 'sighs empty with malignant waiting' for this final commitment to the soul's defeat. The fifth stanza puts the essence of the matter so strongly that the call for a happy resolution at the poem's end hardly affects the theme of refusal to submit to reality here stated:

Friendship I will not, barring you; to have witness does:
Doll birds, dogs with their social nose, by day
Are touchstone. But at night my totem silence
With face of wood refuses to testify.

2. PATRICK KAVANAGH

The lively-spirited Patrick Kavanagh has in his serious poetry become at once simpler and more 'private' than he once was. Without giving us much detail, he communicates a self-weariness and desire for liberation from his own past that seems not unrelated to the closely packed self-searching of Devlin and others. At times the communication comes disguised as boasting that, just when he had thought all was lost, he has come through after all — has learned joy, been loved by women despite his poverty and bohemian character. The poetry then takes on a confidential rather than a confessional tone. He has, at the same time, fallen more and more into the habit of writing satirical verse that on good days approaches that of Austin Clarke — as it sometimes does in 'The Paddiad,' an attack on the superficiality and smugness, the mob-quality, of much Irish criticism. On the many bad days it is facile and self-indulgent. In general, the newer poems are often thinner than his past work although the speaking voice remains interesting and stands in suggestive contrast to the other dominant voices of Irish poetry today.

Kavanagh's early work was highly lyrical and romantic, often impressionistic. Such poems of the 1930's as 'Tinker's Wife' and 'Iniskeen Road: July Evening' are sharp, evocative impressions, and 'A Wind' showed a special promise of ability to encompass opposites while writing freshly and imagistically. In 1942 *The Great Hunger* appeared, a long step forward because the natural gifts displayed from the start were now employed within a sustained narrative poem of relatively free but highly controlled form, in a diction always clear and pointed, sometimes highly colloquial. The poem is in at least a minor aspect a nostalgic recollection, in detail, of traditional rural Irish life. Its major effect, however, is of a three-pronged exposure of the squalor, the emptiness, and especially the sexual deprivation of that life. The pathetic tale of the aging Maguire and his equally frustrated sister — their loyalty to the land and to their chores and economic rituals — was clearly the work of a poet very much coming into his own. This impression was strengthened by a number of the poems in *A Soul for Sale* (1947), particularly the Tolstoyan 'Father Mat,' which lacks the surface bitterness of *The Great Hunger* but presents the polarities of the spiritual life in a manner very true to the workings of Irish sensibility, even Yeats's, in this century. Father Mat is of the world of nature, a figure who, like Yeats's spokesmen for the secular and sexual values of existence, takes over the holiness attributed generally to a more orthodox religiosity and therefore becomes a symbol of the poet's artistic aims as well:

> Father Mat came slowly walking, stopping to
> Stare through gaps at ancient Ireland sweeping
> In again with all its unbaptized beauty:
> In calm evening,
> The whitethorn blossoms,
> The smell from ditches that were not Christian. . . .
>
> His heavy hat was square upon his head,
> Like a Christian Brother's;
> His eyes were an old man's watery eyes,
>
> Out of his flat nose grew spiky hairs.
> He was a part of the place,
> Natural as a round stone in a grass field;
> He could walk through a cattle fair
> And the people would only notice his odd spirit there.
>
> His curate passed on a bicycle —
> *He* had the haughty intellectual look
> Of the man who never reads in brook or book;
> A man designed
> To wear a mitre,
> To sit on committees —
> For will grows strongest in the emptiest mind.
>
> The old priest saw him pass
> And, seeing, saw
> Himself a mediaeval ghost.
> Ahead of him went Power,
> One who was not afraid when the sun opened a flower,
> Who was never astonished

At a stick carried down a stream
Or at the undying difference in the corner of a field.

Another poem in *A Soul for Sale,* 'A Christmas Childhood,' is even more gentle and touching. Like 'Father Mat,' it recalls a rural Garden of Eden full of wonders that were innocent but no less awe-inspiring for that.

One side of the potato-pits was white with frost—
How wonderful that was, how wonderful!

This is a poem of frank sentimentality, in a context of idealization not so much of the past as of a certain tone or set of feeling possible in that past. The volume as a whole is nevertheless far more bitter than *The Great Hunger,* and in it the poet speaks more directly in his own right. The world of childhood, in which the six-year-old Patrick Kavanagh lived with such enthusiasm, was a world of certainties in which, when his father played the melodeon at Christmas,

There were stars in the morning east
And they danced to his music.

The pang of the loss of these certainties comes out in another moving piece, 'Memory of My Father':

Every old man I see
Reminds me of my father
When he had fallen in love with death
One time when the sheaves were gathered. . . .

In 'Stony Grey Soil,' the poet blames the very nature of peasant existence for the loss of his childhood Eden, despite the associations of his beloved father with the land:

O stony grey soil of Monaghan
The laugh from my love you thieved;
You took the gay child of my passion
And gave me your clod-conceived. . . .

We thus see in the most natural facts of human existence the source of the disillusionment that embitters a number of the poems in *The Great Hunger* and later volumes. The family Eden goes under with the aging and death of parents and with the discovery that the preoccupations of peasants can be a blight on the soul's growth. The speaker complains that his speech, his manners, his whole personality, and with them 'the first gay flight of my lyric,' were befouled and bogged down by the 'steaming dunghills' and 'swinish food' of the life of the soil, and that by the same token he was deprived of youthful love. The complaints implied in the objective tale of Maguire in *The Great Hunger* seem restored in this poem to a private source in Kavanagh's own life. In 'A Wreath for Tom Moore's Statue' the attack shifts to the whole of Ireland as passionless, money-minded, and aesthetically indifferent — the peasant-life of 'Stony Grey Soil' writ large, with hypocrisy added as well. Finally, in 'Pegasus,' the poet declares his independence of the world and its institutions and trades:

My soul was an old horse
Offered for sale in twenty fairs. . . .

'Church and state and meanest trade' alike refuse to buy. When the speaker accepts that this condition cannot be changed and decides to cease hawking the 'old horse,' it grows wings and becomes true Pegasus. In the freedom gained through such renunciation we see both the romanticism of Kavanagh and his kinship with the spirit of Yeats and Joyce.

The confession of failure in 'Pegasus' is only partially ironic. It has the pathos of the honest recognition of inadequacy — blame it on what the poet will, whether the barrenness of his upbringing, or whatever it may be. Why, in the poem, do all refuse to bid for the speaker's soul? The 'buyers' for the Church 'were little men who feared his unusual airs.' The State borrows the soul 'for a week or more,' but it 'came back a hurdle of bones' that was 'starved, overworked, in despair.' So the speaker's soul was, then, an old horse with 'unusual airs' that tired quickly. Allegorically speaking, one cannot blame all the buyers who shied away, 'Paudeens' or 'gombeen men' — that is, creatures of the market place, whatever their pretensions — though they might have been. And why, indeed, did the owner want to *sell* his soul so badly? The only 'message' that comes through, beneath the superficially romantic airs, is that in truth the speaker felt he had nothing to offer. The horse became Pegasus only after its master decided: 'No more haggling with the world.' Now it is most unlikely that Kavanagh's genuine poetic inspiration waited upon his practical failure. The poem does suggest, rather tritely, the magic of imagination:

> As I said these words he grew
> Wings upon his back. Now I may ride him
> Every land my imagination knew.

Apart from that, however, and despite its bravado, it speaks a sense of inadequacy. The 'high-paid work in towns' is not for the speaker, though he has made every effort to obtain it.

I stress this point because in Kavanagh's later poetry

his sense of having lost out in the competition is so often brought into the foreground. 'Portrait of the Artist,' for instance, is not *necessarily* a self-portrait yet might well be. The unnamed 'artist' who speaks complains that because he is a man whose life has been uneventful — that is, without scandal or superficial activity — he is not considered a great artist or even an interesting person:

> I never lived, I have no history,
> I deserted no wife to take another,
> I rotted in a room and leave — this message.
>
> The morning newspapers and the radio
> Announced his death in a few horrid words:
> A man of talent who lacked the little more
> That makes the difference
> Between success and failure.
> The biographer turned away disgusted from
> A theme that had no plot
> And wrote instead the life of Reilly.
>
> Great artist, came to town at twenty-one.
> Took a job,
> Threw it up,
> Lived a year with Mrs. Brown. . . .

Not to belabor the point, a number of the later poems indulge in the same sort of not altogether difficult wryness. One of them, 'Sensational Disclosures! (Kavanagh Tells All),' has the exceptional virtue of self-irony, as the title would suggest. He saves himself in it from egocentric solemnity, at any rate — thus raising himself a notch above, say, Robert Graves contemplating the world's injustice to him and 'objectively' noting the inferiority of all other poets. And he does say of himself that he has failed to live up to his own promise. But 'Sensational Disclosures!' also brings his rasping competitiveness right out into the open:

> He frittered away
> A talent that could flay
> D. J. Enright — say;
> He could disburse
> A fabulosity of verse,
> Could swallow without dodgery
> Ted Hughes' menagerie,
> He often spat forth
> Lions of more wrath.
>
> But Kavanagh, the dog,
> Took to the grog
> Leaving Larkin and Logue
> Manufacturing fog,
> And even MacNeice
> Making ground in the race. . . .

Some of the other later poems are serious, and touching, on the subject of feeling that one has not come through. Poems like 'Come Dance with Kitty Stobling' and 'The Same Again' have the grace to desist from complaining about the world's recognition of other poets. The former of these mentions the competition at the very start, indirectly: 'No, no, no, I know I was not important. . . .' Then the speaker goes on to describe himself as 'a tedious man with whom no gods commingle' and who 'once had a myth that was a lie but it served.' The second grants the disappointment of followers who once believed he would be 'their one and only bard' but now have come to see, in spite of themselves, that because of hard drinking 'he's finished and that's definitely.' The simplicity and colloquial vigor of those poetic statements resemble those of an American poet of quite different intelligence and temperament, Paul Goodman, as do some of the poems of sexual failure in the book. But among Kavanagh's poems of self-disillusionment, the most moving, probably, is his 'I Had a Future.' In this poem the evocativeness of his earlier work, based on concrete memory and place, is recaptured but is combined with the sadder notes I have mentioned. The poem is elusive, hard to represent by brief quotation, yet a pure and unusual song of a spirit brought to its knees.

3. THOMAS KINSELLA

Thomas Kinsella shares with his elders whom I have been discussing a savage and nostalgic dismay at the present state of Ireland and of the world, with all that is implied for the subjective life in that dismay. But his work has been more closely assimilated than theirs to the new tendencies that he resists, and he resembles the younger urban poets of England and America the more by that token. I do not mean that this gifted poet lacks a voice of his own. Quite the contrary, he seems to me to have the most distinctive voice of his generation in Ireland, though it is also the most versatile and the most sensitive to 'outside' influences. Only to glance through his first book, *Another September* (1958), is to see the versatility at once. There we find the tragic-romantic lyricism of 'In the Ringwood,' resembling Devlin's 'Ballad of Mistress Death' but far more original in its handling of the ballad form. Shades of Coleridge, Wilde, and Yeats haunt the poem, it is true, but Kinsella's special idiom is present too. In his most recent book, *Wormwood* (1966), he moves toward an uncompromising acuteness of insight into private suffering that has painful confessional dimensions. These are foreshadowed in a stanza of 'In the Ringwood' like the following one:

> 'Many times the civil lover
> Climbed that pleasant place,
> Many times despairing
> Died in his love's face,
> His spittle turned to vinegar,
> Blood in his embrace. . . .'

In *Wormwood* the tone is infinitely less 'debonair,' but we can see how the accomplishment is the perfection of a long-pursued meaning. The rhetoric and vocabulary of a poem like 'Mask of Love' grew out of those of the earlier poem but are the result of a mature and relentless artistry:

> You have seen our nocturnal
> Suicidal dance,
> When the moon hung vast, and seemed
> To wet our mocking mouths:
> She, turning in despair
> Round some tiny mote. . . .

We find, again, in *Another September* at least two more poems of unusual interest both in their own right and for Kinsella's development. One of them, 'Clarence Mangan,' is a gesture of sympathetic identification with the nineteenth-century Irish poet, Poe's nearly exact contemporary whose morbid romanticism and disordered life resembled Poe's in a number of ways. The external details of Kinsella's life are far different from either Mangan's or Poe's. For a number of years an Irish civil servant in the Department of Finance, he accepted an appointment in 1965 as Artist-in-Residence at Southern Illinois University and moved from Dublin to Carbondale, Illinois, with his wife and three young children. But the poetry itself, though often ordered and carefully controlled, can be as we have already observed of a different nature. When Kinsella has Mangan speak of his psychological terror, the voice is similar to that in *Wormwood:*

Back to a wall, facing tumultuous talking faces,
Once I lost the reason for speech. My heart was taken,
Stretched with terror by only a word a mouth had uttered,
Clipped to a different, faceless destroyer.

Long I waited to know what naked meeting would come
With what was moving behind my eyes and desolating
What I touched.

The final lines of 'Clarence Mangan,' too, presage the clinical accuracy of self-observation in certain parts of *Wormwood,* and also the spirit of that book's dedicatory preface. Kinsella has Mangan account for his probing of his own suffering as a necessary self-surgery:

Out of the shadows behind my laughter surgical fingers
Come and I am strapped to a table.

Ultimate, pitiless, again I ply the knife.

Thus 'Clarence Mangan' ends. The passage might be taken as a brief rationale, in another context, for the confessional method. The dedicatory preface of *Wormwood* is an exploration in prose of the same principle, in less familiar images:

> *Beloved,*
> *A little of what we have found . . .*
>
> *It is certain that maturity and peace are to be sought through ordeal after ordeal, and it seems that the search continues until we fail. We reach out after each new beginning, penetrating our context to know ourselves, and our knowledge increases until we recognise again (more profoundly each time) our pain, indignity and triviality. This bitter cup is offered, heaped with curses, and we must drink or die. And even though we drink we may also die, if every drop of bitterness — that rots the flesh — is not transmuted. (Certainly the individual plight is hideous, each torturing each, but we are guilty, seeing this, to believe that our common plight is only hideous. Believing so, we make it so: pigs in a slaughter-yard that turn and savage each other in a common desperation and disorder.) . . .*

The third poem of special interest in *Another September* is 'Baggot Street Deserta.' It is a self-portrait and self-analysis of the poet at work, in stanzas of unequal length that are actually, for the most part, clusters of quatrains with alternately rhyming tetrameter lines. The form, which allows for considerable minor variation, does not always prevent modulation toward doggerel. Nevertheless, it is a form that feeds on its own proliferation and might encourage a poet to carry on courageously in his effort to complete a contemplative poem of some length. At night, in his attic above Baggot Street in Dublin, the young poet examines the nature of his art — its truthfulness and relation to the natural and the sleeping social worlds around him, the subconscious motivations present in it, and the ultimate mystery of the imaginative process. All these topics are handled with a certain intellectual ease and an effect of muted irony and absorbed contemplation somehow working together, but the poem takes on real power only when it touches on the sunken psychological motives in creation.

> Secretly a swollen Burke
> Assists a decomposing Hare
> To cart a body of good work
> With midnight mutterings off somewhere;
> The goddess who had light for thighs
> Grows feet of dung and takes to bed,
> Affronting horror-stricken eyes,
> The marsh bird that children dread.

The next poem of some length and comparable bearing, though quite different in essential subject and tone, was 'A Country Walk,' in *Downstream* (1962). *Poems and Translations* had appeared the year before, containing almost everything in *Another September* together with some newer poems of varying character that were later reprinted in *Downstream.* (Among them are 'Dick King' and 'The Laundress,' two of several poems of Kinsella's that show a warm though unsentimental feeling for common life and experience.) 'A Country Walk' is in blank verse whose surface is roughed over and varied by the active language, the attention to detail, and the tension between a traditional 'music' and the search for an energetic specificity of phrasing and for a note sufficiently conversational to allow for easy pivoting of focus. We move quickly from the quite personal beginning when, 'sick of the piercing company of women,' the speaker leaves for a walk over fields and along the river. Absorbing the landscape as he goes (and quite as sensitive to it as Austin Clarke), his mind dwells on

Ireland's unhappy history from the legendary past through the time 'the first Normans massacred my fathers' and the later time when 'knot-necked Cromwell and his fervent sword' wrought their atrocities in Ireland. From here to the defeat and aftermath of the Easter Rebellion is but a step as it is to contemplation of the shriveled, pedestrian state of the revolutionary tradition in Ireland. The people have exchanged 'a trenchcoat playground for a gombeen jungle.' Once, perhaps, they allowed their task of revolutionary struggle to become too much a playground of emotions and dramatic attitudes, but the net outcome has been worse — the emergence of the new business classes and their purely monetary values. The climactic emphasis comes when the protagonist tells of coming into a square on which are posted signs that say:

> . . . MacDonagh and McBride,
> Merchants; Connolly's Commercial Arms. . . .

These are the names of leading heroes of the Rebellion, and the very phrase 'MacDonagh and McBride' was canonized by Yeats in his 'Easter 1916,' as was the name of Connolly. The 'gombeen' world sees none of the irony here, of course, but the poem sinks downward in a depressed recognition of current realities embodied in the 'otherworldly gloom' of factory windows, the 'lamp switched on above the urinal,' the sight of a car that 'plunged noiselessly and disappeared.' In the closing stanza there is a recovery from the mood as the poet contemplates the rapid river with its myriad surfaces 'that gave and swallowed light' — a sign of change, beauty, power. It suggests the promise, however tragic in its impersonality, of renewal.* The poem ends nobly in a kind of affirmation,

* At this writing Mr. Kinsella is preparing for publication two long poems, 'Matching Silver' and 'Phoenix Park. Dublin,' which are poems

though the inevitable movement of the waters is equally a sign of the irreversible movement of time that has been the source of depression just a little earlier. The final lines contain one obvious though submerged ironic note in the midst of the tragic promise they offer:

> *Venit Hesperus;*
> In green and golden light; bringing sweet trade.
> The inert stirred. Heart and tongue were loosed:
> 'The waters hurtle through the flooded night . . .'

Wormwood is a slender sequence of eight short poems. It is almost entirely inward and at times confessional, as I have already suggested, and we have seen how its dedicatory preface proposes a view of life as 'ordeal after ordeal' — an endless process of growth through the acceptance of suffering and through the self-transcendence required in each phase until the final 'guilt and failure' of death. *'But if we drink the bitterness,'* the preface continues, *'and can transmute it and continue, we resume in candour and doubt the only individual joy — the restored necessity to learn.'* In the poems themselves a private crisis is faced and its bitterness fully drunk; it is a crisis that has shaken the speaker's view of his marriage, whether the relation between husband and wife is its literal cause or only its dramatic center. There are necessary ambiguities in the presentation, for Kinsella is far from being tempted into Edwin Bronk's sort of literal reportage of married life. Rather, we have an attempt to gauge the quality and character of a suffering that emerges within a stable and de-

---

of farewell, temporarily at any rate, to Ireland. Together with 'Baggot Street Deserta' and 'A Country Walk,' these poems form an unintended sequence of contemplative, deeply-felt poems on the poet's conception of the relation between his own art and the cultural state of his country, as well as between these and the meaning of history and tradition on the one hand, the poet's private experience and needs on the other.

voted relationship, as I read the sequence. The whole rationale is stated in the closing sentence of the preface: '*Love also, it seems, will continue until we fail: in the sensing of the wider scope, in the growth toward it, in the swallowing and absorption of bitterness, in the resumed innocence. . . .*' In a very large sense, this sequence is one among a number of poetic expressions of the new sense of private reality that has arisen because of changes in life generally and in our understanding of the nature of love and personal relationship. Like the best overtly confessional poetry, it presents honest and sensitive minds thrown on their own resources in an age when all absolute ideals have had to be abandoned — an old story, of course, but one that becomes more to the point with each passing year as the post-war generations come of age.

The opening piece is the title poem, 'Wormwood.' It is a poem about a recurrent dream in which the speaker stands in a deep thicket, the rain falling heavily, trying to retain the exact tone of a 'wooden echo' that he has heard and to hold intact the vision that is associated with it. The vision, the sound, evoke the whole curve of an experience of shared suffering in love:

> If I can hold it . . . familiar if I can hold it . . .
> A black tree with a double trunk — two trees
> Grown into one — throws up its blurred branches.
>
> The two trunks in their infinitesimal dance of growth
> Have turned completely about one another, their join
> A slowly twisted scar . . . that I recognise . . .
>
> A quick arc flashes sidewise in the air,
> A heavy blade in flight. A wooden stroke:
> Iron sinks in the gasping core.
>
> I will dream it again.

The reader will be aware, of course, that the poem says nothing, literally, about 'an experience of shared suffering in love.' It is the context of the sequence, together with the emotional weight given to the central images of the 'dance' of growth of the intertwined trees with the 'slowly twisted scar' that marks their joining and of the axe that comes to destroy that painfully won stasis, that evokes this interpretation. The form itself, a highly modified *terza rima* with most lines unrhymed but a few half-rhymes at least falling in the expected places occasionally, suggests a Dantean symbolism. So do the presentation of the central image as a dream-vision of compelling force for the dreamer himself and the personified nature of the dance of the trees. If not an archetypal vision in the broadest sense, this is at least an essential pattern of the dreamer's fate that is projected.

I have already quoted from the second poem, 'Mask of Love.' In this poem and the next one, 'Forsaken,' the objective central images are not kept so firmly at a distance from the speaker's subjective state. A certain clarity of detail is sacrificed in them so that the character of the speaker's anguish may receive fuller expression — an anguish perhaps 'in excess of the external facts,' as Eliot wrote in his essay 'Hamlet,' which deals with the kind of artistic problem that confronts Kinsella here. I shall take the liberty of quoting from the fourth stanza a second time, plus a few lines more, so that the way that 'Mask of Love' helps create a context for the opening poem can be clearly seen. In 'Wormwood' we had 'the two trunks in their infinitesimal dance of growth.' In 'Mask of Love' we have

our nocturnal
Suicidal dance,

When the moon hung vast, and seemed
To wet our mocking mouths:
She, turning in despair
Round some tiny mote;
I, doubled in laughter,
Clasping my paunch in grief
For the world in a speck of dust;
Between us, the fuming abyss. . . .

The dilemma of spirit reaches its climax of expression in this penultimate stanza. The first two stanzas pointed the dilemma itself, in two extraordinary images combined in a desperate apostrophe:

Mask of love, staring
Aghast out of unreason,
Do you come to us for peace?
Me, flinching from your stare?
Her, whose face you bear?

Remember how we have come
To stand again and again
On peaks of stress, face
To face, wearied with horror,
Screaming in ecstacy
Across the narrow abyss.

Neither in this poem nor in 'Forsaken' is the literal source of the horror stated, despite the obvious suggestiveness of the language. 'Forsaken' presents the speaker praying to 'a heart of steel and cloth and stone'—signs of the unresponsive deity that will not satisfy the living heart's needs. His burden is too much:

I crush my heart on the stone:
'Choose, O Christ,
One with better strength!'

The order of poems is especially important in this sequence. The dream-poem is profoundly convincing in its introduction of the motif of a grievously hard-earned good life newly menaced by a terrible foreboding. The next two poems insist on present anguish, giving it body through concrete images but holding off a more specific close-up of the scene and exact dramatic conditions of the complex feeling that has been displayed. In the fourth and fifth poems, the effective center of the sequence, these withheld circumstances are provided. 'First Light' opens up the basic scene in three short stanzas that move swiftly, yet in another sense seem exquisitely leisurely. Emotion accumulates, but it is centered (by a kind of psychological transference often found in both reverie and art) in the external data rather than in the human figures, who are seen as being overtaken by the very condition of their existence. The condition resides in surrounding nature: the sky, the sea, the grass. It resides in the literal house: kitchen, stairs, bedrooms. It resides in the abstractions that govern social life: religious tradition, law, marriage, the family. As day dawns, the sleeping innocents begin to be touched once more by all that has wounded them, and that will again. The tight alternate rhymes of the second stanza point up the literal circumstances of the family drama and make for one sort of climax, while in the third stanza the sustained effect of a child's unease in sleep and then in the waking state makes for a more emotional climax of unanswerable authority. This modest poem is a triumph of tact in the use of elements that, uncontrolled, would make the poem degenerate into mere complaining and sentimentality. Instead we have a most original use of familiar elements to bring to life the thought that Yeats once expressed in a refrain: 'All men live in suffering.'

A prone couple still sleeps
While a pale deadly light ascends
Out of the sea: dawn-
Light, reaching across the hill
To the dark garden. The grass
Emerges, soaking with grey dew.

In brutal silence an empty
Kitchen takes form, tidied and swept,
Blank with marriage — where shrill
Unreason and Jew-face Law have kept
Another vigil far
Into the night, and raved and wept.

Upstairs a whimper or sigh
Comes from an open bedroom door
— A child enduring a dream
That grows, at the first touch of day,
Unendurable —
And lengthens to an ugly wail.

The fifth poem, 'The Secret Garden,' shows father and son together in a tangled spot in the garden. Touching the young innocent, 'taking strength,' the father inevitably transfers to the boy something of the corruption of experience, 'the first chill of the curse.' It is the helplessness of the human predicament, whether in Eden or in this world, and no resolution to follow Voltaire's dictum and cultivate one's garden will change it. The earth, as it were, is too coarse — 'corrupt, corrupt, visible, invisible' — to match the need to protect the child's 'innocent energy, light as light.' 'How sweet the kernel of his waiting brain,' the father exclaims. No precautions can be taken, and the man decides to concentrate on awareness and hope, in the

Voltairean sense after all: 'I'll cultivate my garden for the dew.'

One poem only, the next one — 'The Serving Maid' — is in a dramatic voice different from that of the man who speaks in all the others. Its theme follows from that of 'The Secret Garden.' The protagonist is a woman who has given herself entirely to service and accepts her own 'decay' — her 'yellowed skin and eyes' and 'shadowed lips withering' — cheerfully. The cheerfulness is not self-deceiving. She mocks herself in the mirror as 'this squawking busybody' and observes that she has 'too-bright eyes' and a 'wholesome hopelessness' at best and that there is a 'wretched gasp of self-regard' in her devotion to service. Yet she thanks God that she has found someone absolutely helpless to serve —

> Old feathery bones and flesh to tug and turn,
> To lift and wipe, jingling the crumpled bed;
> Every part, from heels to glistening chin. . . .

The 'serving maid' has fear and humiliation and says that she has found her way to reconciliation with life by giving herself to 'soul-consuming Love' of this special kind. In her own way, she has passed through the same torment as that of the protagonist of the other poems. She cries out to the helplessness that depends on her attention: 'I come, I come, in decent skirt and jumper. . . .' When she does so, it is her way of saying, as the speaker in 'The Secret Garden' has said: 'I'll cultivate my garden for the dew.' The poem gives us an objective equivalent, however simplified and pointed, for the subjective state developed in the rest of the sequence.

The final two poems, 'Remembering Old Wars' and 'On a Gift in the Shape of a Heart,' repeat the earlier motifs with a slight difference. 'Remembering Old Wars' recapitulates the scene, apparently, of 'First Light,' but is written in the first person and pictures not a single night and dawn but a recurrent series of exhausted nights of heavy yet desolate sleep and morning awakenings into 'the hells of circumstance.' 'What clamped us together?' the speaker asks at the very start. The answer at the end, insofar as there is an answer in this nine-line poem in the same *terza rima* form as the title poem, is that it was the need to continue and perhaps grow through suffering, as in the tree-dance of 'Wormwood': 'We would renew each other with a savage smile.' The closing poem, in fact, brings back the tree imagery with which the sequence began, although the figure now is of a single 'nearly naked tree.' It is in the form of a penetrable riddle, suggesting a meaning beyond the literal content. The poem ends in a way to send us back over the sequence in search of its full implications:

> *What cannot rest till it is bare,*
> *Though branches crack and fibres tear.*

After this, as epilogue to the sequence, comes a quotation from *Apocalypse,* Ch. 8, vv. 10 and 11, that both accounts for the name of the sequence and stresses the risk of the path the poet has accepted in following the moral and aesthetic direction he has taken in these poems. Here the uncompromising recognition of a tragic state is the important thing; whether or not it will lead to a state of grace is a question deliberately and honestly held in abeyance:

> *and a great star fell from heaven, burning as it were a torch; and it fell on the third part of the rivers and upon the fountains of waters; and the name of the*

> *star is called Wormwood; and the third part of the waters became wormwood; and many men died of the waters, because they were made bitter.*

4. JOHN MONTAGUE

John Montague's poetry is comparable with both Clarke's and Kinsella's in certain ways, though the total amount of it is still fairly slight and the achievement not yet decisive. There are two volumes, *Poisoned Lands* (1961) and *All Legendary Obstacles* (1966). The former book promised an interesting range of style and subject matter. It contains a poem like 'Murphy in Manchester,' a forthright portrayal of an immigrant workman absorbing the English city in the flashing moment between his arrival and the time that the factory prisonhouse and its world will close in on him. On the other hand, it reaches back into the twelve-century-old past in a poem like 'A Footnote on Monasticism: Western Peninsula.' The poem is touched off by the many signs along the rocky coast of former hermit habitation, signs 'weather-beaten but enduring,' and it conjures up a delicately sympathetic though unsentimental picture of one of the 'fiercely dispossessed' hermits at prayer.

> See, among darkening rocks he prayed,
> Whose body was chastened and absurd,
> An earth-bound dragging space in which
> His seeking spirit blundered like a bird. . . .

And the book gives us still another turn in the witty voluptuously imagined half-satire of 'The First Invasion of Ireland.' An explanatory headnote tells us that

> according to *Leabhar Gabhàla,* The Book of Conquests, the first invasion of Ireland was by relatives of Noah, just before the Flood. Refused entry into the Ark, they consulted an idol which told them to flee to Ireland. There were three men and fifty-one women in the party and their behaviour has so little in common with subsequent tradition in Ireland that one must take the story to be mythological

The poem itself is in the same mood:

> Division of damsels they did there,
> The slender, the tender, the dimpled, the round,
> It was the first just bargain in Ireland,
> There was enough to go round.
>
> Lightly they lay and pleasured
> In the green grass of the guileless place:
> Ladhra was the first to die;
> He perished of an embrace. . . .

But the acid-edged realism of 'Murphy in Manchester,' almost muted though it is in that particular poem by compassion, is the clue to Montague at his strongest. The title-poem, 'Poisoned Lands,' has to do with the fact that, as the poet explains, 'in the Irish countryside one often sees crudely painted signs: THESE LANDS ARE POISONED. This indicates that meat injected with poison has been laid down to destroy predatory animals; the practice is not highly regarded.' The beginning is extremely close in spirit to that of a number of Clarke's poems. There is the same closeness to colloquial speech, the same compression and attention to detail, the same air of intelligent but peevish dissatisfaction:

'Four good dogs dead in one night
And a rooster, scaly legs in the air,
Beak in the dust, a terrible sight!'
Behind high weathered walls, his share
Of local lands, the owner skulks
Or leaves in dismal guttering gaps
A trail of broken branches, roots,
Bruised by his mournful rubber boots. . . .

Later in the poem, though, a wild imaginative note takes over as the neighbors' conception of the animal-poisoner as a demon is pursued. The language becomes less true to the colloquial, but in the exuberance and savagery of the statement we sense the power of Montague, never fully realized as yet in his work:

'Children dawdling home from Mass
Chased a bouncing ball and found,
Where he had stood, scorched tufts of grass
Blighted leaves'—and here the sound
Of rodent Gossip sank—'worse by far,
Dark radiance as though a star
Had disintegrated, a clinging stench
Gutting the substances of earth and air.'

Then, in the closing stanza, the poem swings back to a Clarke-like realistic hardness. The speaker tells of meeting the 'demon' on an evening walk, quotes his actual speech (' "I don't like country people," he said, with a grin'), and casually underlines, in conclusion, the relation between the man's wanton murder of animals and his attitude toward human beings:

And behind, a white notice seemed to swing and say:
'If you too licked grass, you'd be dead today.'

Montague's ear for folk-speech and ability to combine the stuff of fantasy and legendry with a kind of flat factuality are seen again in 'The Sean Bhean Vocht' (the poor old woman — 'one of the traditional symbols for Ireland, most familiar in the eighteenth-century patriotic song of that name'). Most of this poem describes an actual old woman whom the poet knew in his childhood and who rather frightened him with her ragged ugliness, her smell ('her clothes stank like summer flax'), and her talk of battles between the fairies of Ireland and the fairies of Scotland and other magical events. Her speech, 'heavy with local history,' had the quality of prophecy and wisdom literature in its rhythm as in its idiom:

'Mrs. McGurren had the evil eye,
'She prayed prayers on the black cow:
'It dropped there and died,
'Dropped dead in its tracks.
'She stood there on the mearing and cursed the Clarkes
'They never had a good day since,
'Fluke and bad crops and a child born strange.'

This is the unconscious sort of incantation that suffuses ordinary speech when uttered by someone who sees supernatural force at work in the plainest events. The poet, in the final stanza, speaks of striding 'through golden light' among the local hills and fields 'in high summer.' Though it had been logical to point out a few lines earlier that 'age is neither knowledge nor authority,' he cannot help wondering 'what illusive queen lay dust' in the grounds where the old woman now lies buried. The balance of elements in this poem is like that of 'Poisoned Lands,' but Montague's love of the sound of Irish speech and his deep engagement with Irish tradition come through more beautifully and genially. In *Poisoned Lands* as a whole, indeed, that sense of involvement with the whole of Irish reality, at once nostalgic and critical, appreciative and uncompromising, is what gives the work its authority. One feels it even in a poem as modestly unsensational as 'Irish Street Scene, with Lovers,' an impressionist composition that gets the precise ambience of a 'rainy quiet evening' in Dublin when lovers walk 'linked under the black arch of an umbrella' through 'this marine light.' The restraint and confidence of 'Irish Street Scene, with Lovers' are as true to that urban ambience as the released whimsy and fantasy of some of the other poems are to their motives in legendry and folk-tradition.

In his second book, *All Legendary Obstacles,* Montague has made a leap toward the confessional in some crucial ways very much like Kinsella's. Apart from one poem, 'The Trout,' the most striking poems in this volume are three poems of difficult, even terror-filled, marital love. The title poem is the least drastic. It concerns the reunion of two people, either husband and wife (as seems most likely) or lovers of long standing, who had been separated by 'all legendary obstacles.' The specific 'obstacles' noted in the poem are those of distance, weather, and time, for its literal situation is that of the speaker waiting all day in a railroad station for the woman who eventually arrives at midnight. However, the moment of reunion suggests deeper obstacles:

> At midnight you came, pale
> Above the negro porter's lamp.
> I was too blind with rain
> And doubt to speak, but
> Reached from the platform
> Until our chilled hands met.

Why they have been so long separate we are not told, but the portentousness of the mood throughout the poem militates against the more harmless reasons. If we take the piece as a controlled series of dramatic perspectives which reveals less than it withholds, it approaches the character of the other two poems of married love that I have mentioned, 'That Room' and 'A Private Reason.' The first stanza focuses on the physical distances and obstacles between the actors at the start, 'the long imaginary plain,' the 'monstrous ruck of mountains,' the 'hissing drift of winter rain.' The second presents the waiting man, 'shifting nervously from station to bar' as he waits all day. He does not know when to expect her — a sign, one surmises, of the failure of communication that makes the relationship an uncertain one. The great trains 'sail by,' a subtle effect of dislocation of time and expectation. Then we have the moment of arrival, in the quoted stanza, with a light literally focused on the woman, and at the same time the words 'blind,' 'doubt,' and 'chilled' — though not literally attached to the relationship — frame that focused picture. In the last stanza, we are placed inside the railway car with the 'old lady' who has been the younger one's companion. With her we focus on the relationship from yet another viewpoint, not that of the waiting speaker and lover but of one who watches, apart, a disappearing moment of vivid life. The old woman in the train, we are told,

> marked
> A neat circle on the glass
> With her glove, to watch us
> Move into the wet darkness
> Kissing, unable to speak.

The poem may be simply one of anxious waiting for a beloved woman, and then of the inarticulable joy of having her finally arrive. But the very structure of the poem subordinates any notion of pure joy in the relationship to effects that interfere with this feeling — the sheer geographical barriers presented at first, then the nervous uncertainties of waiting, then the words to which I have already referred ('blind,' 'doubt,' 'chilled'), and finally the 'wet darkness' and inability to speak of both central figures. Especially, the shift of viewpoint from that of the husband-lover to that of an onlooker who will herself disappear and who watches them disappear emphasizes more the darkness and inarticulateness that surround the protagonists than the ecstasy of their reunion.

'That Room,' in which there are two figures of undefined relationship (who nevertheless seem to be husband and wife) begins almost like Kinsella's 'Mask of Love.' In the course of its first sentence, though, it directs our attention to some dreadful predicament in which these figures are involved together. Once the fact of that predicament comes into view, we have in intensified form the sort of thing we had in 'All Legendary Obstacles,' a secret whose existence is forced upon our attention while its nature is kept hidden.

> Side by side on the narrow bed
> We lay, like chained giants,
> Tasting each other's tears, in terror
> Of the news which left little to hide
> But our two faces that stared
> To ritual masks, absurd and flayed.
>
> Rarely in a lifetime comes such news
> Shafting knowledge straight to the heart

Making shameless sorrow start —
Not childish tears, querulously vain —
But adult tears that hurt and harm,
Seeping like acid to the bone.

Sound of hooves on the midnight road
Raise a romantic image to mind:
Someone riding late to Marley?
But we must suffer the facts of self;
No one endures a similar fate
And no one will ever know

What happened in that room
But that when we came to leave
We scrubbed each other's tears
Prepared the usual show. That day
Love's claims made chains of time and place
To bind us together more: equal in adversity.

What have they discovered? What terrifying 'facts of self,' so rare and so unmentionable? The mind plays over the possibilities, then refuses to pry where it has been so explicitly warned not to. Here, as in 'A Private Reason' (where husband and wife are seen walking together, 'both of us sad, for a private reason'), the reader is probably willing to grant the authenticity of the emotion but is also compelled to dissociate himself from it because he is asked to share but not to understand it. Short of the reader's ultimate commitment, the poems are powerfully moving. They show, as it were, what Montague is perhaps capable of doing. But insofar as they throw us into the need to satisfy vulgar curiosity before we can sympathize fully, their very power is self-defeating rather than self-transcendent.

A number of other poems in *All Legendary Obstacles* seem related to the central three. For instance, 'Obsession,' the opening piece in the book, states the theme of inarticulateness both directly and symbolically. It projects a state of darkness in which the protagonist cannot respond to the fresh, naked challenge of the life-force:

> My tongue
> Lies curled in my mouth—
> My power of speech is gone.
>
> Thrash of an axle in snow!
> Not until the adept faun-
> Headed brother approves
> Us both from the darkness
> Can my functions return. . . .

'A Charm,' too, expresses the same challenge and darkness through the figure of a falcon obsessed with its master yet feeling 'the dark hood' descend, always, 'when you step near.' Montague has left the relatively sure ground of his early work for the exploration of an irresistible yet defeating relationship. Like the falcon of this poem, the predicament 'describes a circle' around his work that he is not yet ready to break out of and dominate through a more impersonal art.

Yet in 'The Trout,' already mentioned in passing, we have his most beautifully achieved poem thus far. His mastery of the literally fluid medium (recalling the ambience of 'Irish Street Scene, with Lovers' and of 'All Legendary Obstacles') and of his own ability to establish sensitive empathy with another form of being than his own does this time transcend the emotions that enter into the poem, emotions that are not unrelated to those of the marriage poems. The fish 'in his fluid sensual dream' embodies motives far beyond those of fisherman and trout:

> I was so preternaturally close
> I could count every stipple
> But still cast no shadow, until
>
> The two palms crossed in a cage
> Under the lightly pulsing gills.
> Then (entering my own enlarged
> Shape, which rose on the water)
> I gripped. To this day I can
> Taste his terror on my hands.

5. RICHARD MURPHY

Of the significant Irish poets to emerge since the last war, Richard Murphy is the least introspective or tempted toward confessional writing. He shows exceptional narrative and elegiac powers, and his poems are highly local, sentimentally so when they are not rescued by his talent for loading every rift with objective details—and quite deliberately not with Romantic ore, especially of the psycho-mined variety. Fundamentally, he is an old-fashioned, rather conventional poet. Reading his 'The Cleggan Disaster' and 'Sailing to an Island,' both poems about stormy sailing off the Connemara coast, one wants to check back to poems like Masefield's neglected *Dauber* or even to the relevant passages in Hopkins's 'The Wreck of the *Deutschland*' for comparison. Mr. Murphy knows sailing—it has almost become his trade—and these accounts are sparklingly concrete and exciting. They serve a timeless artistic purpose in the way they repossess a particular kind of experience and life-style. Nostalgia for a lost and (sayeth the poet) a nobler past, as seen from the viewpoint of the Ascendancy, is heavy in these pieces. It is even heavier in 'The Last Galway Hooker,' the tale of Mr. Murphy's own ship the *Ave Maria,* and in 'The Woman of the House,' a poem about his grandmother that is at the same time about his whole family's and his country's past as well. These poems are all printed in his *Sailing to an Island* (1963). 'The God Who Eats Corn,' a long poem published in *The Reporter* of May 7, 1964, carries this quality of aristocratic nostalgia controlled by a refined narrative and descriptive technique to its highest point yet in his work.

'The God Who Eats Corn' is about the poet's father, Sir William Murphy, a classical scholar and civil servant who, after years as colonial secretary in Bermuda and governor in the Bahamas, retired to Central Africa. There, after a time, he was recalled from retirement to act as governor-general of the Central African Federation, which came to an end in 1963. 'He is noted,' writes the poet in the account in *The Reporter* from which I have taken this information, 'among both races as a liberal and a supporter of African advance, to which he has contributed in a practical way on his farm, where white paternalism is perhaps to be seen at its best.' The style of the poem is well illustrated by the lines describing Sir William in his Southern Rhodesian garden with which the poem begins:

In his loyal garden, like Horace's farm,
He asks his visitors to plant a tree.
The black shadow of the African msasa
Squats among the lawn's colonial company.

In honour among the watersprays that spin
Rainbows over the cool English rose-beds

Hand-weeded by a pink-soled piccanin
The Queen-Mother's cypress nods in a straw hood. . . .

The deliberate formality and restraint enable the poet to enter into an extended account of the relation of this honored figure to the Central African situation and to the people of the area in all its complexities of injustice, suffering, and genuine service.

Tall in his garden, shaded and brick-walled,
He upholds the manners of a lost empire.
Time has confused dead honour with dead guilt
But lets a sunbird sip at a gold creeper. . . .

On the game-cleared plateau the settlers say
'This is our home: this is white man's country.'
Dust-storms gather to hide their traces
Under boulders balanced in a smouldering sky.

The shout for 'Boy!' from the dinner table
Long after their exodus will be recalled:
The black male hanged for a white woman's rape,
For loving a Negro, the fair girl gaoled. . . .

Violence of love deprived of communion
Begins to bud like trees before the rains.
The safari is over: the earth needs planting.
But the planters are hunting each others' skins. . . .

Irish poets are constantly faced with the pressure to choose between native, traditional perspectives and 'larger' ones. All serious poets everywhere, doubtless, are faced with similar issues. For obvious reasons, though, the poet in Ireland seems to find the issue more acute than it is elsewhere, at least on the surface. We can see, in 'The God Who Eats Corn,' one way in which Murphy has resisted becoming bogged down in provincialism and self-repetition. In *Sailing to an Island,* we see earlier evidences that he had no great temptation in any case to settle for this state. The lovely, sad, brief 'Girl at the Seaside' — in its way the rarest thing in that collection — and the gently understanding portrait of the American poet Theodore Roethke on a not too happy visit to the Irish poet's village ('The Poet on the Island') round out the volume. In his forthcoming long narrative poem *The Battle of Aughrim,* a crucial confrontation of Ireland's past, long the theme of patriotic literature, is re-examined in the light of a sophisticated, relativistic intelligence:

> Deep red bogs divided
> Aughrim, the horses' ridge
> Of garland hedgerows and the summer dance,
> Ireland's last defence
> From the colonists' advance.
> Each saw his enemy beyond
> A broad morass
> Of godly bigotry and pride of race,
> With a causeway two abreast could cross. . . .

VII Epilogue: American Continuities and Crosscurrents

Inevitably, we have scanted certain figures not directly related to the central concerns of preceding chapters. The versatile American poet Howard Nemerov, for instance, has an extraordinarily varied body of excellent work to his credit. It ranges from light but telling satirical comment to the very serious, morbidly brilliant sequence 'The Scales of the Eyes,' and includes touching buffoonery such as 'Lot Later' (in which the biblical Lot tells his story in the language of a modern American-Jewish businessman) and the archaically elegant, eerie formality of 'The Goose Fish.' Sheer humane intelligence with a sharply ironic edge carries Nemerov a good distance, and 'The Scales of the Eyes' reveals a sensibility such as marks the best of the confessional poets — here turned away from the particular events that have scarred the poet's life to the symbolic dream-data of the inward life. Throughout the sequence, the speaker wrestles with the grossness of existence and with the inevitability of death and its omnipresence:

Around the city where I live
Dead men in their stone towns
Wait out the weather lying down. . . .

The terror of the poem seems in some degree a total retention of the first awareness and horror of death felt by children. Many of the specific memories the speaker calls upon in the course of the poem are of a comparable nature — unforgotten shocks and depressed responses of childhood. Thus, the opening of the fifth section, called 'A Can of Dutch Cleanser':

The blind maid shaking a stick,
Chasing dirt endlessly around
A yellow wall, was the very she
To violate my oldest nights;
I frighten of her still.

Birth-trauma, the ominousness of all things — snow, an empty house, the sea — viewed in certain moods: many of the notes of the poem are a reaching back toward childhood and even toward a pre-natal condition, as well as an opposing effort to grasp the actual feel and import of literal death. The acceptance of life in joy toward which the poem ultimately strives must wait upon the demanding discipline of these efforts and is well-earned when it comes through. In 'The Scales of the Eyes' and a few other poems, Nemerov holds his cleverness in check and discovers his deeper possibilities.

Nemerov is one of a number of poets whom we might call 'independents,' though the term would be something of a misnomer. It is easy enough to see their place in the whole modern picture; they are 'independents' in the sense that they have worked on their own, in the manner of many artists, without being closely involved with the momentary 'centers' of most intense poetic influence and perhaps without attracting much critical attention. Theodore Weiss is such an independent, a writer who combines exuberance of spirit and diction with rigorous formal self-discipline. His recent poem 'In the Round' will illustrate:

> Catching yourself, hands lathery
> and face ajar, inside the glass,
> you wryly smile; watching, you know
> you're in for it:
>   and in the twinkle
> of your eye the horny butting goat
> and jutting horny bull, the weasel,
> goose bedraggled and the wren
> with greedy bill go flashing by. . . .

These lines introduce a poem which moves with the speed of leaping association of a truly poetic mind (in the essential sense of 'poetic,' comparable with 'musical'—that is, a mind that seems to take naturally to a plastic sense of language and rhythm and even thought as materials for design). 'In the Round' begins with the 'wryly' smiling insight of the speaker, under the influence of the glimpse of his mirrored face disguised by lather, into the presence of every other kind of animal nature in his own. Soon he reverses the comparison, thinking of the human implications of lower forms of life:

>   What gusto
> can it be that blows its violence
> through a locust's violin, mad summer
> burnishing in such midge mouths?

As the poem races along, it plays with sound both for its own sake and for the kind of relationships and meanings that can be highlighted by it — as in the echoing of 'horny butting goat' and 'jutting horny bull' or of 'goose bedraggled' and 'greedy bill' or, more obviously, 'violence' and 'violin.' At the next stanza we are in the realm of Keats's 'Ode on a Grecian Urn' as the thought of an eternal heroic music played by the locust or some other insect recalls the equally unchanging realm of art that brings human and animal figures together 'on a vase.' What mere clay can hold (itself miraculously surviving) in a single marvelous vision is amazing, and the life-force out of which art grows, and which is the source of the myriad resemblances of man and beast, is still more amazing:

> Still, though clay crack, necks
> break, twitchy as a cock, they stand,
> engrossed and going on, a Bach
> of a beetle, strutting like a yokel,
> nightlong at its tongs and bones.

Weiss's volatile, restless imagination and his energy contribute to a conscientious artistry. He has tried various forms, most daringly a long poem named *Gunsight* (1962) that seeks to present the thoughts, memories, and feelings of a wounded soldier undergoing an operation. The conception itself is an act of sympathetic identification, in which the soldier soon is thought of as a human being far from any stereotype, full of guilt, resolutions, and intelligence.

Among other 'independents' whose work is not yet widely enough known are Paul Goodman, Galway Kinnell, Ramon Guthrie, James Schevill, Henry Rago, Howard Moss, Carolyn Kizer, and William Stafford. Goodman's poetry, as one might expect from his career as a critic of American mores and institutions, is filled with forthright political statement, following the model of Wordsworth and Shelley in such matters. His 'April 1962' begins:

> My countrymen have now become too base,
> I give them up. I cannot speak with men
> not my equals. . . .

This is Goodman at his bluntest. One sees a subtler, though equally heartfelt, expression of his views in 'The Lordly Hudson,' title poem of his 1962 collected volume. For many years he has advanced a half-mystical conception of the relation between our civilization and its neglect of the resources that should be made available to the citizenry. The passionate outcry of this poem is an indirect protest but at the same time a spontaneous outburst of love for the river — patriotic love, in fact — and pain at its neglect:

> Be still, heart! no one needs your passionate
> suffrage to select this glory,
> this is our lordly Hudson hardly flowing
> under the green-grown cliffs. . . .

One might view Goodman's work as in some degree a throwback to the romantic and polemical style of the best popular poets of the last century. To some extent his refusal to internalize the ills of the age as thoroughly as many other modern poets do, obliterating their character as social issues and offering up their own psyches as more interesting symbolic substitutes, points toward such a throwback. But there is a thoroughly contemporary side to his poetic style and thought as well. It is seen in the lighthearted sequence 'Poems of My Lambretta,' which has to do with the poet and his motorbike. The doughty, slangy tone Goodman employs is not merely for the sake of humor and immediacy. He is, rather, presenting himself as a chivalric figure, vulnerable and dauntless despite his weaknesses and despite the demeaning world he inhabits — a New York Don Quixote, in short. The bike has a pennant, sewn for him by his lady; he prays to Castor and Pollux ('from cops preserve me') and rides out for adventure. His pride is provincial but noble:

> I never had to jam the brakes
> for I am a New Yorker bred,
> the light is green all my road. . . .

A more introspectively moving note is introduced in the third poem of the sequence, which begins confessionally and ends in exaltation; the speaker here is at once Paul Goodman and the poet of this age, swiftly carried through the débris of the modern with his head still full of the past:

> Dirty and faded
> is the banner of my bike
> and tattered in the winds
> of journey like
>
> my self-esteem my soiled
> repute my faded hope. . . .

But at the end:

> on glad our windy way
> nowhere, going forty!
> *Flapping* is my flag,
> faded torn and dirty,
>
> and on the buddy-seat
> there rides Catullus dead

and speaks to me in gusts of shouts,
I dare not turn my head.

Finally, Goodman has written still more inward poems that bring his work into rapport with the confessional tendency of the age — particularly his poems about love, both homosexual and normal, and poems like 'Long Lines' that recall the sonnets of Wordsworth (or the tone of his and Coleridge's odes) but are thoroughly modern in their dislocations of syntax and of the hexameter pattern, their shifts of focus, their specific diction, and, most important, their essential attitude:

The heavy glacier and the terrifying Alps
that simply I cannot, nor do I know the pass,
block me from Italy. As winter closes in,
just to survive I hole up in this hovel
with food that has no taste, no one to make love to
but fantasies and masturbating, sometimes sobbing
South! South! where white the torrent splashes down
past Lugano. . . .

The exuberance tinged with melancholy of Goodman's Lambretta poems can be matched in some of the work of Galway Kinnell, especially his long poem 'The Avenue Bearing the Initial of Christ into the New World' (Whitman brought up to date in the modern big city), and of Ramon Guthrie and Carolyn Kizer. It is the mark of Guthrie above all the others, however. He has an extraordinarily well-stocked mind, the mind of a scholar to whom the data of his learning are living, relevant facts of experience. Guthrie resembles Pound in this respect, although his poetry makes no effort at large formal invention. It exists, however, within the atmosphere of freedom to draw on many traditions and frames of thought that

Pound helped to create, and the level of consciousness and spirit is comparable.

There is so much gaiety in Guthrie that one almost misses the common, brooding humanity his gaiety leavens. Like all good scholars of a *spirituel* cast, he loves toying with language, or with languages: 'Dieu knows or God sait'; 'You an' me, bister, been giraffes'; 'Mr. Eliot posteriorly acquiring pew-sheen.' And like all the better scholars, he has a bright and happy eye for feminine beauty:

> Everything about her
> bounced:
> It was like early Spring
> fresh from the Forêt de Chantilly
> coming around a corner at full tilt
> with its arms full of daffodils.
> ('Fragment of a Travelogue')

The common, brooding humanity is there, though. In 'Postlude: For Goya,' the poet sees dark signs for the age in the sky:

> two skinned bulls, motionless, backed off
> from goring one another. . . .

The landscape of this poem has the same desolate, post-catastrophic quality:

> You stare at a dry hollow and your lips
> peel back from your teeth
> and your shoulders mean laughter,
> remembering it lately was a brook.

Guthrie is of that company who have looked starkly at the Goya-like scene of our generations of war, as Williams does in 'To a Dog Injured in the Street' (quoted in the first chapter), who have made their peace with none of it, and who yet have steadfastly nourished the impulse to affirm.

> . . . after a while
> we will creep forth and search among the crevices
> for seeds and cover them with dust
> and try for tears to quicken them.
> Remember only this is not an end.
> We have won if we can believe
> that this is not an end.

The relation between his poetic worlds of gaiety and of pain is by way of Guthrie's assumed character of the buffoon or clown. A number of his poems take on the rôle directly, but perhaps the most brilliant of the clown-pieces in Guthrie's collection of his post-war work, *Graffiti* (1959), is one which does so indirectly: 'The Clown: He Dances in the Clearing by Night.' In this poem, art is seen as a moment's undoing of the inexorable oppressions implicit in actual experience. The liberation is not 'escape' but the realization of a power at once disengaged and transforming:

> The Tyger in the forest stared,
> chin sunk upon his powered paws
> while pirouette and caper dared
> the awesome sinews of the Laws
> his stripèd humors improvise —
> Immutabilities laid down
> by conclaves of eternities —
> *revoked an instant by the Clown.*

The whole of this poem just about sizes up the truth of things as a poem in this perspective has to present it.

Realization has arrived at a certain pitch, and buffoonery discovers a higher dignity than all the 'conclaves of eternities' possess. The connection between this dignity and that of ordinary humanity, dauntless in its ability to survive the blows of history and the dull torment of neglect, should be obvious.

A brave company of still other 'independents' comes to mind here. It includes the elusively impressionistic William Stafford, whose poetry is unobtrusively regional and whose restraint gives to his more self-portraying psychological insights the emotional coloration of Chinese and Japanese poetry. His fellow West Coast poet James Schevill has a keenly active intelligence that broods over an unusually wide range of observations — from reading, travel, personal experience, and the contemplation of art and philosophy. Schevill and Nemerov resemble many British poets in their sometimes journalistic eagerness for stimulation through incidental bits of knowledge from the day's news or from casual reading. Both, though, move freely into realms of meditation, reverie, and pure poetic discovery that have little in common with their lighter verse-essays except an easy deployment of vernacular effects.

Among our more purely contemplative American poets, who seek above all to close in on some perfectly tranquil, mystically attuned state of inner peace or balance, is Henry Rago. This poet, like Weiss and a few other figures — the explosively witty Carolyn Kizer, for instance, or the fastidiously precise and intense Howard Moss — has suffered a certain muting of his reputation because of his duties as an editor.* He has for a number of years been

* Weiss is editor, with his wife Renée, of *Quarterly Review of Literature.* Carolyn Kizer, until recently, edited *Poetry Northwest.* Howard Moss is poetry editor of *The New Yorker.*

editor of *Poetry* magazine, a position which uniquely requires tactful relationship with many poets of outstanding ability and — ideally at least, for some editors of *Poetry* have not had this talent — the knack of keeping his own gifts and predilections sufficiently in the background to make all others with genuine gifts feel welcome.

One group of poets who have made themselves felt, largely outside the central tendencies discussed in earlier chapters, is that loosely associated with the magazine *The Sixties* (formerly *The Fifties* and soon, no doubt, to change its title once again in what is perhaps the most convenient way of all to meet the demands of changing times). In one sense this group, which includes Robert Bly, Donald Hall, Louis Simpson, James Wright, and James Dickey, is seeking to affect the aims of American poetry in much the same way as Robert Conquest, Kingsley Amis, and others actually did affect those of British poetry. That is, it has taken stands opposed to the central tendencies of which I speak, and in favor of a new simplicity and directness. At the same time, it has occupied itself salutarily with translation — this is particularly true of Bly, the most active 'theorist' of the group, who has tried valiantly to propagandize for the poetry of Lorca and Neruda, among other European and Latin-American poets. From Lorca especially, the group has learned to value the surrealist image highly. An incidental concern related to this attempt seems to be the desire to create a new 'social' poetry of a strongly critical character. This poetry should, ideally, have the political effectiveness of Neruda's writing without embodying any of the feeling that the speaker is simply another variant of *poète maudit* that emanates from most current poetry in which a hostile assessment of our society is offered. (Of course, my comparison of the

Bly group with The Movement refers neither to their interest in translation as a clue to effective use of imagery nor to their desire for a renewed poetry of social protest.) Meanwhile, in the usual blessed course of events, the individual poets have developed — theory aside — in varying ways.

The characteristic feeling of Bly's more interesting poems is suggested by the title of his book *Silence in the Snowy Fields* (1962). He does at times catch the inhumanly cold atmosphere of the Minnesota winter, say: a sparse landscape, the isolation of human beings in the countryside, the importance (and treacherousness) of one's automobile and of the roads that will get one to the post office in the village and back again. Bly's poems have the makings of an essentially regional art, if that were the direction he finally wished to take:

As the snow grows heavier, the cornstalks fade farther away,
And the barn moves nearer to the house.
The barn moves all alone in the growing storm. . . .

Under the influence of the interest he shares with Bly in this kind of writing, Donald Hall has slowly evolved from a poet whose work was derivatively intellectual and verbose without organic life into one able to make a poem move in a simple, self-creating curve. His latest book at this writing, *A Roof of Tiger Lilies* (1964), contains passages and whole poems that are among the firmest work anyone in the group has yet produced. 'Wells,' for instance, unfolds in six unrhymed couplets of exquisite movement, each image along the way a touchstone against which the speaker tests the genuineness of the growth of the private liberation he is describing. At the center is the dominating sexual image toward which the early stanzas move and from which the joyously simple ending derives:

> I crouched by the wall ten years
>
> until the circle of a woman's darkness
> moved over mine like a mouth. . . .

Hall's new realization of what actually makes a poem can be seen even more clearly in three stanzas from 'The Snow' that move surely from abstract argument and analogy to literal statement and then to a new level of vision, both concrete and symbolic:

> Snow is what must
> come down, even if it struggles
> to stay in the air with the strength
> of the wind. Like an old man,
> whatever I touch I turn
> to the story of death.
>
> Snow is what fills
> the oak, and what covers
> the grass and the bare garden.
> Snow is what reverses
> the sidewalk and the lawn
> into the substance of whiteness.
>
> So the watcher sleeps himself
> back to the baby's eyes.
> The tree, the breast, and the floor
> are limbs of him, and from
> his eyes he extends a skin
> which grows over the world. . . .

While none of these poets achieve that kind of ultimate immediacy which makes a whole poem, perhaps complex, seem a single *aperçu* developing in time only because that is what the medium of language requires, the quality of this work is self-evident. Louis Simpson, who has a natural conversational and narrative style, has perhaps been less affected than Bly and Hall by his association with a group seeking a style and impress of its own. His engaging manner is half his style in any case, and the serious use to which he can put it is well illustrated by his poem 'A Story About Chicken Soup.' The phrase 'chicken soup' becomes the refrain element, and the fact is important in the way that Simpson moves from a rich, Chagall-like Jewish whimsy to the sudden introduction of horror in the first three stanzas:

In my grandmother's house there was always chicken soup
And talk of the old country—mud and boards,
Poverty,
The snow falling down the necks of lovers.

Now and then, out of her savings
She sent them a dowry. Imagine
The rice-powdered faces!
And the smell of the bride, like chicken soup.

But the Germans killed them.
I know it's in bad taste to say it,
But it's true. The Germans killed them all.

The poem is divided into three sections, each in three short stanzas. The second section is about an incident in Germany after the victorious American troops had marched into Berchtesgaden. A German child, so reduced to skin and bones that there was 'not even enough to make chicken soup' of her, ran out of a doorway and laughed at the soldiers (who had killed, made 'chicken soup' of her 'mechanical' brothers). Because they were replete after that killing, they 'forgave her.' And now, says the third section, long after the deaths of those affianced lovers, the speaker feels that their eyes are all fixed on him. 'They want me to be more serious than I want to be,' 'to be poor, to sleep in a room with many others,' 'to live in the tragic world forever.' The 'chicken soup' symbolism has become too obvious and too frightful to be repeated explicitly.

Simpson has cultivated his ability to speak directly and unpretentiously about dead-serious matters, and he carries it furthest in his best known poem, 'Carentan O Carentan.' This is a war-poem in an old-fashioned sense, with many traditional antecedents. It is written in ballad-stanzas, but with an added rhyme — *abab* rather than the familiar *abcb* — and describes the ambushing of untried invasion troops near Carentan in Normandy. Though his style is quite unlike Wilfrid Owen's, the spirit of Simpson's poem is precisely the same, and so by implication is the poem's artistic rationale: 'The poetry is in the Pity.'

> Carentan O Carentan
> Before we met with you
> We never yet had lost a man
> Or known what death could do.

Of the other two poets whom I have named in connection with this group, James Wright is closer in practice to the theoretical positions described. At first a typically edgy poet of the age, disturbed by the terror in the air and finding a half-masochistic release in projecting it, he has turned the unease into several channels. The first is political — for instance, 'Eisenhower's Visit to Franco' or 'Two Poems about President Harding.' The irony and bitterness of these pieces and others like them do take to a certain degree, though there is a facile, unearned quality to the emotion. The second is quietistic, the speaker deriving strength by 'turning to nature' in the good old-fashioned way.*

> I climb a slight rise of grass.
> I do not want to disturb the ants
> who are walking single file up the fence post,
> Carrying small white petals,
> Casting shadows so frail that I can see through them. . . .

A third channel is the continuation of his earlier mode of thought, but in a simplified style that stresses the naked pain and fear of natural existence and brings social criticism into the poem almost incidentally. This is Wright's most sympathetic vein, because closest to the state of his own sensibility. In his work, as in Simpson's, we have interesting examples of the artistic gain that can sometimes be won through a relaxing of discipline and self-consciousness in writing. The raw materials, at least, of a genuine art are thus allowed to come to the surface (as Ginsberg discovered more drastically); and poems that are still to be perfected formally begin, by that token, to discover their voice and direction.

An attempt to be guided by afflatus marks James Dickey's work. He is the most expansive and energetic of these poets, and his poetry is alive with fugitive notes of compassion, fantasy, empathy with personalities that sometimes hold, sometimes flicker in a poem and then disappear. He seems capable of great compression, of an economy that could hold within deliberately contrived limits diverse elements working together. But language for Dickey is a form of energetic action that does not

* The title, however, of the poem from which the lines that follow come is not quietistic: 'Depressed by a Book of Bad Poetry, I Walk Toward an Unused Pasture and Invite the Insects to Join Me.'

necessarily allow him to work his materials into achieved formal shape and meaning. The poems tend to grow more than to be shaped; their expansion is a necessary aspect of his discovery of what he wishes to say and to release through them. It is actually a method of letting the materials come to the surface, comparable to the relaxation of tension that gives Wright his insights and the effortless surface of his poems. Certainly in poems like 'The Firebombing' and 'The Being' Dickey does make discoveries. 'The Firebombing' is too long for full effectiveness, and its movement almost loses dramatic force in its rapidity. Nevertheless, as with Simpson's 'Carentan O Carentan,' it is a true war (or rather, post-war) poem. At once extremely concrete and somehow bland in its narrative emphasis on external detail, it catches accurately the mentality and guilt of the former American bomber-pilot who speaks in it — his repressed hysteria and guilt buried under his desire not to contemplate the human results of his actions, and also buried under his narrow absorptions as a suburban family man and under his pride in American prowess and technique:

Combat booze by my side in a cratered canteen,
Bourbon frighteningly mixed
With GI pineapple juice,
Dogs trembling under me for hundreds of miles, on many
Islands, sleep-smelling that ungodly mixture
Of napalm and high-octane fuel,
Good bourbon and GI juice.

Rivers circling behind me around
Come to the fore, and bring
A town with everyone darkened.
Five thousand people are sleeping off

An all-day American drone.
Twenty years in the suburbs have not shown me
Which ones were hit and which not.

Of all Dickey's poems, 'The Being' comes closest to discovery of its own proper form in addition to discovery of the character of an experience. The experience in question is a mystical one, possession of and by an invisible being vaguely like a succubus. This 'being' awakens a dreamer to full sensuous awareness of the physical, miraculous, blazing quality of existence and of life. The stages of the experience, from the first realization of what is happening through submission to 'utter delight' to a state of frozen terror and then the revitalized awakening, constitute a series of six beautifully paced movements. The poem shows that, when his materials are entirely subjective and therefore demand tight formal control in order to emerge with any clarity and effect, Dickey is capable of doing the full job of being a poet.

Curiously, the tendency to subordinate the kind of constructive energy that makes for highest formal achievement to a state of mind that allows what I have called the raw materials to emerge is shared today by poets whose writing is otherwise of the most diverse character. The discovery of the 'final' form of a work is a second discovery, as it were, which takes its clues from the first, less disciplined emergence of an insight, with its organic possibilities. It is a pursuit of those possibilities demanding, finally, a far more impersonal discipline, such as we see superimposed on the materials of Lowell's *Life Studies*. Among the American poets of the present generations, there is now a considerable range of work, sometimes exciting, sometimes pathetic or shocking, and very often profoundly absorbing and sympathetic, at the primary level. It is, to distort a quotation and its original point, 'waiting to be born.' More than that, it is already on its ways to birth. The names of at least three poets come to mind at once to illustrate: Gary Snyder, Brother Antoninus, W. D. Snodgrass. Their most interesting poems are a tuning in on their own experience and voices: Snyder's rather deep plunge into the life of those who work for logging companies in Western forests and mountains, his study of American Indian lore and of Chinese and Japanese literature and religion, and his years of study in Kyoto under a Zen master; Brother Antoninus's religious struggle to come to terms with himself; Snodgrass's psychological problems, particularly as described in his most successful poem, the long 'Heart's Needle,' which details the excruciating period of a father's relation to his little daughter while he is in process of being divorced and then of remarrying. It is commonly said that the poetry of recent years represents a process of consolidation of the gains made by the great innovators earlier in the century. This is only partly true. It is to a greater degree marked by the exploration of new areas of personal experience while their new implications for form gradually make themselves felt.

In emphasizing the more dynamically influential tendencies and figures of recent poetry, and in seeking to give the reader 'news' (about British and Irish poetry of the last two decades especially), I have omitted a number of accomplished poets of established reputation. Our modern generations are many, and there are poets writing interesting new work who were born in the last century, as well as younger figures from Muriel Rukeyser to Richard Wilbur who have been the subjects of many critical studies since the war.* As a girl in the 1930's, Miss Rukeyser was already a pioneer in various kinds of poetic exploration that have come into their own in the present period. Her *Waterlily Fire: Poems 1935–1962* (1962) gives full evidence of her experiments with the poem sequence, of her efforts to find the right means to express intimate and even humiliating private experience, and of her sense of an essential bearing — if only one could close in on it — of social and international problems on that experience and therefore on her artistic concerns. In the recent poem 'Waterlily Fire' she sums up these efforts in the image of the 'long body' ('an idea from India of one's lifetime body as a ribbon of images, all our change seen in process'):

This journey is exploring us. Where the child stood
An island in a river of crisis, now
The bridges bind us in symbol, the sea
Is a bond, the sky reaches into our bodies.
We pray : we dive into each other's eyes.

Whatever can come to a woman can come to me.

This is the long body : into life from the beginning. . . .

At the opposite end of the process from Miss Rukeyser's poetry is the poetry of the late Randall Jarrell. He hardly ever spoke in his own person about his own sufferings and circumstances. Though his poetry is filled with sheer pity for the vulnerable of the earth, in war and in peace, the voice has usually been that of someone else, a voice overheard, of a dead soldier, a desolate child, a woman

* Many of these figures are discussed in my book *The Modern Poets: A Critical Introduction* (N.Y.: Oxford University Press, 1960; Galaxy Edition, 1964).

without hope. Or else it has had a protective covering of cool irony and objectivity, though the subject has been, say, a German concentration camp in the Prussian forest. In his last books, *The Woman at the Washington Zoo* (1960) and *The Lost World* (1965), a change had begun to take place, heralded by three poems in the former book: 'In Those Days,' 'The Elementary Scene,' and 'Windows.' These are poems of private memory — of a time in the past that seemed, often was, 'poor and miserable' (and yet 'everything was better'); of the sadness of what appears, in 'The Elementary Scene,' to have been an unsatisfactory childhood, with a last ironic allusion to the speaker's adult condition ('I, I, the future that mends everything'); and of the impossibility of recovering the dead, simple past of parents who

> have known nothing of today,
> That time of troubles and of me. Of troubles.
> Morose and speechless, voluble with elation,
> Changing, unsleeping, an unchanging speech.
> These have not lived. . . .

This kind of personalist immediacy is precisely avoided by poets who, like Richard Wilbur, are still primarily concerned to absorb their 'secret' motivations into relatively impersonal and objective structures, or else have not yet found the key to unlock them. It is not quite avoided by a writer like Karl Shapiro, who has sought through wit and candor about his own predicaments and embarrassments — for instance in *Poems of a Jew* (1958) and in *The Bourgeois Poet* (1964) — to expose his own problems and his confusions as an artist. Although very much of the era and of the 'literary establishment,' Shapiro would like to free himself of all false airs and associations as Allen

Ginsberg has tried to do. Brightly sardonic, he reveals the ambiguities of the situation again and again in *The Bourgeois Poet:*

> The sea of subjectivity comes at you like a tidal wave, splashing the cuffs of middle-aged monuments. War is written on their unwritten faces. They try out wet dreams and wandering mind. They're rubbing Aladdin's lamp in the locker room. They pray for moments of objectivity as drunkards pray for the one that puts you out. They've captured the telephone centers, the microphones, the magazine syndicates (they've left the movies to us). I wait behind the wheel and spy; it's enemy territory all right. My daughter comes, grows taller as she approaches. It's a moment of panic. . . .

And:

> Lower the standard: that's my motto. Somebody is always putting the food out of reach. We're tired of falling off ladders. Who says a child can't paint? A pro is somebody who does it for money. Lower the standards. Let's all play poetry. Down with ideals, flags, convention buttons, morals, the scrambled eggs on the admiral's hat. I'm talking sense. Lower the standards. Sabotage the stylistic approach. Let weeds grow in the subdivision. Putty up the incisions in the library façade, those names that frighten grade-school teachers, those names whose U's are cut like V's. Burn the *Syntopicon* and *The Harvard Classics.* Lower the standard on classics, battleships, Russian ballet, national anthems (but they're low enough). Break through to the bottom. Be natural as an American abroad who knows no lan-

> guage, not even American. Keelhaul the poets in the vestry chairs. Renovate the Abbey of cold-storage dreamers. Get off the Culture Wagon. Learn how to walk the way you want. Slump your shoulders, stick your belly out, arms all over the table. How many generations will this take? Don't think about it, just make a start. (You have made a start.) Don't break anything you can step around, *but don't pick it up.* The law of gravity is the law of art. You first, poetry second, the good, the beautiful, the true come last. As the lad said: We must love one another or die.

Attracted toward what he rejects (a phrase that can, like these quotations, be taken either way), Shapiro points up the cultural and personal crisis within which it is increasingly hard to be 'assured of certain certainties.' I have cited his work and that of others in this chapter, not with any hope of representing them completely or even altogether justly, but merely to suggest once again the convergence of the whole drift of the modern, from almost any starting point one chooses. Of course, there are exceptions, but by fate and by choice the involvement of most of our vital poets is with the simultaneous exercise of an almost helpless identification and sympathy with the victimized psyche of the present cultural moment, and of the will to define the situation clearly, to insist on the poet's meaningful relation to it, and to seek the way to transcendent meaning in the process. As another passage of Miss Rukeyser's 'Waterlily Fire' has it:

> This moment in a city, in its dream of war.
> We chose to be.

Becoming the only ones under the trees
when the harsh sound
Of the machine sirens spoke. There were these two men,
And the bearded one, the boys, the Negro mother feeding
Her baby. And threats, the ambulances with open doors.
Now silence. Everyone else within the walls. We sang.
We are the living island.
We the flesh of this island, being lived,
Whoever knows us is part of us today.

Whatever can happen to anyone can happen to me. . . .

Selective Bibliography: Individual Volumes by Poets Discussed

Note: See also the anthologies by Donald M. Allen, A. Alvarez, Robert Conquest, Edward Lucie-Smith, M. L. Rosenthal, David Wright, and others referred to in the preceding chapters and in the Index.

Abse, Dannie, *Tenants of the House* (London: Hutchinson, 1957).

———, *Poems, Golders Green* (London: Hutchinson, 1962).

Amis, Kingsley, *A Case of Samples* (N.Y.: Harcourt, Brace, 1957).

Antoninus, Brother (William Everson), *The Crooked Lines of God* (University of Detroit Press, 1959).

———, *The Hazards of Holiness* (Garden City, N.Y.: Doubleday, 1962).

Barker, George, *The True Confession of George Barker* (Denver: Alan Swallow, 1950).

———, *Collected Poems* (N.Y.: October House, 1965).

Berryman, John, *The Dispossessed* (N.Y.: William Sloane Associates, 1948).

———, *Homage to Mistress Bradstreet* (N.Y.: Farrar, Straus & Cudahy, 1956).

———, *77 Dream Songs* (N.Y.: Farrar, Straus and Giroux, 1964).

Betjeman, John, *Collected Poems* (London: John Murray, 1958; Boston: Houghton Mifflin, 1959).

Blackburn, Paul, *The Dissolving Fabric* (Highlands, N.C.: The Divers Press, 1955).

Bly, Robert, *Silence in the Snowy Fields* (Middletown, Conn.: Wesleyan University Press, 1962).
Bronk, Edwin, *An Attempt at Exorcism* (Northwood, Middlesex: Scorpion Press, 1959).
———, *A Family Affair* (Northwood, Middlesex: Scorpion Press, 1960).
———, *With Love from Judas* (Lowestoft, Suffolk: Scorpion Press, 1963).
Carruth, Hayden, *The Crow and the Heart* (N.Y.: Macmillan, 1959).
———, *Nothing for Tigers* (N.Y.: Macmillan, 1965).
Clarke, Austin, *Later Poems* (Dublin: Dolmen Press, 1961).
———, *Flight to Africa* (Dublin: Dolmen Press, 1963).
———, *Mnemosyne Lay in Dust* (Dublin: Dolmen Press, 1966).
Connor, Tony, *With Love Somehow* (London: Oxford University Press, 1962).
———, *Lodgers* (London: Oxford University Press, 1965).
Creeley, Robert, *For Love: Poems 1950–1960* (N.Y.: Scribner's, 1962).
Davie, Donald, *A Winter Talent* (London: Routledge and Kegan Paul, 1957).
———, *New and Selected Poems* (Middletown, Conn.: Wesleyan University Press, 1961).
———, *Events and Wisdoms* (London: Routledge and Kegan Paul, 1964; Middletown, Conn.: Wesleyan University Press, 1965).
Devlin, Denis, *Selected Poems* (N.Y.: Holt, Rinehart and Winston, 1963).
———, *Collected Poems* (Dublin: Dolmen Press, 1964).
Dickey, James, *Buckdancer's Choice* (Middletown, Conn.: Wesleyan University Press, 1965).
Duncan, Robert, *Selected Poems* (San Francisco: City Lights Books, 1959).
———, *The Opening of the Field* (N.Y.: Grove Press, 1960).
———, *Roots and Branches* (N.Y.: Scribner's, 1964).
Enright, D. J., *Addictions* (London: Chatto and Windus with Hogarth Press, 1962).
———, *The Old Adam* (London: Chatto and Windus with Hogarth Press, 1965).
Fainlight, Harry, *Sussicran* (London: Turret Books, 1965).
Finlay, Ian Hamilton, *Glasgow Beasts, An a Burd* (Edinburgh, Scotland: Wild Flounder Press, 1961).

———, *The Dancers Inherit the Party* (Ventura, California, and Worcester, England: Migrant Press, 1962).
———, *Telegrams from My Windmill* (Edinburgh, Scotland: Wild Hawthorn Press, 1964).
Fuller, Roy, *Collected Poems 1936–1961* (London: André Deutsch, 1962).
———, *Buff* (London: André Deutsch, 1965).
Ginsberg, Allen, *Howl and Other Poems* (San Francisco: City Lights Books, 1956).
———, *Empty Mirror: Early Poems* (N.Y.: Totem/Corinth, 1961).
———, *Kaddish and Other Poems* (San Francisco: City Lights Books, 1961).
———, *Reality Sandwiches* (San Francisco: City Lights Books, 1963).
———, *Jukebox All'Idrogeno* (Milan: Arnoldo Mondadori Editore, 1965).
Goodman, Paul, *The Lordly Hudson: Collected Poems* (N.Y.: Macmillan, 1962).
Gunn, Thom, *The Sense of Movement* (London: Faber and Faber; University of Chicago Press, 1957).
———, *My Sad Captains* (London: Faber and Faber; University of Chicago Press, 1961).
Guthrie, Ramon, *Graffiti* (N.Y.: Macmillan, 1959).
Hall, Donald, *A Roof of Tiger Lilies* (N.Y.: Viking, 1964).
Hamburger, Michael, *The Dual Site* (London: Routledge and Kegan Paul, 1958).
———, *Weather and Season* (London: Routledge and Kegan Paul; N.Y.: Atheneum, 1963).
Holloway, John, *The Minute and Longer Poems* (Hessle, East Yorkshire: Marvell Press, 1956).
Hughes, Ted, *The Hawk in the Rain* (London: Faber and Faber; N.Y.: Harper, 1957).
———, *Lupercal* (London: Faber and Faber; N.Y.: Harper, 1960).
Jarrell, Randall, *Little Friend, Little Friend* (N.Y.: Dial Press, 1945).
———, *Losses* (N.Y.: Harcourt, Brace, 1951).
———, *The Seven-League Crutches* (N.Y.: Harcourt, Brace, 1951).
———, *The Woman at the Washington Zoo* (N.Y.: Atheneum, 1960).
———, *The Lost World* (N.Y.: Macmillan, 1965).

Jennings, Elizabeth, *A Sense of the World* (London: André Deutsch, 1958).
Jones, LeRoi, *Preface to a Twenty Volume Suicide Note* (N.Y.: Totem/Corinth Books, 1960).
———, *The Dead Lecturer* (N.Y.: Grove Press, 1964).
Kavanagh, Patrick, *Collected Poems* (London: MacGibbon and Kee, 1964).
Kinnell, Galway, *What a Kingdom It Was* (Boston: Houghton Mifflin, 1960).
———, *Flower Herding on Mount Monadnock* (Boston: Houghton Mifflin, 1964).
Kinsella, Thomas, *Another September* (Dublin: Dolmen Press, 1958).
———, *Downstream* (Dublin: Dolmen Press, 1961).
———, *Poems and Translations* (N.Y.: Atheneum, 1961).
———, *Wormwood* (Dublin: Dolmen Press, 1966).
Kizer, Carolyn, *The Ungrateful Garden* (Bloomington: Indiana University Press, 1961).
Larkin, Philip, *The Less Deceived* (Hessle, East Yorkshire: Marvell Press, 1955).
———, *The Whitsun Weddings* (London: Faber and Faber, 1964).
———, *The North Ship* (London: Dent, 1945: Faber and Faber, 1966).
Levertov, Denise, *Overland to the Islands* (Highlands, N.C.: Jonathan Williams, 1958).
———, *With Eyes at the Back of Our Heads* (N.Y.: New Directions, 1959).
———, *The Jacob's Ladder* (N.Y.: New Directions, 1961).
———, *O Taste and See* (N.Y.: New Directions, 1964).
Lowell, Robert, *Land of Unlikeness* (Cummington, Mass.: Cummington Press, 1944).
———, *Lord Weary's Castle* (N.Y.: Harcourt, Brace, 1946).
———, *The Mills of the Kavanaughs* (N.Y.: Harcourt, Brace, 1951).
———, *Life Studies* (N.Y.: Farrar, Straus and Cudahy, 1960).
———, *For the Union Dead* (N.Y.: Farrar, Straus and Giroux, 1964).
———, *Near the Ocean* (N.Y.: Farrar, Straus and Giroux, 1967).
MacBeth, George, *The Broken Places* (Lowestoft, Suffolk: Scorpion Press, 1963).
———, *A Doomsday Book* (Lowestoft, Suffolk: Scorpion Press, 1965).

MacCaig, Norman, *Riding Lights* (London: Hogarth Press, 1956).
———, *The Sinai Sort* (London: Hogarth Press, 1957).
———, *A Round of Applause* (London: Chatto and Windus with Hogarth Press, 1962).
———, *Measures* (London: Chatto and Windus with Hogarth Press, 1965).
———, *Surroundings* (London: Chatto and Windus with Hogarth Press, 1966).
MacDiarmid, Hugh, *Collected Poems* (N.Y.: Macmillan, 1962).
Middleton, Christopher, *Torse 3* (N.Y.: Harcourt, Brace, 1962).
———, *Nonsequences: Selfpoems* (N.Y.: Norton, 1965).
Montague, John, *Poisoned Lands* (London: MacGibbon and Kee, 1961).
———, *All Legendary Obstacles* (Dublin: Dolmen Press, 1966).
Moss, Howard, *A Winter Come, a Summer Gone: Poems 1946–1960* (N.Y.: Scribner's, 1960).
———, *Finding Them Lost and Other Poems* (N.Y.: Scribner's, 1965).
Muir, Edwin, *Collected Poems* (N.Y.: Oxford University Press, 1965).
Murphy, Richard, *Sailing to an Island* (London: Faber and Faber; N.Y.: Chilmark Press, 1965).
Nemerov, Howard, *New and Selected Poems* (University of Chicago Press, 1960).
———, *The Next Room of the Dream* (University of Chicago Press, 1962).
Olson, Charles, *The Distances* (N.Y.: Grove Press, 1960).
———, *The Maximus Poems* (N.Y.: Jargon/Corinth Books, 1960).
Plath, Sylvia, *The Colossus and Other Poems* (N.Y.: Knopf, 1960).
———, *Ariel* (London: Faber and Faber, 1965; N.Y.: Harper & Row, 1966).
Porter, Peter, *Once Bitten, Twice Bitten* (Northwood, Middlesex: Scorpion Press, 1961).
———, *Poems Ancient and Modern* (Lowestoft, Suffolk: Scorpion Press, 1964).
Rago, Henry, *A Sky of Late Summer* (N.Y.: Macmillan, 1963).
Redgrove, Peter, *The Collector* (London: Routledge and Kegan Paul, 1960).
———, *The Nature of Cold Weather* (London: Routledge and Kegan Paul, 1961).

———, *At the White Monument* (London: Routledge and Kegan Paul, 1963).
———, *The Force and Other Poems* (London: Routledge and Kegan Paul, 1966).
Roethke, Theodore, *Words for the Wind* (Garden City, N.Y.: Doubleday, 1958).
———, *The Far Field* (Garden City, N.Y.: Doubleday, 1964).
Rukeyser, Muriel, *Waterlily Fire: Poems 1935–1962* (N.Y.: Macmillan, 1962).
Schevill, James, *Private Dooms and Public Destinations: Poems 1945–1962* (Denver: Alan Swallow, 1962).
Schwartz, Delmore, *Summer Knowledge: New and Selected Poems, 1938–1958* (Garden City, N.Y.: Doubleday, 1959).
Sexton, Anne, *To Bedlam and Part Way Back* (Boston: Houghton Mifflin, 1960).
———, *All My Pretty Ones* (Boston: Houghton Mifflin, 1962).
Shapiro, Karl, *Poems 1940–1953* (N.Y.: Random House, 1953).
———, *Poems of a Jew* (N.Y.: Random House, 1958).
———, *The Bourgeois Poet* (N.Y.: Random House, 1964).
Simpson, Louis, *A Dream of Governors* (Middletown, Conn.: Wesleyan University Press, 1959).
———, *At the End of the Open Road* (Middletown, Conn.: Wesleyan University Press, 1963).
Snodgrass, W. D., *Heart's Needle* (N.Y.: Knopf, 1957).
Snyder, Gary, *A Range of Poems* (London: Fulcrum Press, 1966).
Stafford, William, *Traveling Through the Dark* (N.Y.: Harper & Row, 1962).
Thwaite, Anthony, *The Owl in the Trees* (London: Oxford University Press, 1963).
Tomlinson, Charles, *Seeing Is Believing* (N.Y.: McDowell, Obolensky, 1958).
———, *A Peopled Landscape* (London: Oxford University Press, 1963).
———, *American Scenes* (London: Oxford University Press, 1966).
Wain, John, *Weep Before God* (London: Macmillan, 1961).
———, *Wildtrack* (London: Macmillan, 1965).
Weiss, Theodore, *Outlanders* (N.Y.: Macmillan, 1960).
———, *Gunsight* (New York University Press, 1962).
———, *The Medium: New Poems* (N.Y.: Macmillan, 1965).

Wilbur, Richard, *The Beautiful Changes and Other Poems* (N.Y.: Reynal and Hitchcock, 1947).

———, *Ceremony and Other Poems* (N.Y.: Harcourt, Brace, 1950).

———, *Things of This World: Poems* (N.Y.: Harcourt, Brace, 1956).

———, *Advice to a Prophet and Other Poems* (N.Y.: Harcourt, Brace, 1959).

Wright, David, *Monologue of a Deaf Man* (London: André Deutsch, 1958).

———, *Adam at Evening* (London: Hodder and Stoughton, 1965).

Wright, James, *Saint Judas* (Middletown, Conn.: Wesleyan University Press, 1959).

———, *The Branch Will Not Break* (Middletown, Conn.: Wesleyan University Press, 1963).

Index